Architecture of Network Systems

Architecture of
Network Systems

Dimitrios Serpanos

Tilman Wolf

AMSTERDAM • BOSTON • HEIDELBERG • LONDON
NEW YORK • OXFORD • PARIS • SAN DIEGO
SAN FRANCISCO • SYDNEY • TOKYO
Morgan Kaufmann Publishers is an imprint of Elsevier

Acquiring Editor: Todd Green
Editorial Assistant: Robyn Day
Project Manager: Andre Cuello
Designer: Kristen Davis

Morgan Kaufmann is an imprint of Elsevier
30 Corporate Drive, Suite 400, Burlington, MA 01803, USA

Library of Congress Cataloging-in-Publication Data
Serpanos, Dimitrios Nikolaou.
  Architecture of network systems / Dimitrios Serpanos, Tilman Wolf.
    p. cm. – (The Morgan Kaufmann series in computer architecture and design)
  Includes bibliographical references and index.
  ISBN 978-0-12-374494-4 (pbk.)
1. Computer network architectures. I. Wolf, Tilman. II. Title.
  TK5105.5.S4234 2011
  004.6–dc22

                                                                                2010045063

British Library Cataloguing-in-Publication Data
A catalogue record for this book is available from the British Library.

ISBN: 978-0-12-374494-4

Printed and bound by CPI Group (UK) Ltd, Croydon, CR0 4YY

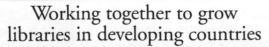
For information on all MK publications visit our website at www.mkp.com

To the memory of my father Nikolaos. -DS
To Ana and our daughter Susana. -TW

Contents

Preface

WHY WRITE THIS BOOK?

Data communication networks are widely used today and are an integral part of our daily life. The Internet is a medium for business, personal, and government communication, and it is difficult to envision today's society without this essential infrastructure. The continued success of the Internet is dependent on our ability to maintain and improve the functionality, performance, and scalability of these networks. As a basis for obtaining the necessary knowledge about networks, there is a clear need for textbooks that provide an introduction to the foundations of this topic as well as a detailed understanding of more advanced issues.

While many available books cover the design of network protocols and their operation, there has been preciously little focus on the systems that implement networks. Early data communication networks struggled with the scarcity of transmission bandwidth, which led to significant efforts to improve management and efficient use of this resource. Over the last three decades, advances in transmission technology have led to the availability of vast amounts of bandwidth, thus shifting the main bottleneck of networks from the transmission medium to the switching and processing of transmitted data. As a result, modern networks and the Internet are not only in need of appropriate protocols for the wide deployment of applications and services, but also in need of efficient systems that enable the timely processing and forwarding of network traffic.

TARGET AUDIENCE

This book aims to serve as a textbook and reference for designers and implementers of networking technology, networking students, and networking researchers. The goal of the book is to present the systems issues of network systems, approaching them from the architecture, design, and implementation point of view. Considering that network systems are embedded systems that implement network protocols, readers of the book would benefit from being familiar with the basic concepts of networking, embedded systems, and computer systems organization and architecture.

APPROACH

This book is about computing systems or, more specifically, about a class of special-purpose embedded systems used in networking devices. As such, the main thrust of the book is the promotion of systems architectures and designs. Therefore, this book can be classified as a computing systems book.

In contrast to typical architecture and computing systems books, this book follows a structure analogous to those of typical networking books. Following the OSI reference model for network protocols, a model that has been proven highly valuable from an education point of view, we classify and present network systems and their designs. Later in the book, we also discuss specific components of network systems, similarly to books on system architecture.

Since this book is the first systematic effort to present the architecture of the complete range of network systems as a whole, we focus on promoting key concepts for all types of network systems. We attempt to present the main architectures and designs of systems and components that cover this area. Clearly, the book does not and cannot cover all existing material in this area, which has experienced fast growth in recent years. Instead, the book focuses on major concepts. In addition to presenting state of the art, we have tried to demonstrate the progress in the field during the last couple of decades through specific examples that illustrate the improvements of technology and indicate the path of evolution for network systems in the future.

COURSE USE

This book has been specifically developed for use in college courses at the upper undergraduate level and graduate level. Much of the material presented in this book has been used previously by the authors in a graduate and advanced undergraduate course on network systems architecture of the Department of Electrical and Computer Engineering at the University of Patras and in a graduate level networking course of the Department of Electrical and Computer Engineering at the University of Massachusetts Amherst. It is expected that students taking a course based on this book have some prior exposure to computer networks and computer system organization. While the Appendix of the book provides a brief overview on the network protocols used in the Internet, a more detailed course on this topic may be of value.

It is not necessary to cover the entire book in a course. While there are some dependencies between chapters, different courses can emphasize different characteristics of network systems. For courses that address the networking aspects of network systems, we suggest a focus on Chapters 4 through 10, while for courses that address the embedded system aspects of network systems, we suggest a focus on Chapters 11 through 14.

WE WANT TO HEAR FROM YOU

We would appreciate receiving any feedback you may have about the book. Tell us if you find mistakes, if you have suggestions for improvements, what you like about the book, how you have used it in a course, etc. You can contact the authors via email at serpanos@upatras.gr (Dimitrios Serpanos) and wolf@ecs.umass.edu (Tilman Wolf).

ACKNOWLEDGMENTS

We thank the many individuals who have helped us in making this book a reality. First and foremost, we thank our editor Todd Green and Nancy Hoffmann for guiding us through the publication process and helping us meet our deadlines. We are also grateful for the technical input and editorial comments by current and former students, specifically C. Datsios, G. Keramidas, A. Papalambrou, and A. Voyiatzis. In addition, we thank the anonymous reviewers of book chapters, whose valuable comments enabled us to address and promote the appropriate technical concepts and to deliver a more readable book. Any failure to achieve these goals is, of course, the responsibility of the authors. Last, but definitely not least, we acknowledge the support and patience demonstrated by our families during the long process of developing this book. Without their understanding and extreme patience, this book would never have been completed.

About the Authors

Dimitrios Serpanos is a Professor of Electrical and Computer Engineering at the University of Patras, Greece, and the Director of the Industrial Systems Institute (ISI/RC Athena). Currently, he is also the chairman of the governing board of the newly founded University of Western Greece. His research interests include embedded systems, with focus on network systems, security systems and multimedia systems, computer architecture, and parallel and distributed systems.

Serpanos holds Ph.D. and M.A. degrees in Computer Science from Princeton University, Princeton, since 1988 and 1990, respectively. He received his diploma in Computer Engineering and Informatics from the University of Patras in 1985.

Between 1990 and 1996 he was a research staff member at IBM Research, T.J. Watson Research Center, New York. Since November 1996 he has been a faculty member in Greece. Between 1996 and 2000 he was with the Department of Computer Science, University of Crete. Currently, he is with the Department of Electrical and Computer Engineering, University of Patras, where he is a professor. During his term in Crete he conducted research at ICS-FORTH; while in Patras he has been conducting research at ISI. Professor Serpanos' research has received funding from the EU, the Greek government, and the private sector in Europe and the United States.

Serpanos is a senior member of the IEEE, a member of the ACM, a member of the New York Academy of Sciences, and an educational member of USENIX. He is serving or has served as associate editor for technical journals, including *ACM Transactions on Embedded Computing Systems*, *IEEE Transactions on Industrial Informatics*, the *Journal of Internet Engineering*, and *International Journal on Computers and Their Applications*. He has served as general chair and TPC chair of several conferences and workshops, as well as a TPC member of more than 120 conferences and workshops. In addition, he has served as guest editor to special issues of *IBM Journal of Research and Development*, *IEEE Network*, *ACM Transactions on Embedded Computing Systems*, IEICE/IEEE joint issues, and *Telecommunication Systems*.

Tilman Wolf is an Associate Professor in the Department of Electrical and Computer Engineering at the University of Massachusetts Amherst. He is engaged in research and teaching in the areas of computer networks, router design, embedded systems, and network and system security. Wolf received a diploma in Informatics from the University of Stuttgart, Germany, and holds a D.Sc. in Computer Science and two M.S. degrees from Washington University in St. Louis.

Wolf started working in the area of router design and network processor design in the late 1990s when commercial interest in routers with programmable data paths started taking off. His worked focused on the design of high-performance routers that use programmable port processors to provide dynamically changing functionality, with an emphasis on performance modeling and benchmarking.

Since joining the University of Massachusetts in 2002, Wolf and his students in the Network Systems Laboratory have designed and prototyped run-time systems for workload management across multiple embedded processor cores in packet processors. Their work also addresses the question of how to redesign Internet architecture to balance the need for custom networking functions with the need for simplicity and manageability. More recently, he and his students have explored security vulnerabilities in processing components of network systems that require embedded protection mechanisms.

Wolf is a senior member of the IEEE and the ACM. He has served as associate editor for the *ACM/IEEE Transactions on Networking*, as program committee member and organizing committee member of numerous professional conferences, including IEEE INFOCOM and ACM SIGCOMM, and as TPC chair and general chair for ICCCN. He has served as treasurer for the ACM SIGCOMM society for several years. He has received several recognitions for his educational activities, including a college outstanding teacher award.

Architecture of network systems overview

Computer networks have become critical infrastructure on which we rely for personal, business, and government use. Network systems are the hardware and software components from which these networks are built. Network systems determine what functionality a computer network can provide and what performance it can achieve. Due to this critical role, we believe it is important to study the architecture and operation of these network systems.

Network systems draw from concepts and technologies in computer networks, embedded systems, computer organization, and distributed computing. The convergence of these very diverse technical areas makes the study of network systems particularly exciting. This diversity also requires a thorough understanding of the relationship between these areas and how they influence network system design. We hope to provide these insights in this book.

COMPUTER NETWORKS

The advances of transmission technology for more than two decades have brought significant changes in networking as well as computing. In the 1970s and 1980s, standard networks provided limited connectivity, achieving bandwidth in the order of kilobits per second (kbps) up to a few megabits per second (Mbps) for local area networks, where the maximum speed reached 10 to 16 Mbps. From the middle of the 1980s, the development and commercialization of high-speed links that provided bandwidth of several Mbps for point-to-point connectivity enabled development of a new generation of networks and protocols that enable communication at very high speeds, reaching today hundreds of gigabits per second (Gbps).

In parallel with the dramatic progress in transmission technology, in the last decade of the 20th century the Internet was commercialized, moving it from research use to commercial use. The need to provide Internet connectivity to end users at home and at work not only exploited the high-speed transmission technology that had been developed, but also led to significant progress in access technologies. This trend led to development of a wide range of access protocols to connect end users to the Internet through telephone lines, cable TV infrastructure, satellites, and so forth.

The deployment of high-speed links and networks, as well as the Internet, provided the infrastructure for the development of new computing paradigms, mainly network-centric computing. In this paradigm, newly developed system infrastructures are used to support computing and storage-intensive applications and services. An early characteristic example is the development of networks of workstations, a multiprocessor architecture that relies on high-speed connectivity among workstations. This multiprocessor model is a natural advance of traditional distributed systems, which connected autonomous computing systems; the single view of the network of workstations as one system, necessary for a multiprocessor, was enabled by the high-speed networks that had become available. This abstraction enabled the efficient management of distributed resources through appropriate computing models and enabled a unified view of the networked workstations to the users. In a different direction, the ability to provide access to data and computational resources over the Internet enabled a vast number of new services for users and customers of commercial enterprises. These services are based on the well-known client/server distributed computing model and include examples ranging from banking to news feeds and from video conferencing to digital libraries.

The provision of all these services and applications over networks, including the Internet, requires technological advances at two fronts: protocols and network systems. Network protocols define the methods and mechanisms necessary to achieve reliable communication between two parties (or more than two in the case of multicasting or broadcasting). For example, network protocols define methods with which data units are encoded for transmission, mechanisms to detect transmission errors, methods for retransmission of data in case they are lost or transmitted with errors, and methods for regulating the flow of information between communicating peers to ensure that the receiver is not flooded with incoming data. Importantly, network protocols do not define any aspect of the systems that execute these protocols in order to implement data communication. For example, protocols do not define the type of processors, their speed, the size of memory, or any other systemic characteristic of the devices that implement these protocols.

Network systems are the systems and subsystems that realize the implementation of network protocols. Network systems need to be designed to meet the functional requirements specified by protocols. They also need to meet the performance requirements determined by the ever-increasing speed of transmission links. This relationship between network systems and related areas is illustrated in Figure 1-1. The demands for executing protocols at high speed led to the need for advanced, sophisticated system architectures, component designs, and implementations. These network systems constitute the focus of this book.

Network systems represent a distinct area of embedded systems architecture. Network systems are embedded systems because they are embedded in autonomous systems and devices that have specific purposes. For example, network systems are present in the infrastructure of networks, such as in switches, bridges, routers, and modems. Importantly, network systems also include network adapters,

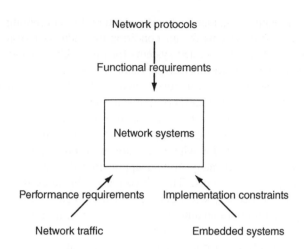

FIGURE 1-1

Requirements and constraints for network system design.

which are used in general-purpose computing systems, as well as in special-purpose systems, such as mobile phones.

The importance of network systems is increasing continually, driven by the dramatic growth in network-centric services developed and deployed. The expansion of broadband services has led to the continuing exponential growth of Internet users and the increasing adoption of services on the go (e.g., mobile banking, mobile TV), as well as the increasing deployment of large, networked sensing and monitoring systems (e.g., transported goods containers, environment monitoring systems). Importantly, these services are differentiated from traditional data connectivity services because they also provide real-time communication for voice and video services. Therefore, network systems have become critical components of the overall network infrastructure.

The design of network systems is challenging not only due to the increasing requirements to execute several complex protocols, but also because of the need to achieve efficient protocol execution within the resource limitations of embedded systems (i.e., size, power). Thus, the architecture of network systems constitutes a significant area of embedded systems architecture.

EMBEDDED SYSTEMS

Embedded systems are special-purpose computing systems embedded in application environments or in other computing systems and provide specialized support. The decreasing cost of processing power, combined with the decreasing cost of memory and the ability to design low-cost systems on chip, has led to the development and deployment of embedded computing systems in a wide range of application environments. Examples include network adapters for computing systems and mobile phones, control systems for air conditioning, industrial systems, and cars, and surveillance systems. Embedded systems for networking include two types of systems required for end-to-end service provision: infrastructure (core network) systems and end systems. The first category includes all systems required for the core network to operate, such as switches, bridges, and routers, while the second category includes systems visible to the end users, such as mobile phones and modems.

The importance of embedded systems is continuously increasing considering the breadth of application fields where they are used. For a long time, embedded systems have been used in many critical application domains, such as avionics and traffic management systems. Their broad use illustrates the importance of embedded systems, especially when considering the potential effects of their failure. For example, a failure of an automatic pilot system or a failure of a car braking system can lead to significant loss of life; failure of an electric power system may lead to loss of life or, if not to that, to loss of quality of life; and failure of a production control system in a factory may lead to a significant loss of revenue. Our dependence on embedded systems requires development and adoption of new architectural and design techniques in order to meet the necessary performance requirements and to achieve the required dependability using their limited resources in terms of processing, memory, and power.

The importance of embedded systems has led to the emergence of a strong industry that develops and uses them. Their criticality for services on all fronts and for technological and thus economic growth has led to significant efforts to address the challenges placed by embedded systems development and deployment. One important effort is the ARTEMIS initiative of the European Commission [1]. This program started with a Strategic Research Agenda (SRA) [8] and has grown to a significant activity, including a strong industrial association, named ARTEMISIA, which conducts research and development in the area of embedded systems. Figure 1-2, a figure from the ARTEMIS SRA [8], shows one view of the embedded systems area organized by research domains and application contexts. In Figure 1-2, horizontal bars constitute technological areas involved in embedded systems development and vertical bars indicate application contexts where embedded systems are used and are expected to penetrate applications in the future. Considering the differentiated requirements of embedded systems adoption in different application areas, Figure 1-2 groups in application contexts the services and applications that have common characteristics; different application contexts have significant differences among them. For example, the application context of private spaces includes systems and services for the home environment, the car, and private environments in general, where comfort and safety are the highest priority, while the context of industrial systems focuses on safety-critical systems for industry, avionics, and others. Clearly, the organization and semantics of application contexts change as time progresses and new applications and services are developed. One can organize the vertical bars with different criteria, such as, for example, the industrial sectors involved in the development of embedded systems.

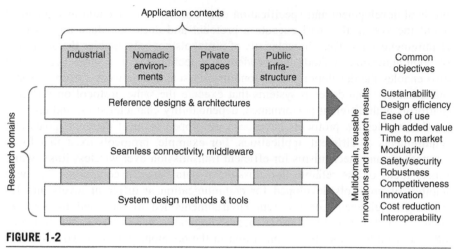

FIGURE 1-2

ARTEMIS research domains and application contexts.

PROTOCOLS AND NETWORK SYSTEMS

As noted earlier, the networking field has focused mostly on the development of protocols for communication among network nodes. Considering the high bit error rates of early transmission media and methodologies, as well as their low throughput, special attention was paid to the development of communication mechanisms that achieved efficient and reliable transmission. The need for voice services led to development of a range of protocols for voice and real-time traffic, using a centralized communication model where a single entity had centralized control. This centralized network paradigm with its single point of failure led to reliability problems, which is a significant drawback.

The non-real-time requirements of data traffic for computer-to-computer communication enabled development of a noncentralized communication model where data could follow alternate paths in order to avoid failed network systems. This model, also employed by the Internet, leads to more robust networks in terms of the ability to transmit data successfully between nodes, even in the presence of intermediate network system failure.

These communication paradigms and requirements influence network protocols as well as the systems that execute them. It is important to differentiate, however, protocols from the systems that execute them, for several reasons. Protocols define communication methods, as explained previously, while network systems execute these protocols. In general, protocols include mechanisms that accommodate systems with different performance and reliability characteristics, with methods that regulate traffic flow among systems and mechanisms to detect transmission errors and lead to data retransmission. Thus, the activity of protocol development and specification does not take into account any specifics about the system that will execute a protocol and does not place any specific requirements on it. This characteristic of protocols not only enables the definition of communication methods independently of technology to a large degree, but also enables the development of economically scalable network systems, where manufacturers can develop systems that execute the same protocol on different platforms with different performance, dependability characteristics, and cost.

Communication protocols have been developed to meet different goals and requirements of different applications. For example, protocols exist that focus on methods and mechanisms for efficient transmission over wireless links, while others focus on the reliable transmission of data between computers. The vast number of protocols developed for communication at different levels and for meeting requirements of different environments led to the need to organize protocols and their functionalities methodologically. In addition to this structuring, the need to enable free competition in the development of network systems that execute protocols led to development of a standardized reference model for protocols.

As discussed in the following chapter and in the Appendix in more detail, the functionality of most computer networks is structured using the layered protocol stack as a reference model. This model was introduced as the Open System Interconnection (OSI) model [79] and is still at the core of today's Internet architecture. Each layer provides particular communication functionalities while drawing on the functionalities provided by the layer below. The architectures of network systems reflect this layered protocol architecture. The layer at which a network system operates (i.e., its placement within the network architecture) determines what functionalities need to be built into the system.

This book focuses on network systems that operate at the link layer, the network layer, the transport layer, and the application layer. Specifically, we do not consider any details of the lowest layer, the physical layer, which deals with the coding and transmission of individual bits over a medium. Interested readers are referred to the large body of work on wired and wireless communication.

ORGANIZATION OF THIS BOOK

This book discusses the architecture of network systems as a class of embedded systems, that is, systems with limited resources. The book presents system structures and architectural techniques for all types of network systems, ranging from network adapters to routers and gateways. Considering the synergy between protocols and the systems that execute them, this book presents network system architectures and design techniques where network protocols are part of the system specifications. However, we do not present new protocol concepts or protocol techniques since our focus is on systems. Instead, we consider standard protocols and explore architectural space for the development of efficient network systems that meet their performance requirements. The input to these systems is network traffic that is consistent with the protocols stated in the system specification.

This book follows a systematic approach to network systems based on the protocols they implement. Considering the large number of existing and emerging protocols defined for different purposes, we use the OSI reference model for our presentation. The OSI reference model has well-defined and well-understood layers, which match the popular Transmission Control Protocol (TCP)/Internet Protocol (IP) protocol stack as a special case, and enables us to easily identify the functionality and requirements of specific network systems. It must be stressed that adoption and use of the OSI reference model in the book does not promote or limit the presented architectures and systems to specific protocols. Rather, this approach provides a basis for a systematic classification of network systems and avoids the complexity of considering the wide landscape of protocols standardized by several bodies and groups.

The book is organized in the following three parts:

- The first part of the book, constituted by Chapters 2 and 3, addresses the types and general structure of network systems, as well as evaluation techniques for the resulting architectures and designs. Chapter 2 presents and classifies network systems on the basis of the OSI reference model and describes the general architectural structure of network systems. Chapter 3 presents the requirements placed on network systems, focusing on performance and the methods used for the evaluation of developed systems.

- The second part of the book, composed of Chapters 4 through 9, presents architectures of the types of systems defined in Chapter 2. Each chapter addresses a different class of systems, starting with link layer systems (switches) up to application layer systems. We discuss different design alternatives within each layer and how they impact the performance and functional requirements established for network systems. We also present several algorithms and data structures for the main performance-critical operations in network systems, including packet forwarding, packet classification, and payload inspection.

- The third part of the book, Chapters 10 through 15, addresses special requirements and subsystems of network systems, such as security, low power, and networks-on-chips. Chapter 10 addresses how requirements for quality of service and network security are reflected in network system designs. Chapter 11 describes network processors and other special hardware components used in network systems to achieve high-throughput performance. Chapter 12 describes architectures and techniques for subsystems of network systems, which address power issues, that is, target the execution of specific network operations, such as table lookups, optimizing for power consumption. Considering the rapid growth of networks-on-chips and the resulting inclusion of network systems in these highly integrated components, Chapter 13 presents an overview of system and technology issues that influence the design of network systems in this technology. Chapter 14 discusses software considerations from the perspective of software development for network systems and runtime management. Chapter 15 provides an outlook on emerging technologies, including network virtualization.

In addition, the Appendix provides a brief overview on common protocols used in the Internet. It focuses on Ethernet, IP, and TCP. Because many readers are likely to be familiar with these protocols, discussion on their design and implementation details is limited to this Appendix.

The specific topics covered in each chapter of this book are as follows.

- Chapter 1 introduces the motivation for this book and discusses how network systems are influenced by technologies from computer networks and embedded systems.
- Chapter 2 presents the architectural structure of network systems. We discuss how the layering of network functionality in protocol stacks relates to network systems and what the key components of a network system are.
- Chapter 3 discusses functional and performance requirements in network systems. Throughput preservation is introduced as a design paradigm and techniques for performance evaluation are presented.
- Chapter 4 introduces switching fabrics and interconnects, which are the center of any switch and router system. Interconnects provide the ability to transfer network traffic between ports of the network system. We discuss different designs and how they are able to meet performance and scalability requirements.
- Chapter 5 presents network adapters, which provide the interface between transmission medium and network system. We discuss how design alternatives for memory management in network adaptors affect system performance.
- Chapter 6 introduces bridges and switches as the first complete network system discussed in this book. This chapter focuses on system architecture, as well as bridge operation within the network.
- Chapter 7 presents topics on router design and operation. We distinguish between control path and data path and discuss different algorithms and data structures for routing and forwarding.
- Chapter 8 looks at network systems that operate at the transport layer systems, that is, those that consider individual connections and flows. We discuss algorithms and data structures for packet classification and examples of network systems that use them.
- Chapter 9 discusses network systems in the application layer. These systems process the payload of packets to provide support for application-layer functions. We discuss different content inspection algorithms that can be used to provide security in high-performance network systems.
- Chapter 10 shows how performance guarantees and security issues need to be addressed in all layers of a protocol stack and a network system. We show how link-scheduling techniques can be used to ensure fair sharing of networking resources. We also show how network protocols can be used to meet security requirements in communication.

- Chapter 11 presents specialized hardware components that can be used in network systems to meet performance requirements. The main focus of this chapter is on programmable network processors and their use in network systems.
- Chapter 12 discusses how power consumption can be addressed in network system design. We present this issue in the context of memory designs for lookups and network processors.
- Chapter 13 presents networks-on-chip, a key technology component of embedded networks systems. We discuss different design network-on-chip architectures and designs.
- Chapter 14 addresses the software aspects of network systems. Specifically, we focus on the issues of software development and run-time management.
- Chapter 15 concludes this book with an outlook on emerging network architectures and their impact on network system design. In particular, we discuss the need for programmability and how network virtualization can help in accommodating new protocols and communication paradigms.
- The Appendix provides a review of common network protocols used in the Internet and can be used as an introduction for readers who are new to those topics and as a reference for readers who are more experienced.

Overall, these topics cover the key aspects of architecture, design, implementation, and operation of network systems.

Network protocols and network systems

INTRODUCTION

The technical area of telecommunications and networking is a mature area of engineering that has experienced significant contributions for more than a century. The continuous evolution of cost-effective media, communication protocols, network designs, and network systems has led to dramatic changes in communications and networking. The effects have been particularly remarkable during the last few decades, when advances in fiber optics and high-speed transmission techniques in wire-based and wireless networks have brought significant amounts of bandwidth to users at the office, at home, or on the go, enabling a wide range of applications and services.

The technological progress of physical media, transmission methods, and communication needs over a long period has led to a rich and complex landscape of network architectures and network systems. The different engineering approaches to the problem of networking, the diverse application areas, and the quest for proprietary solutions have resulted in a large number of complex network designs that differ significantly among them. In order to reduce complexity in network design, most networks are organized in layers, where each layer represents a level of abstraction focusing on the communication/networking services it provides.

In a layered network of communicating nodes, every protocol layer of a node communicates with the equivalent protocol layer of another node. The set of rules that specify the structure and semantics of the exchanged information at a given layer is denoted as the corresponding communication (network) protocol. In an effort to minimize proprietary solutions, to create an open market in network systems, and to enable management of communications complexity, the International Organization for Standardization (ISO) has developed a reference model for open communications [78]. This reference model, called the ISO Open Systems Interconnection (OSI) Reference Model, proposes an abstract and layered model of networking. Specifically, it defines seven layers of abstraction and the functionality of each layer. However, it does not define specific protocols that must be used at every layer, but gives the concepts of service and protocol that correspond to each layer. ISO has published protocols and prototypes for every layer of the OSI reference model but these are not parts of the reference model itself.

The abstract nature of the OSI reference model is the motivation for using it as a basis in the presentation of systems in this book, although the Internet era has established the dominance of the Transmission Control Protocol (TCP)/Internet Protocol (IP) reference model. The OSI reference model is not oriented to a certain protocol set, which makes it more generic. The TCP/IP reference model became a de facto model after its protocols had been introduced. Interestingly, the TCP/IP reference model has embraced the paradigm of the OSI model, using almost direct analogies for the four lower layers and the highest layer of the OSI model and discarding the other ones. Thus, it can be considered as a special case of the OSI reference model. We discuss the TCP/IP reference model and specific details of its protocols in the Appendix.

A network system, which is the basic building block of a network, executes a protocol stack composed of protocols of a layered network architecture. Some layers are implemented in hardware modules, whereas others are implemented in software. This chapter describes the OSI reference model, gives the definition of a network system, distinguishes its various types, and presents the basic structure of a network system.

THE OPEN SYSTEMS INTERCONNECTION REFERENCE MODEL

Communicating systems execute protocols that implement the specific communication mechanisms used in the information exchange. As mentioned earlier, the protocols are organized as stacks of protocol, following the OSI reference model with up to seven layers, where each layer provides a different level of abstraction and performs a set of well-defined functions. These seven layers are as follows.

1. Physical layer: These protocols employ methods for bit transmission over physical media and include such typical functions as signal processing, timing, and encoding.
2. Data Link Control (DLC) layer: Its protocols establish point-to-point communication over a physical or logical link, performing such functions as organization of bits in data units (frames) organization, error detection, and flow control.
3. Network layer: These protocols deliver data units over a network composed of the links established through the DLC protocols of layer 2. Part of these protocols is identification of the route the data units will follow to reach their target.
4. Transport layer: Transport protocols establish end-to-end communication between end systems over the network defined by a layer 3 protocol. Often, transport layer protocols provide reliability, which refers to complete and correct data transfer between end systems. Reliability can be achieved through mechanisms for end-to-end error detection, retransmissions, and flow control.
5. Session layer: This layer enables and manages sessions for complete data exchange between end nodes. Sessions may consist of multiple transport layer connections.

6. Presentation layer: This layer is responsible for the presentation of exchanged data in formats that can be consumed by the application layer.

7. Application layer: The application layer includes protocols that implement or facilitate end-to-end distributed applications over the network.

Layer 1, the physical layer, is considered the lowest layer in the OSI reference model, and layer 7, the application layer, is considered the highest layer. It is important to note that layer 2 (DLC) of the reference model is usually considered to be divided into two sublayers: the Media Access Control (MAC) sublayer above the physical layer (layer 1) and the Logical Link Control (LLC) sublayer above the MAC sublayer. This structure of layer 2 is influenced mostly by the IEEE standardization effort for local area network (LAN) technology [66], which has specified that all compliant LANs may differ at the physical layer and MAC sublayer, but should operate under a specific protocol at the LLC sublayer; this protocol is the 801.2 LLC protocol.

The purpose of the OSI reference model has been to specify layers of protocols employed by network nodes to communicate successfully. Thus, two communicating end systems need to have implemented at least one common protocol per corresponding layer. However, communicating systems do not need to implement full seven-layer protocol stacks, as described later. The number of layers implemented in communicating system stacks is influenced by the functionality of the systems, that is, the level of abstraction they provide, depending on their goals. For example, systems that target to deliver packets between two networks do not need to implement end-to-end reliable transmission or application layer protocols because of their specified and intended functionality.

PROTOCOL STACKS AND PROTOCOL ELEMENTS

In a complete configuration, compliant with the OSI Reference Model, two communicating systems need to implement one protocol stack each, as shown in Figure 2-1. Data that need to be transmitted between systems are provided by the transmitting end system to the top protocol (layer 7 protocol) of its protocol stack. They are processed by the seven protocols of the protocol stack and then transmitted over physical media to the receiving system. The receiving system performs the protocol operations in reverse order: transmitted data are received by the physical protocol (layer 1 protocol) of the receiving stack and are processed in turn by the seven protocols of the receiving protocol stack. At the end of this process, data are delivered to the appropriate process of the receiving end system.

Considering the properties of the stacks and the protocols, as defined in the OSI Reference Model, it is easy to deduce that communication between the two systems requires both protocol stacks to have the same protocols at each layer, enabling the node-to-node communication at all layers. Any violation of the protocols, that is, any differentiation in the structure or the semantics of the exchanged

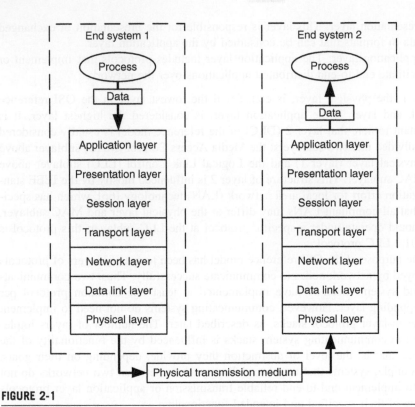

FIGURE 2-1

Node-to-node communication using the OSI Reference Model.

information, at any layer renders the correct processing of that information impossible and thus makes communication infeasible.

An important property of the OSI Reference Model is that it enables standardization of the protocols used in the protocol stacks, leading to the specification of interfaces between layers. Furthermore, an important feature of the model is the distinction it makes between specification (layers) and implementation (protocols), thus leading to openness and flexibility. Openness is the ability to develop new protocols for a particular layer and independently of other layers as network technologies evolve. Openness enables competition, leading to low-cost products. Flexibility is the ability to combine different protocols in stacks, enabling the interchange of protocols in stacks as necessary. For example, consider the stack configurations shown in Figure 2-2. Figure 2-2(a) shows a typical stack with four layers, including Transmission Control Protocol at the transport layer, Internet Protocol at the network layer, IEEE 802.2 LLC at the logical link sublayer and IEEE 802.3 (Ethernet) MAC at the MAC sublayer of the data link control layer, and IEEE 802.3 (Ethernet) at the physical layer. This stack configuration is typical in conventional enterprise end systems due to the wide adoption of Ethernet technology at end

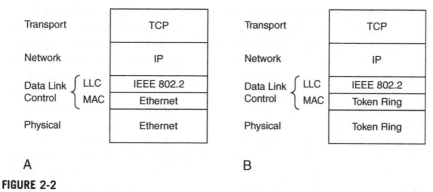

FIGURE 2-2

Typical protocol stacks.

systems and local area networks, as well as the prevalence of the TCP/IP protocol suite in the Internet. The openness of a layered reference model enables users to develop alternative protocols to the ones mentioned previously and replace them at the appropriate layer of the stack, assuming compliance of the interfaces. As the example in Figure 2-2(b) indicates, one can replace the bottom two protocols of the stack, that is, Ethernet protocols, with an alternative, for example, IEEE 802.5 Token Ring protocols, and create a functional, alternative stack.

A layered reference model for protocols enables the interconnection of heterogeneous networks, that is, end systems and networks that use different technology, through network systems, as shown in Figure 2-3. As Figure 2-3 illustrates, reliable end-to-end connectivity is typically achieved at the transport layer (layer 4), while

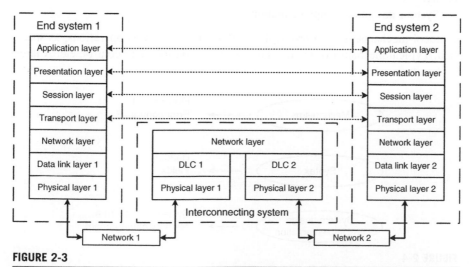

FIGURE 2-3

Protocol stacks in a network with heterogeneous links.

interconnection of networks can be established at lower layers. In Figure 2-3, an end system transmits data packets to a receiving end system traversing two different networks. The networks are interconnected through a system that implements two protocol stacks, one per network, and delivers packets of lower layer protocols between the networks. This is a typical configuration, following the layered OSI Reference model where different DLC protocols are used to establish two logical links and the network system enables the interconnection of the two links into a single network at layer 3 (network layer).

Developments in recent decades have been led by standardization efforts in communications as a follow-up of OSI models and needs of the market. Proprietary protocols and network architectures have been reducing steadily due to economic reasons, as well as the progress of LAN technology and the spread of the Internet. As a result, most of the protocols used today have been standardized, and a large number of companies build systems that provide these standardized protocols. Protocols are being standardized by several organizations, such as ISO [77], the Institute of Electrical and Electronics Engineers (IEEE) [67], and the ATM Forum [23].

Considering the standardization process and the resulting specifications, which have to be obeyed by networks and network systems, we need to specify the options of network and network system designers, which enable product differentiation and lead the definition of new network architectures and network protocols.

A systematic approach to network protocols enables us to identify that protocol implementations are composed of three elements as shown in Figure 2-4 [118]. These three elements are:

1. Mechanisms
2. Syntax
3. System design and implementation

Protocol mechanisms are a protocol's methods to perform its operations, as specified. Typical mechanisms include those for flow control, error control, etc. A large

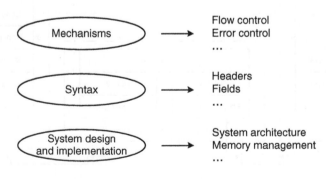

FIGURE 2-4

Protocol elements.

body of networking and communications literature is dedicated to the study of protocol mechanisms in various protocols and environments in order to identify the appropriate methods and the specification of their parameters, for example, flow control window size, rate or credit-based flow control, and CRC polynomials for error checking [35, 154]. Protocol syntax specifies the structure of packets (data units), enabling the correct interpretation of each transmitted information bit. In a packet protocol, for example, the syntax specifies the use of headers or trailers, the fields in a header or trailer, the packet size, and so on. System design and implementation refer to the structure of the system that executes the protocol itself and implements communication as defined by the protocols of the protocol stack it implements.

Standards typically define the first two protocol elements, that is, the mechanisms and the syntax of protocols. Standards do not specify the structure of the systems that implement protocols. Thus, a network system developer is able to develop any architecture and implementation one considers appropriate and will be standards-compliant as long as it implements the mechanisms defined for the protocol and follows the syntax. This is a very important observation because it enables a developer to implement any necessary function by any appropriate means (hardware or software) and to specify any structure suitable for correct execution of the protocols. Importantly, considering that network systems execute protocol stacks, the developer's ability to specify system structure is extremely valuable because it enables the development of subsystems that execute protocols of different layers and thus different levels of communication.

This systematic view of the elements enables us not only to identify the areas where system designers can contribute, but also to research more efficient protocols and network architectures. A clear direction for research is the development of new mechanisms for protocols, which exploit the characteristics of new technologies as they appear. The adoption of reliable fiber-optic media, for example, can be exploited by protocols with new mechanisms that take into account the low bit error rates—developing new error control mechanisms—and the high bandwidth (e.g., DWDM) through use of new more efficient flow control mechanisms. Another direction is development of a new protocol syntax that enables more efficient protocol processing as, for example, proposed in the Xpress Transport Protocol (XTP) protocol [172], which is designed to overcome some shortcomings in the widely used TCP. Finally, a clear research direction is the development of new architectures and designs for network systems, especially since they are not influenced by the protocol standardization efforts, giving many options to network system developers.

NETWORK SYSTEMS: DEFINITION AND TYPES

Network systems are computational systems that implement connectivity among networks or between a network and an end system. In general, a network system is a system attached to two or more communication links, wired or wireless.

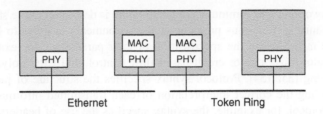

FIGURE 2-5

Layer 2 interconnection of different layer 1 networks.

Each communication link is associated with a network architecture and thus with a related protocol stack, as shown in Figure 2-5. As Figure 2-5 indicates, the goal of such a network system is to deliver information from one communication link to another, implementing connectivity among networks. In this view, a network system executes a set of protocol stacks, one associated with each attached link, and delivers data among appropriate stacks. Based on the discussion earlier, we will employ the following definition: a network system is a computational system that executes protocol stacks and switches data among the protocol stacks. Clearly, this definition covers all network systems used to interconnect networks. In addition, we include in our definition a computational system that executes a single protocol stack; this boundary case for our generic definition covers the case of end-system network adapters that deliver transmitted data between an end-user system and a network.

Network systems are classified according to the size of the stacks they implement and switch data among. Before presenting this classification, two important issues need to be clarified.

1. Protocol stacks in a network system can have any size (i.e., one up to seven layers), but all stacks in a single system need to have the same size, as their highest layer is the same.
2. The protocol of the highest layer needs to be the same for the stacks among which data are switched.

The first issue is important to emphasize so that a network system architect knows that networks can be interconnected at all available layers of the OSI Reference Model. For example, Ethernet standards define a maximum length for the coaxial cables that can be used; if one wants to connect two such cables to create a longer network (basically, a longer cable), the standard allows that and a network system needs to be used to interconnect the two cables. This network system will implement functionality defined in the physical protocol of Ethernet, that is, it will implement a stack with size equal to one layer (to be precise, it will not even implement the whole physical protocol but a subset of it; however, this is consistent with our layer-based view and definitions). The decision to use such a network system is feasible because the two cables are Ethernet networks, that is, homogeneous networks. If they were heterogeneous networks, though, for example, an Ethernet and a Token Ring, such a network system could not be designed to interconnect the networks at the physical layer because their protocols are not consistent. In that case, the network system would need to implement stacks with more layers per stack (two or more), as shown in Figure 2-6.

When data are switched between two stacks, as shown in Figure 2-6, data are produced by the protocol at the highest layer of one stack and consumed by the highest layer of the receiving stack. These data must have semantics that is understood by both protocols, leading to the requirement that these two protocols have to be the same protocol. If the protocol is exactly the same, for example, IP in an IP router, then data can be switched among stacks directly without any processing related to protocol conversion. However, some network systems exist where the highest layer protocols are not exactly the same in all stacks. In that case, data conversion is necessary in order to make data meaningful to each stack. This is achievable only for protocols of the same layer, although considering the functionality of the layers and thus, data are switched among protocols of the same stack layer, for example, routing protocols of layer 3, or MAC protocols of layer 2, and so on. This leads to the consideration that all stacks in a network system have the same size, that is, number of protocol layers; however, the heterogeneity of some protocol stacks, which do not have a one-to-one correspondence to the OSI reference model, may lead to stack size differences. For simplicity, we assume that all protocol stacks of a network system have the same size, unless explicitly stated.

Network systems are classified and named according to the layer of the top protocol in the protocol stacks, that is, the layer of the protocol at which data are

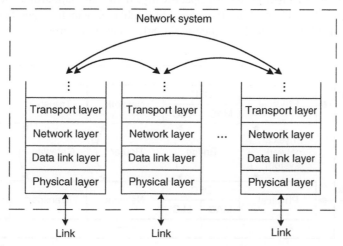

FIGURE 2-6

Switching of data between network stacks in network system.

switched among the stacks. Specifically, typical classification and naming of network systems are as follows:

1. Physical network systems: systems that switch data among physical layer protocols
2. Bridges: systems that switch data among stacks at the DLC layer
3. Routers: systems that switch data among stacks at the network layer
4. Gateways: systems that switch data among stacks at the transport layer or a higher layer

Figure 2-7 illustrates the operation of network systems in reference to the OSI Reference Model stacks, using two stacks.

Physical network systems cover a wide range of devices, which transfer data among physical layer protocols. Considering the rich set of media used, including air, twisted copper wires, coaxial cables, and fiber links, as well as the transmission methods employed by existing protocols, physical network devices implement a variety of functions, ranging from signal amplification to bit encoding. Examples of these systems include repeaters, amplifiers, multiplexers, and hubs.

Bridges are network systems that switch DLC layer data among stacks. Although previous definitions led to the concept of a bridge switching packets among DLC protocols, as defined by the OSI Reference Model, this is not the case in most existing bridges. Most conventional bridges actually switch packets over the MAC sublayer of the DLC layer due to the way LAN protocols have evolved, especially through the IEEE standardization effort [66]. As mentioned previously, the Data Link Control layer (layer 2) is divided into two sublayers: the Media Access Control sublayer and the Logical Link Control sublayer. This division of layer 2 was introduced and adopted by IEEE in an effort to provide a unified framework for the standardization of link layer protocols. Specifically, IEEE has standardized a protocol, 801.2 Logical Link Control, for the logical link sublayer, which is specified to operate above all MAC protocols defined in the 801.x family of protocols. This family

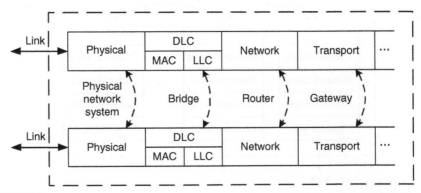

FIGURE 2-7

Network system classification.

includes all popular MAC protocols, ranging from the traditional Ethernet and Token Ring to wireless LAN (WLAN), hybrid fiber-coax (HFC), and Worldwide Interoperability for Microwave Access (WiMAX). Because all such MAC protocols are specified to operate under 801.2 LLC, they provide a normalized interface to LLC and thus data can be switched easily and efficiently among MAC protocols without making it necessary to switch layer 2 data over LLC. These bridges, known as MAC bridges, constitute the main thrust of bridging architecture.

Routers are well-known network systems, especially due to the wide adoption of the Internet. Clearly, the best-known concept is that of the IP router, as IP is the protocol used by the Internet. Routers exist for several other protocols as well, considering the legacy systems and networks that are deployed today. Importantly, the main operation of routers is the same as in IP routers.

The term gateway is used to describe a large number of network systems, as it refers to systems that switch data among protocols of layers 4 through 7.

In addition to the systems mentioned earlier, network systems exist that have limited functionality and are denoted using different terminology. The most widespread of these systems are layer 2 switches and IP switches. Layer 2 switches switch MAC layer data units without a bridging protocol, as described in Chapter 6. IP switches perform IP routing (layer 3) functions but switch data at a lower layer, exploiting Asynchronous Transfer Mode (ATM) switching technology (corresponding to layer 2). Furthermore, systems exist that provide combined functionality: brouters (from bridge/routers) combine bridging and routing functionality in one system.

Finally, network systems include network adapters, that is, network attachments of end systems. Network adapters implement stacks so that end systems can connect to networks and communicate with other end systems over the network(s).

STRUCTURE OF NETWORK SYSTEMS

Network systems implement protocol stacks and switch data units among them. As such, network systems need to include memory for data storage, processing power for protocol processing, and link interface(s) for attachment to network links. This indicates that network systems are computational systems with subsystems analogous to those of a typical computing system: processing element, memory, and an input/output (I/O) subsystem for the link attachment.

The simplest network system is the network adapter, as it implements a single protocol stack. Considering the requirements mentioned previously, the structure of a typical network adapter is illustrated in Figure 2-8. The adapter includes a processor, memory, and two I/O subsystems, one for attachment to the network link and one for the appropriate bus of the end system. It is important to note here that in typical adapters the link attachment subsystem is composed of circuitry that implements the physical and the MAC sublayers of the corresponding DLC protocol. For example, if one builds an Ethernet adapter, the basic hardware component

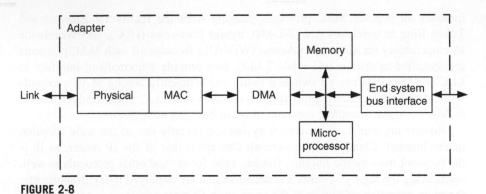

FIGURE 2-8

Typical network adapter structure.

used as the link attachment implements the Ethernet physical and MAC protocols. This is due to the fact that physical protocols require significant signal processing, which is typically implemented in hardware that often integrates the analog components required for signal transmission and reception. Furthermore, because MAC protocols group data in meaningful data units for higher level processing and often implement protocols with demanding performance requirements, they are also implemented in hardware, providing to system designers a straightforward byte-level or word-level interface, exchanging MAC data units with the remainder of the system. Given that the requirements and functionality of physical and MAC protocols differ significantly from higher layer protocol requirements and functionality, we always consider in our architectural descriptions and analyses that link attachments are designed with components that implement physical and MAC protocols at the I/O subsystem of adapters and network systems, similar to the structure of Figure 2-8.

The adapter illustrated in Figure 2-8 constitutes a typical computational system, which performs computations on data delivered to and from its two interfaces with the end system and the network link. Its operation is simple in general. When receiving data from the network, the I/O link subsystem executes the physical and MAC protocols and produces packets that are delivered to the adapter's memory. The packets are processed by the processor, which executes the remainder of the protocol stack, and the resulting data are delivered to the end system. Data transmitted to the network follow the reverse path, being delivered to the adapter memory, processed by the protocol stack up to the point where MAC packets (frames) are produced, and then delivered to the link attachment subsystem, which executes the MAC and physical protocol and transmits data on the link. Apparently, the architecture of the adapter can and should employ computer architecture techniques and methods to result in an efficient, low-cost system; such techniques include memory management units and direct memory access subsystems, as discussed in subsequent chapters.

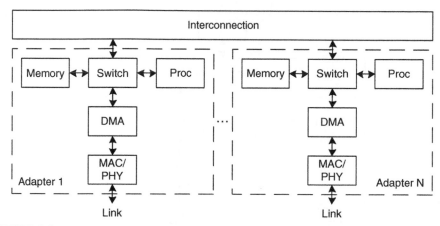

FIGURE 2-9

Simple network system architecture.

Considering the definition of network systems as systems that switch data units among protocol stacks, one can easily develop a network system employing the adapter architecture of Figure 2-8. Figure 2-9 illustrates a simple network system structure, which employs one network adapter per protocol stack of the network system. As Figure 2-9 shows, one can use a set of adapters, one per attached network, and interconnect them through a backplane interconnection, providing a system that is functional, flexible, and scalable if implemented appropriately. Specifically, the structure of the network system maps directly to the system's functionality: an incoming packet is processed by the protocol stack of the receiving adapter and then is delivered over the backplane to the adapter of the transmitting network where it is processed by the protocol stack of that adapter and placed on the attached network link. Because of its simplicity, this simple architecture has been a basic architecture of the first generation of network systems. A typical router architecture, for example, has been developed using a personal computer (PC) with several network adapters—one per connected network. In that architecture, adapters implement the lower layers of protocol stacks, while the main processor of the PC executes the higher layers of the protocol stacks for all stacks and performs data packet switching.

The backplane of the network system can be any appropriate interconnection network: a bus, a crossbar switch, or a multistage interconnection network [190]. The decision is made based on performance requirements, scalability, and cost.

The architecture shown in Figure 2-9 is the architecture of a multiprocessing system with multiple processing elements, distributed memory, and I/O subsystems (the link attachments). More specifically, based on its structure and operation description, the architecture can be classified as a message-passing multiprocessor, where each processor has its own memory space and messages are the exchanged packets. When viewing the network system as a multiprocessor, a system architect

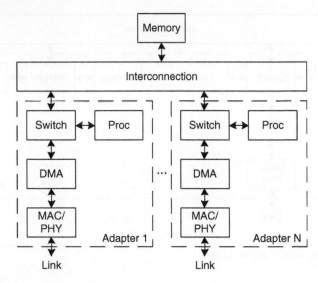

FIGURE 2-10

Shared memory architecture for network systems.

can exploit multiprocessor architecture and design techniques to develop alternative structures, which may provide benefits in several configurations. Such an alternative architecture is shown in Figure 2-10, where a shared memory multiprocessor architecture is employed.

Shared memory architecture employs a centralized memory, shared by all network attachments to store packets and by all processors to execute protocols. This architecture provides several benefits over the previous one. Data packets are stored once in the system and are kept in place before transmission, while in the distributed memory architecture each packet needs to be stored twice, once in the receiving adapter and once in the transmitting adapter. This shared memory architecture leads to more efficient use of memory and to lower packet delay in the system. Clearly, one can develop several alternatives to these two architectures, employing concepts and methods from multiprocessor architecture and design.

SUMMARY

This chapter reviewed the OSI reference model and related protocol stacks. Subsequently, we defined the functionality and the terminology of network systems. We introduced the basic architecture of network systems, including adapters, establishing their need and suitability for advanced computer architecture techniques. Our view of network systems as multiprocessor systems, in general, establishes a basis for the development of more sophisticated architectures, as described in following chapters.

Requirements of network systems

INTRODUCTION

Network systems are embedded, special-purpose computational systems that implement one or more protocol stacks. The set of network systems in a network configuration constitutes the infrastructure over which end systems communicate to implement distributed applications. Thus, network systems need to meet the requirements set by these applications. Similarly, network systems may need to meet requirements set forth by network operators. Due to the diverse needs of emerging network applications and services and operational concerns, requirements for network systems span a range of issues and parameters from performance to cost and power consumption. In general, these requirements can be divided into functional requirements and performance requirements.

To determine if network systems meet their requirements, it is necessary to have suitable evaluation methods. To verify that functional requirements are met, the operation of a network system can simply be compared to protocol standards (e.g., using test cases). To verify that performance requirements are met, a variety of performance evaluation techniques are used. Performance evaluation of network systems requires specification of appropriate parameters to be measured, as well as development of suitable evaluation methods. For example, in network systems, when one measures performance at the application layer, one has to account for bandwidth loss due to protocol overhead (packet headers, control packets, etc.) as well as for protocol processing overhead.

Computational systems, in general, have several parameters that characterize their performance and functionality. The general approach to evaluating a computational system is to evaluate either the parameters of its architecture, design, and implementation, such as clock rates, memory sizes, and bus widths, or the operation and performance of the system for the execution of a *typical* application. This latter approach provides more valuable information, considering that it captures the characteristics and performance of all subsystems, including their overall interaction. In this direction, typical applications are considered either benchmarks (real, synthetic, or combined code) or model-based operations, taking into account models that are assumed to capture the operational characteristics of applications.

This chapter presents the different types of network applications, the requirements they place upon network systems, and how these requirements influence the underlying protocol stacks. Additionally, we describe how protocol layers reduce the provided physical link bandwidth. Finally, we describe methods for network system performance evaluation and the tools used for that.

REQUIREMENTS OF NETWORK APPLICATIONS AND SERVICES

Network systems implement protocol stacks, as explained in detail in Chapter 2. The functional specifications of network systems seem fairly easy to define, as network systems implement protocol stacks: one needs to define the size of the stack(s), the protocols of each stack, and the performance characteristics of the network links used. Given our approach to consider standardized protocols, the specification of stacks and protocols is easily deduced from the corresponding standards.

The performance specification of a network system is driven by the needs of the parties involved in data communication: end-system applications, users, and network operators. For example, network applications and services often deliver data to a human interface (e.g., telephony, TV, and multimedia applications). In these cases, special parameters have to be taken into account in order to enable application and service delivery to humans with appropriate *quality* so that the service is acceptable to the user.

Communications and networking have evolved in a (relatively) small number of years from telephony to broadband services. Originally, telephone networks dictated the development of circuit-switched networks, which establish end-to-end connections (circuits) before voice communication takes place. These networks require a significant amount of resources, for example, bandwidth and switching, which are allocated per call (per connection). The high cost of the original approaches to implement circuit switching was one of the main reasons that led to the development of packet-based networks. Packet-switched networks transfer packets independently through the networks and implement applications and services of all types, including those that are traditionally connection oriented (e.g., voice and video). An example of a packetized network is Asynchronous Transfer Mode (ATM) technology, which uses packets as primary data units transmitted in the network and can deliver all types of applications and services, real time or nonreal time [39]. Considering the progress of packet switching technologies and the development and adoption of Internet Protocol (IP)-based real-time applications, such as IP telephony [64] and IP TV [167], we consider only packet switching networks for the rest of this chapter, as we do for the whole book. Thus, when considering real-time applications, such as telephone services, we assume a packet network.

The two facets of network systems, that is, the engineering side as well as the quality of the delivered services, allow us to classify the requirements of network applications and of network systems in two categories: functionality (qualitative) and performance (quantitative).

Qualitative requirements

Qualitative parameters capture the characteristics of the network overall rather than the network systems themselves, as they include clients, servers, switches, and other network systems as well as links. Thus, they are considered as network characteristics overall. Characteristic qualitative parameters include correct operation, work conservation, in-order packet delivery, graceful degradation, etc. Correct operation implies that the network behaves as expected and as specified by the protocol of the application/service it executes; furthermore, it implies that the network can handle any type of valid traffic data. The network needs to be work conserving, avoiding loss of data or augmentation of work in the network. In terms of human users, as well as applications, data packets may need to be delivered to the receiver in order (i.e., without reordering the packet sequence sent by the sender); this property is a critical characteristic of the vast majority of applications and services. Finally, graceful degradation is an important requirement that leads to systems and users perceiving gradual degradation of network performance under load. That is, the network exhibits a gradual "slow down," as traffic increases or system components fail, but avoids a collapse of services and systems; graceful degradation is an important characteristic to ensure service acceptance and use.

Quantitative requirements

Qualitative characteristics of network applications and services can be described with combinations of quantitative parameters, such as admission control (the acceptance of connections or packets in the network), fault tolerance (the ability to continue operation despite component or link failures), out-of-order statistics (the number of packets that arrive in different order than the one sent), and so forth. Clearly, these parameters are not sufficient and, although useful, do not provide a clear description of the characteristics of the network and its services. In contrast, there are quantitative parameters of high interest and importance because they influence services in a direct fashion and constitute fundamental requirements of services in the sense that their lack leads to an inability to provide the necessary services provisioning. These quantitative parameters include throughput, delay, jitter, and packet loss.

Throughput is a parameter that measures completion rates of fundamental data units and has been used in a wide range of measurements for various systems, for example, bits per second in links, packets per second in interconnections, and instructions per second in processors. The important issue related to throughput is that it is analogous to bandwidth, with the only difference that it refers to effective bandwidth rather than aggregate. In the case of links, for example, bandwidth is measured in bits per second counting all transmitted bits, while throughput may be measured also in bits per second, but counting only the bits that are delivered successfully to the application or a protocol at a specified layer; thus, throughput measures the fraction of the bandwidth that is offered to the application or to a layer of the protocol stack, as a fraction of the bandwidth is used by protocol control information, etc.

Network delay is the time latency to deliver a unit of data over a link or a network. Delay is composed of four components: (i) transmission delay, that is, the delay to transmit (insert) the data unit in the network; (ii) propagation delay along the path; (iii) switching delays by the network systems along the path; and (iv) queuing delays at the intermediate network systems due to traffic load and destination conflicts among the data units (packets) transmitted by different sources over the network simultaneously. When considering network services and applications, though, it is important to note that application performance is affected not only by network delay as defined previously, but by additional delay as well, such as network control delays, necessary for network configuration or reconfiguration in light of a change, and application execution delays at end systems [56].

Network jitter is the fluctuation (variation) of delay; typically, it is due to fluctuations in queuing and scheduling delays at network systems across network paths [56]. Finally, packet loss is the measurement of packets that are lost in transmission, that is, they are transmitted but never received. There are several causes for packet loss, mainly network congestion, transmission errors, and network system failures [56].

Example requirements

Practical applications and services are affected by several parameters overall. Table 3-1 lists a set of applications, including interactive and noninteractive, as well as real-time and nonreal-time ones. Applications are listed as rows of the table, while columns show quantitative parameters and their influence on each application. Clearly, popular services are influenced by all parameters to a larger or smaller degree.

Table 3-1 Network Services and Quantitative Parameters

Application	Throughput	Delay	Jitter	Packet loss
Internet browsing	Low	Large	Insensitive	Unacceptable
Scientific data archiving	High	Medium	Indifferent	Unacceptable
Telephony	Low	Minimal	Sensitive	Low
Internet TV	High	Minimal	Sensitive	Low
First-person shooter game	Low	Minimal	Very sensitive	Unacceptable
Real-time surgery	High	Minimal	Very sensitive	Unacceptable
Delay-tolerant networking	Low	Large	Insensitive	Acceptable

Qualitative and the quantitative parameters need to be supported by both protocols and network system implementations. Often, the main target for the provision of appropriate performance characteristics has been the development of appropriate protocols that enable the delivery of appropriate applications. For example, traditionally, a significant problem targeted by the networking community has been the provision of voice and video services over packet switching networks; this major issue has been addressed in ATM networks, for example, in the last couple of decades [120]. Additionally, one can meet these requirements through efficient design and implementation of the network systems that execute protocols. Importantly, requirements at the network system must be met carefully by their architects and designers. Consider, for example, a network supporting voice services, which have strong real-time requirements in terms of delay, jitter, and data loss. Even if protocols address all these parameters appropriately, the network needs to employ network systems that are designed in such a way that the strict requirements are supported and delivered to the application level. It is impossible, for example, to execute a delay-bounding protocol on a system that does not or cannot provide bounds on delays for processes and protocol execution.

THE THROUGHPUT PRESERVATION CHALLENGE

Ultimately, network systems enable the end-to-end delivery of application data, that is, from one end system to another. Applications running atop network layers define the requirements for an acceptable user experience: throughput, delay, jitter, and packet loss can severely affect this experience. Importantly, protocols of the stacks implemented in network systems add extra information to the application data due to packet headers and trailers. The sum of application and protocol-related data has to be transmitted over physical media, leaving a fraction of the link bandwidth to actual application data, as Figure 3-1 depicts. Furthermore, additional overhead is added due to protocol processing, packet queuing, and control interaction among protocols in a stack. Thus, the throughput preservation problem is "to preserve the high bandwidth of a communication link through the various protocols layers to an application" [118].

Throughput preservation is an important topic in network design. It is not sufficient to address it in a specific layer but rather it involves engineering solutions in all layers, including cross-layer system optimization in order to retain the high speed of the communication link up to the application layer. It is important to note that throughput preservation may involve meeting requirements of real-time and non-real-time applications and service, both concurrently and independently. That is, a network system may be engineered for meeting only real-time service requirements while another system may be engineered to satisfy requirements of mostly non-real-time applications.

Advances in communication technologies in recent years demonstrate that the speed of processors has not caught up with the speed of links and that the speed

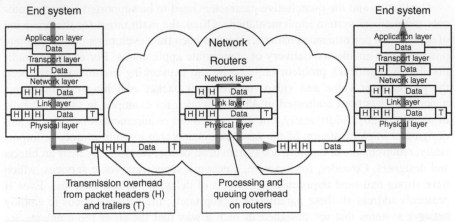

FIGURE 3-1

Traffic flow through network systems and protocol layers.

increase rate of links is still higher than that of processors [97, 113, 118]. This means that even a generous resource overprovisioning strategy cannot easily achieve scalability and preserve throughput from high-speed links up to the applications. Thus, careful system design and clever engineering approaches must be exploited to preserve the throughput with a fractional cost leading to high-performance network systems capable of coping with high-speed network links.

Network throughput can be measured by two metrics: bits per second (or bytes per second) and packets per second. The most appropriate metric in each scenario depends on the nature of the application and the network layer under examination. For example, a file transfer application usually measures throughput in average bytes per second in order to derive how much time it takes a file to reach a destination. However, real-time applications, such as IP telephony, are mostly interested in packets per second throughput, where each packet contains some milliseconds' worth of voice. Such applications require a steady packet delivery rate in order to present a continuous stream of human voice.

A network system consists of several internal components that need to interact when handling network traffic. We briefly discuss the operation of an example network system to illustrate how network system design can impact the throughput needed to meet performance requirements. A generic model of a processing system for networks includes at least four components, as Figure 3-2 depicts:

1. A link adapter, through which packets are sent and received to/from the network.
2. A processor or microprocessor, executing a set of network protocols (and possibly end-user applications).
3. A memory unit, for storing information, including network packets.
4. A Direct Memory Access (DMA) unit, responsible for transferring data to/from the link adapter.

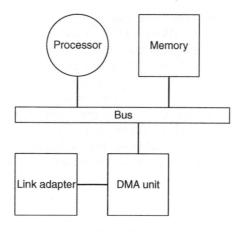

FIGURE 3-2

Generic adapter architecture.

The flow of events for packet reception from the network is as follows:

- A packet is received from the link adapter.
- An interrupt is issued to the processor, which results in a task switch.
- A DMA operation transfers the packet to the main memory.
- The processor performs a set of memory operations for queuing the packet for later processing by the various network protocols.
- The processor switches back to the task it was executing before the interrupt occurred.

Clearly, the sequential flow of events results in delays; the more network layers the system implements, the more delays that are introduced. Memory management is identified as the first and most significant bottleneck in a network system [118]. Two factors affect network protocol processing costs: per packet and per byte. The first factor refers to costs for processing a packet independently of size; these are mostly functions related to packet header processing, such as address lookup and header checksum checks. The second factor refers to costs for processing each byte of a packet; these are mostly related to memory operations, such as moving data to/from the adapter and deep inspecting its contents (also see Chapter 5). These costs differ among protocols, and the dominant factor may be either one of the aforementioned, depending on the operations and the packet size; for example, cyclic redundancy check (CRC) operations on long packets are very expensive, leading to high cost per byte, whereas packet costs are the dominating factor in networks with short, fixed-size packets.

The sequence of events sets an upper limit on the number of packets and bytes the system can process in a given amount of time. Smaller packets can reach the application more quickly due to smaller per-byte costs. However, smaller packets result in more packets per second for a specific amount of information. This can slow down the system due to larger amounts of per-packet processing and thus introduce delays.

An example of this behavior is the case of 1-Gbps Ethernet links. The typical maximum transmission unit (MTU) for Ethernet frames is 1500 bytes. This means that a system to preserve throughput must be able to fully process one frame every 12 ms; as we increase link bandwidth or add more links to the system, these numbers become prohibitive for current processor capabilities. However, should we allow the MTU to increase to 9000 bytes, as in the case of so-called "jumbo frames," then the same system must process one frame every 72 ms. The combination of per-byte and per-packet costs on each layer sets an interesting trade-off that the network designer must address. The following chapters explore how we can achieve higher performance in all layers, up to the application, and thus preserve the throughput.

TRAFFIC MODELS AND BENCHMARKS

To determine if network systems meet qualitative and quantitative requirements, several evaluation techniques are used. Evaluation of network systems is performed with the typical methodologies for performance evaluation of computational systems at the corresponding level of abstraction. Analysis and simulation are used for architectures and designs, whereas measurements are performed for real, implemented systems. A significant question in all methods and at all levels of abstraction is regarding the *traffic* or *application* used for the evaluation. For example, when evaluating the architecture of a switch, what is the best traffic to consider?

Evaluation in networking is often based on analytical techniques developed for evaluating protocols and networks under various theoretical traffic scenarios. In contrast, evaluation of networks and systems using real traffic traces is less common, as only few trace files are widely available (e.g., from National Laboratory for Applied Network Research [115]). Drawing an analogy to classical evaluation of computational systems, we deduce that, in networking, evaluation is performed mostly with theoretical traffic models that have been developed in an effort to capture generic characteristics of various applications; importantly, commonly used benchmarks do not exist or at least are not widely available. Considering the models that exist in the literature for capturing characteristics of real applications, we do not discuss such models further. Architects and developers can choose among several traffic models to evaluate their systems, identifying the model that best approximates the targeted applications.

Importantly, developments in embedded computing systems and the need for effective evaluation methods have led to significant steps in the establishment of widely accepted, and hopefully standardized eventually, benchmarks. The Embedded Microprocessor Benchmark Consortium (EEMBC) [49] leads an effort to establish and promote benchmarks that enable system developers to choose the appropriate embedded microprocessor for their designs. Considering the dramatically different characteristics and requirements of network services, as shown also in Table 3-1, EEMBC partitions the benchmarks and scores in application areas, such as automotive, consumer, entertainment, telecom, networking, office automation, etc. Networking constitutes a significant component of the EEMBC benchmark suite. Specifically, it includes benchmarks for the most critical network applications where embedded microprocessors are typically used: IP packet processing, IP packet reassembly, IP network address translation, route lookup, OSPF protocol, quality of service (traffic shaping), and Transmission Control Protocol (TCP) execution [50]. The EEMBC efforts seem to be influenced by target environments where Ethernet and TCP/IP technology prevail. Clearly, these technologies are so widespread that they cover a significant majority of network systems, such as network adapters, routers, etc. However, they definitely do not cover all network protocols and applications and they need to be augmented. Importantly though, the telecom benchmarks of EEMBC enable evaluation of end network systems, such as mobile phones, etc.

The focus of existing efforts on microprocessors is part of the work needed to develop benchmarks for networking, as there is a need for benchmarks for other components as well, such as memory managers, switching fabrics, schedulers, etc. Benchmarking efforts are still in their first steps, but constitute a significant direction for the future, where a wider range of real traffic data is necessary for the development and evaluation of real network systems.

SUMMARY

Network systems are special-purpose embedded systems addressing requirements of networks and related services and applications. The wide range of services developed and envisioned for future networks include data transmissions, telephony, video services, and so forth. These applications and services place significant requirements on network systems, both quantitative and qualitative. Furthermore, these requirements must be satisfied in a demanding context with practical constraints that include low cost, low power consumption, configurability, and manageability.

This chapter identified the requirements on network systems, which are placed for a range of services, including real-time and non-real-time, human oriented, or automated. We have associated these parameters with the driving problem of performance preservation through protocol layers, and we have discussed the need for traffic models and benchmarks for evaluating the performance of current network systems.

Interconnects and switching fabrics

INTRODUCTION

Network systems and computing systems employ interconnections to deliver data among their components. In computing systems, an interconnection is necessary to enable data transfer among the processor, the memory system, and input and output (I/O) subsystems. This use of interconnects is common for all computing systems, including network systems. The design of interconnects has a big impact on the performance and functionality of network systems. Therefore, interconnects are an important aspect of network system architecture.

The most typical interconnection for component communication is the well-known bus, which is composed of a set of wires delivering data, address information, and control information (e.g., timing, arbitration). Busses are shared interconnections among a number of attached components, implementing a point-to-point communication path between any two components. The typical operation of a bus is as follows: components that need to transmit information to another component request access to the bus, an arbiter selects the component that will transmit (in case of several requests), and then the selected component transmits its data. Considering the operation of the bus, it is clear that all data transmissions among the components of the system are multiplexed over the bus. This multiplexing may delay some communications over the bus and limits the aggregate system throughput to the peak throughput of the bus. Despite these drawbacks, busses are quite simple and have significantly lower cost relative to alternatives; this is the key to their success and wide adoption in systems to date. Furthermore, their peak throughput has increased significantly, reaching gigabits per second in the last couple of decades, as conventional bus technologies demonstrate (e.g., PCI [165], VME [80]).

The high peak throughput and low cost of busses make them good candidates for the interconnection of components in low-cost systems and in systems that have low data traffic requirements among their components. These characteristics constitute the motivation that has made bus-based architectures also attractive in the first generations of networks, especially the first generations of local area networks (LANs) and metropolitan area networks (MANs). LAN architectures, such as Ethernet [75], token ring [73], and token bus [68], as well as MAN architectures such as FDDI [150] and DQDB [72], employ shared media, with low cost and high peak performance analogous to system busses. They are useful and successful in environments where traffic requirements are such that the multiplexing of all traffic over the single medium leads to acceptable delays and throughput per connected user or system. However, the increasing requirements for low latency point-to-point communication and for high throughput lead to a need for multiple concurrent interconnections among pairs of communicating components or systems.

Switches and networks of switches constitute alternative interconnections to busses, implementing parallel, nonconflicting paths among communicating components and systems. Figure 4-1(a) shows a switch with N inputs and N outputs, employing a typical architecture to implement input-to-output connections dynamically. This switch, able to implement any combination of N parallel, nonconflicting input-to-output connections, is called a crossbar switch and constitutes the building block of several switch-based networks. Figure 4-1(b) shows a network of switches, composed of crossbar switches and employing a mesh topology, which is able to achieve several paths of communication in parallel and in contrast to shared media networks.

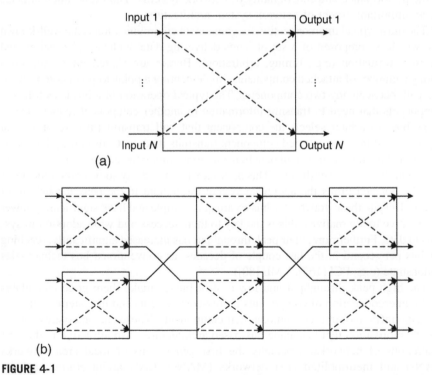

(a)

(b)

FIGURE 4-1

Crossbar switch and mesh network of crossbar switches.

Crossbar switches can employ any transmission link technology and are thus useful in several environments. An interesting and important use of crossbar switches emerged soon after it was realized that shared media LANs were not sufficient for emerging applications that require high point-to-point throughput and low latency. In that case, crossbar switches emerged that used LANs as their links. In environments with structured deployed cabling for specific LANs, most commonly Ethernet, switches were inserted, reducing traffic conflicts and enabling high-speed switching among systems, as shown in Figure 4-2; this was the first generation of LAN switches. Also, new network technologies that employ switches were developed for various environments and applications; these technologies and related protocols include ATM [103], Fiber Channel [89], and InfiniBand [164]. Importantly, switches emerged not only for networks but for intersystem interconnection as well. For example, the evolution of multi-core processors led to the employment of interconnection networks (multiple data paths) of various types, such as switch interconnects, HyperTransport [179], and multiple networks, such as the EiB of the Cell BE [27]. Furthermore, switched backplanes are introduced for network systems, such as routers [31, 180, 181].

This chapter focuses on switches and analyzes their architecture, their requirements for scheduling, and their performance. We consider ATM as the driving network technology for switches because it is an important switched network technology employed in LANs, MANs, and WANs and because it captures the characteristics of several switches in computing systems due to its cell-based operation, where all cells have equal size. First, we describe switches and interconnection networks and then we present the main switch organizations. We focus on structures with multiple input queues and analyze the scheduling problem that

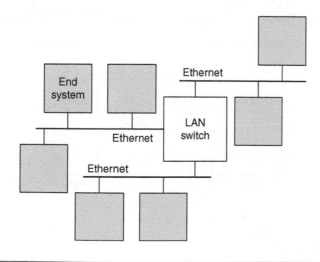

FIGURE 4-2

Local area network (layer-2) switches.

emerges. Finally, we address the issue of randomization in switch scheduling, which is an important tool to not only achieve high performance, but to enable analysis of switches and networks as well.

CROSSBARS AND INTERCONNECTION NETWORKS

Crossbar switches are designed to implement all permutations of connections among inputs and outputs. Crossbars constitute an important component of emerging interconnections among system components and in networks of all types: local, metropolitan, and wide area. Their ability to establish multiple parallel data paths makes them attractive building blocks for high-performance interconnections and networks. However, the high design complexity of crossbars limits their scalability in size, that is, the number of input and output terminals they interconnect. Thus, networks of crossbars are employed to interconnect a large number of terminals and also when longer distances have to be accommodated.

The basic crossbar switch was originally developed for interconnection networks of multiprocessors. It is a 2×2 buffer-less switch, which was named crossbar because it could be in one of two states, cross or bar, as shown in Figure 4-3(a). The concept of crossbar switching was extended to switches of larger sizes as well, where switches implement any input-to-output permutation with more inputs and outputs. The design of a crossbar switch is simple but expensive, in terms of resources, as it has to

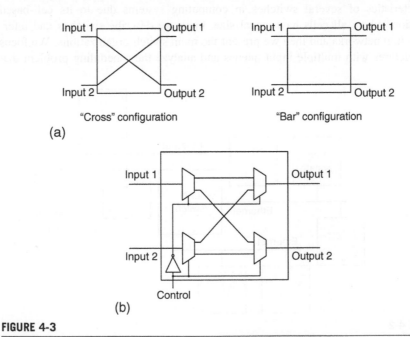

(a)

(b)

FIGURE 4-3

(a) Crossbar switch states. (b) Typical design of crossbar switch.

implement all potential permutations of inputs to outputs. A typical design of a crossbar switch is shown in Figure 4-3(b), which shows a Register Transfer Level design. This crossbar design can be and has been implemented in various technologies, including specialized VLSI implementations with Domino logic.

The high cost of crossbar switches, growing as $O(N^2)$, where N is the number of switch terminals, as well as the need to interconnect physically separated systems over variable distances, has led to the development of networks of crossbar switches. These networks employ various topologies, each offering different characteristics in terms of ease of routing, node connectivity, fault tolerance, etc. Thus, these interconnection networks are efficient for different communication patterns and thus are preferable for specific classes of applications and services. Figure 4-4 shows two characteristic interconnection networks: a mesh and a

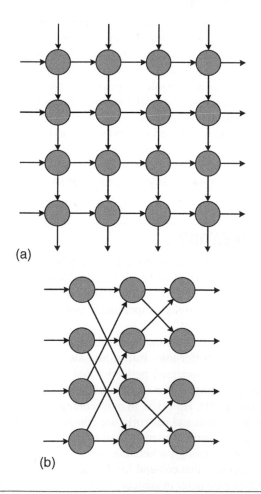

(a)

(b)

FIGURE 4-4

Interconnection networks: (a) mesh and (b) butterfly.

butterfly interconnection. Interconnection networks such as the butterfly, Omega, and other similar networks are commonly used in multiprocessors and backplanes of systems that are in physical proximity and enable uniformity in link lengths; furthermore, their regular structure enables their efficient use in exploiting parallelism of applications and thus are attractive for use in parallel processing systems in general. The main characteristic of networks such as the ones shown in Figure 4-4 is their ability to establish and exploit parallel active paths between several pairs of communicating parties. However, not all combinations of parallel active paths are feasible, as in the case of the crossbar switch or a fully connected network. Analysis of such interconnection networks is beyond the scope of this book and thus we focus on switches in the remaining part of the chapter. The interested reader can find several fairly complete presentations of interconnection networks in the literature [37, 45].

Crossbar switches are attractive for a wide range of network systems because many systems require a modest number of link attachments, either in switched networks or within network systems interconnecting components. Crossbar switches with a modest number of inputs and outputs, for example, 8 to 64 inputs and outputs, have reasonable cost and enable all possible input-to-output connections in parallel, enabling exploitation of parallelism in data transfers. The development of high-speed, serial point-to-point connections that can be used as a basis for intrasystem and intersystem switched networks leads to the expectation of crossbar switches that accommodate more inputs and outputs in the future as technology progresses. For these reasons, we focus on crossbar switches in the remainder of the chapter; reference to a switch implies a crossbar switch.

SWITCH ORGANIZATION

Crossbar switches are characterized by a large number of parameters: (i) use of memory or not, (ii) transmission of fixed- or variable-size packets, (iii) synchronous or asynchronous operation, (iv) equal number of input and output (I/O) terminals, and (v) internal connectivity. Importantly, switches are classified according to these parameters.

One of the most important parameters is the use of memory, that is, whether switches are buffered or buffer-less. Buffer-less switches are typically employed in synchronous, connection-oriented networks that implement their input–output connections before any transmission of data, avoiding the need for buffering data in the switch due to conflicts. However, in most communication systems where data transmission is asynchronous and networks are composed of autonomous switches, buffered switches are the norm. The main goal of memory in switches is to provide temporary storage for incoming packets that need to wait for transmission due to conflicts with other packets that contend for the same output link and high load.

Another important parameter in switches is the size of the packets they transfer. There are two approaches: (i) fixed-size packets and (ii) variable-size packets. Switches with fixed-size packets receive and transmit packets that have equal length. Network traffic that consists of variable-size packets at higher layers in the protocol stack is broken down into fixed-size packets within the switch. These fixed-size packets are reassembled at the output port to recreate the original variable-size packets. Not all fixed-size packet switches accommodate the same packet length, but their operation requires a single packet size. In contrast, variable packet switches accommodate a wide range of packet lengths. Clearly, switches accommodating variable packet sizes require more elaborate circuitry and need to take into account several network parameters in order to enable networks to meet their goals; such parameters include fairness, end-to-end delay requirements for short and long packets, and others. The trends of networking technology, however, are focusing more on fixed-size packets in switches, which enable multiplexing of higher level traffic, provide good average performance in terms of packet delays, and enable more straightforward and thus efficient switch designs. The trade-off between fixed-size switching and variable-size switching has been addressed [129] and still provides a good source of debate. However, as network technologies based on fixed-size packet transmission, such as ATM [103], are still progressing and being adopted into a wider network base, we focus on fixed-size packet switching.

The structure and the placement of memory in switches enable a range of possible switch architectures, each with different requirements and performance characteristics. In the following, we focus on $N \times N$, synchronous, cell-based crossbar switches with memory because they capture the characteristics of most widespread technologies, such as ATM [103], and cover a wide range of switching technologies. In the synchronous model, we assume that all packets arrive simultaneously (and synchronous to the global clock) and that their transmission time is equal to the global clock cycle. Synchronous operation is widespread in such switches because it leads to simpler circuits with lower cost and easier verification of correct operation. The assumption of an equal number of input and output ports is also typical. Although $N \times M$ switches, with a different number of inputs and outputs, exist, the difference of the number of input and output ports is not significant at the architectural level. A switch with fewer outputs than inputs operates as a switching multiplexer, whereas a switch with fewer inputs than outputs operates as a switching demultiplexer. In either case, the architectural principles are similar, as can be deduced easily from Figure 4-3(b), as switch designs employ (de)multiplexers.

Figure 4-5 shows the main switch memory architectures. Figure 4-5(a) shows a switch with one queue per input. Incoming packets to an input are inserted to the queue corresponding to the incoming port. At every time interval, a scheduler looks at the packets at the heads of all queues and chooses the packets that will be served (delivered to their output) next; this scheduling is necessary because several packets may be directed to the same output port and thus need to be sequenced. Figure 4-6 plots the average delay of packets for an input queuing switch, assuming a traffic pattern that is typical for switch analyses: incoming packets are assumed to be generated by Bernoulli independent and identically distributed (i.i.d.) processes and each packet arriving at the switch is assumed to

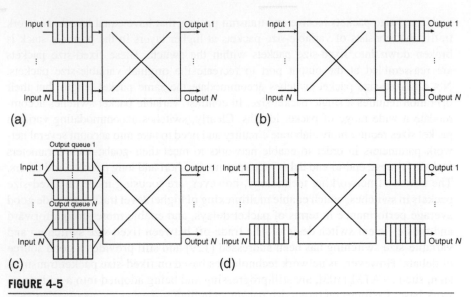

FIGURE 4-5

Input and output queuing switches.

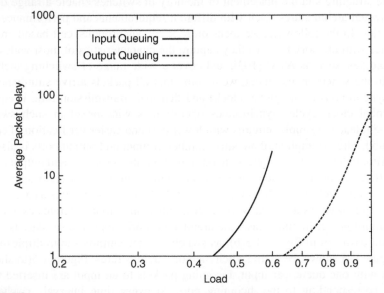

FIGURE 4-6

Average packet delay for input and output queuing switches.

be targeted to a specific output with a uniform probability distribution among all outputs. As Figure 4-6 indicates clearly, input queuing switches cannot achieve output throughput more than (almost) 60%, even under heavy load conditions. This occurs because input queuing switches suffer from a blocking phenomenon, called Head-of-Line (HoL) blocking, which limits switch performance. HoL blocking is due to the fact that a head packet that is not served blocks all packets in its queue, even ones that are targeted toward outputs that may be idle [85].

The HoL blocking phenomenon is avoided with alternative memory architectures. Figure 4-5(b) shows one such architecture where N queues are attached to the outputs, one queue per output, rather than to the inputs. As Figure 4-6 shows, this architecture avoids HoL and achieves 100% throughput under heavy load conditions. It is important to realize, though, that this performance improvement is achieved with increasing the cost of the switch because the internal fabric of the switch needs to operate with a clock that is N times faster than the clock of the overall switch. One can realize the need for this internal speedup, when considering the traffic scenario, when N incoming packets are targeted to the same output; in this case, N packets must be inserted to one outgoing packet queue in one switch clock cycle, requiring queue accesses that are N times faster than the switch clock cycle in order to avoid loss of data. An alternative architecture that avoids HoL blocking is the one shown in Figure 4-5(c), where input queues are divided to N queues each; this enables the scheduler to choose any available queue for transmission. This configuration, known as advanced input queuing or virtual output queuing, avoids HoL blocking at the cost of using multiple (N^2) input queues, relatively to the N used in the simple input queuing scheme. However, each of the N^2 input queues has the same cost as each of the N simple input queuing switch queues. Also, Figure 4-5(d) illustrates an alternative method that avoids HoL blocking at a lower cost than that of output queuing: the combined input–output (CIO) queue architecture combines input and output queues and employs an internal fabric of small or no speedup.

SWITCH SCHEDULING

Scheduling is necessary in switches because high load and routing conflicts lead to contention for resources. In switches that employ input queuing, scheduling is necessary to choose the input queues that will be served at every clock cycle; in switches that employ output queuing, packets contend for output queues and need to be serialized for buffering and transmission over a link. The scheduling problem in switches with input queuing is straightforward: there may be up to N requests in an $N \times N$ switch, which may have conflicts on some outputs; because the selection of any request to serve does not affect any other request or output in any way, the scheduling problem can be solved easily by employing independent schedulers at each output, which select a request—among candidates—independently with any typical scheme, such as random selection, round robin, etc. [85].

Considering the resources that require scheduling, the most demanding scheduling requirements emerge in switches with multiple input queues (advanced input queuing or virtual output queuing switches). In these switches, the scheduler needs to choose at most N input queues—as many as the outputs—among N^2 input queues, with the requirement that each input with N queues can forward at most one packet per cycle and each output can transmit at most one packet per cycle. Thus, scheduler decisions need to satisfy restrictions per input and output. In contrast, in switches with simple input queuing, the scheduling problem is straightforward because the input queues that contend for each output are disjoint from any input queues that contend for any other output; this enables independent scheduling per output without the need for any coordination as mentioned earlier, in contrast to switches with multiple input queues, which require coordination. In the following, we focus on the scheduling problem for switches with multiple input queues due to its complexity. The model of multiple input queues per input of a switch fits well in network systems, considering their structure as described in Chapter 2. In a system configuration where the backplane is a switch, multiple input queues can be organized and configured in the adapters, in their packet memory, minimizing the cost of input queue establishment and management.

We describe the scheduling problem in virtual output queuing switches considering a synchronous model of switch operation for a switch that receives and transmits fixed size packets. The switch is considered to operate in clock cycles, where the duration of the cycle is the transmission delay of one packet. The scheduler operates using the same clock, calculating a schedule in every cycle, that is, choosing the input queues that will transfer packets to the corresponding output links during the next cycle. In every cycle, the scheduler of an $N \times N$ switch can choose up to N different transfers among all the requests, which can be up to N^2 overall. Because the number of potential choices of the scheduler in every cycle can be up to $N!$, a large number of scheduling algorithms exists for calculation of a schedule.

We need a model for switch scheduling, which represents the requests of inputs for transmission through the switch and which enables us to express the restrictions of the system. Typical models are suitable: (i) the request matrix and (ii) the bipartite graph. Figure 4-7 shows these two models. Figure 4-7(a) shows a request matrix, RM, which represents inputs as rows and outputs as columns. The model originates from the well-known traffic matrix used in traffic engineering and has binary values in its entries. A value of 1 at $RM[i,j]$ represents the existence of a packet at input $In[i]$ requesting transfer to output $Out[j]$; a value of 0 indicates that the corresponding queue is empty and thus there are no requests for packet transfer from $In[i]$ to $Out[j]$. The bipartite graph model, shown in Figure 4-7(b), represents requests with a bipartite graph, where the two parts represent inputs and outputs correspondingly. An edge from one part to the other represents the corresponding request. Figure 4-7 shows models of the same requests with both models; thus, the request $RM[i,j]$ in the request matrix is represented with the edge going from node $In[i]$ to node $Out[j]$. Clearly, the two models are equivalent and one representation leads to the other in a straightforward way. However, each model enables us to conceptualize the requests differently and to develop and understand different algorithms better. For this reason, we will use them both, each one to describe a different scheduling algorithm.

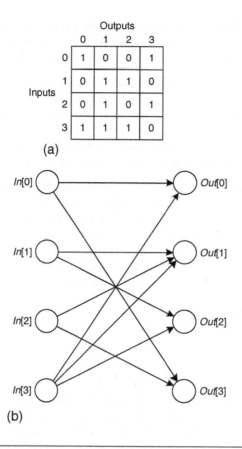

Outputs

	0	1	2	3
0	1	0	0	1
1	0	1	1	0
2	0	1	0	1
3	1	1	1	0

Inputs

(a)

(b)

FIGURE 4-7

Switch scheduling model.

The use of the two models, despite their equivalence, also originates from different approaches used to develop scheduling algorithms. In general, two different categories of scheduling algorithms exist based on the decision method used to choose the transfers that will be performed. The first category, central schedulers, makes decisions centrally, using all available information, typically represented with a data structure such as the Request Matrix. The second category, distributed schedulers, uses a distributed algorithm that calculates matching based on local input and output information and after exchange of messages between inputs and outputs. Because message exchange follows the paths of the requests, as represented pictorially by the bipartite graph model, the bipartite graph is typically used to illustrate the operation of distributed schedulers. An important characteristic of distributed schedulers is that they are iterative, that is, they calculate a first matching and then augment it through iterations that add new requests to outputs that remain idle after the previous iteration(s).

The potentially large population of choices a scheduler can make results in a large number of candidate scheduling algorithms. Independently of the methods used by the schedulers, the goals of all schedulers are basically the same:

1. High throughput: to maximize the number of requests per time unit
2. Low latency: to minimize the average packet latency
3. Fairness: to avoid starvation of requests and serve all input queues in a fair manner
4. Low-cost implementation: to enable an efficient implementation that will calculate an effective schedule within one cycle of the switch's operation.

Among these goals, the first three are typical algorithmic goals. The fourth one, though, is quite important in network systems as they have emerged through the last decades. The increasing link speeds and the adoption of cell-based networks, such as ATM, lead to very small transmission delay per cell (packet). Thus, the scheduling cycle decreases as well, considering the synchronous operation of switches, leading to a need for low-cost, efficient implementations of scheduling algorithms that can complete a schedule within one switch cycle.

Centralized scheduling

Centralized schedulers model transfer requests with a single data structure, such as the Request Matrix, and execute a sequential algorithm to calculate a schedule. A schedule is a subset of the requests, which can be served in parallel; in reference to the Request Matrix, the calculated schedule includes at most one request per row (input) and at most one per column (output) in order to satisfy the requirement that each input and each output can transfer one packet per cycle.

Several algorithms can be employed to calculate a correct schedule. Straightforward algorithms calculate the schedule in the following iterative fashion:

```
for (I = 0; i < N; i++) {
        Choose a row (different from the previous iterations)
        Choose a column with a request
    }
```

Use of any selection method for the steps given earlier leads to calculation of a correct schedule; selection methods include random, round-robin, etc. Although all these algorithms lead to a correct schedule, they are not efficient and are unable to provide finite average packet delay as the switch load approximates 100%. It must be noted that traffic considered for performance evaluation is generated by Bernoulli i.i.d. processes with uniform distribution among outputs for each generated packet.

More sophisticated scheduling algorithms are necessary to achieve bounded average packet delay under heavy load. Such algorithms maximize the average number of requests served per cycle, while achieving fairness. One such algorithm is the Two-Dimensional Round-Robin (2DRR) algorithm, which is a two-dimensional generalization of the one-dimensional round-robin scheme used in allocation problems with a single shared resource [95].

The 2DRR examines in parallel subsets of the N^2 cells of the Request Matrix *RM* that can be served in parallel, that is, cells that belong to different rows and columns; such subsets include up to N different cells for an $N \times N$ switch. Looking at *RM* as a two-dimensional structure, one clear such choice is a (geometric) diagonal, such as cells labeled D_0 in the 4×4 Request Matrix shown in Figure 4-8(a). If one examines cells of a diagonal and there exist requests in them, one can serve the requests in parallel and the schedule is calculated in a single step.

Examining the same diagonal in every cycle may lead to starvation of requests. Furthermore, there may be no requests in the cells of *RM* for the examined diagonal. Because of this, 2DRR defines N different diagonals, which cover all cells in *RM*, and in every cycle it examines the cells of a different diagonal. Figure 4-8(a) shows four diagonals, $D_0, \ldots, D_3$, for a 4×4 switch. All four diagonals cover all 16 (N^2) cells. Diagonals D_1, D_2, and D_3 are produced from D_0 by shifting D_0 to the right by one, two, or three columns, respectively. In general, for an $N \times N$ switch, the $N \times N$ Request Matrix is organized in N diagonals.

The 2DRR avoids starvation and provides fairness in the sense that it guarantees to serve any input queue within N cycles, as each queue is examined by one of the N diagonals and each of the N diagonals will be examined during a sequence of N cycles. Using one diagonal per cycle, though, leads to low performance in many traffic scenarios because the examined diagonal may have a few requests or even

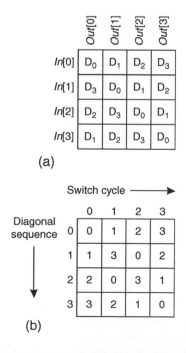

(a)

(b)

FIGURE 4-8

Two-Dimensional Round-Robin diagonals and Pattern Sequence Matrix.

none, while there may be additional requests in *RM* that can be served. In order to improve performance, we need to identify such additional requests. The 2DRR achieves this in the following fashion: after examining ("applying") the selected diagonal as described earlier, if there are idle inputs and outputs, it "applies" the remaining diagonals, one at a time and within the same cycle, in order to identify additional requests to be served. The application sequence of the remaining diagonals is critical for fairness: if they are applied in a fixed sequence, for example, $D_0, \ldots, D_{N-1}$, requests that lie in the cells of D_0 are preferred over ones that belong to the other diagonals $D_1 \ldots D_{N-1}$, the requests that lie in the cells of D_1 are preferred over the ones in $D_2 \ldots D_{N-1}$, and so on. This unfairness is alleviated by changing the order in which the diagonals are applied in every cycle. In 2DRR, this order is defined through a Pattern Sequence Matrix (*PSM*), which dictates the sequence in which the N diagonals must be applied in a sequence of N cycles. The *PSM* for a 4×4 switch is shown in Figure 4-8(b). As the figure indicates, during the first cycle of operation the diagonals will be applied with the sequence specified in the first column of *PSM*; in the second cycle, they will be applied as specified in the second column; and so on. After four cycles, *PSM* is reused starting from the first column, etc. The *PSM* of Figure 4-8(b) has two important properties that provide fairness among diagonals. These properties are:

1. The maximum direct ordering of diagonals is 1, where maximum direct ordering is the maximum number one diagonal index follows another index.
2. The maximum row and column frequency is 1, that is, the maximum number a diagonal index appears in a row or column of *PSM* is 1.

The two properties basically indicate that every diagonal is examined only once per cycle, that its order is different in every cycle, and that, for any pair of diagonals, the number that one precedes the other one is exactly 1. This indicates clearly that no diagonal is preferred over another one when examining requests; that is, all requests are treated equally. These two properties result from the way that matrix *PSM* is constructed. Specifically, *PSM* is calculated using the following algorithm:

```
for (j = 0; j < N; j++) {   /* sequence through N columns*/
    offset = j + 1;
    v= - 1;          /* setup to make j first pattern in sequence "/
    for (i = 0; i < N; i++) {
        while (v ≥ M) v=(v + offset) mod M;
        PSM[i,j] = v
        }
    }
```

Taking into account everything just discussed, the 2DRR operates using three matrices: (i) the Request Matrix (*RM*), which specifies the nonempty input queues in every cycle; (ii) the Diagonal Matrix (*DM*), which partitions the set of N^2 queues to N diagonals, each with N matrix entries (cells); and (iii) the Pattern Sequence Matrix (*PSM*), which specifies the sequence in which all N diagonals are examined during each cycle of the switch's operation. The result of execution of the 2DRR is calculation of a matrix, called Allocation Matrix (*AM*), whose entries have binary values with the "1" indicating that the corresponding queue is selected for service (the value is "0" otherwise). The operation of 2DRR is described fully later, considering the aforementioned four matrices. For the description we consider that the switch cycles accommodate the examination of all N diagonals in one cycle, that the switch cycles are numbered (indexed) starting from "0," and that the described operation is for a cycle with index k:

```
for (i = 0; i < N; i++)
     for (j = 0; j < N; j++) AM[i,j] = 0;
k = k mod N;
for (i = 0; i < N; i++) {
     Dm = PSM[i,k]
     for (all AM[r,c] that belong to Dm, that is, such that DM[r,c] = Dm) do {
          if (RM[r,c] = 1 AND (input r and output c are available)
     then AM[r,c] = 1
     }
}
```

Figure 4-9 shows an example from the original 2DRR description [95], which illustrates operation of the 2DRR. Figure 4-9 shows all the matrixes involved—Request, Diagonal, and Pattern Sequence—and operation of the 2DRR for the specific traffic scenario included in the specific Request Matrix.

The 2DRR achieves fairness and high performance. Figure 4-10 shows the average packet delay for the 2DRR next to the delay achieved with output queuing. Although inferior to the performance of output queuing, 2DRR achieves high performance at all loads, with delay that is bounded for all loads up to 1.

It is important to note that the 2DRR is not a completely unbiased algorithm despite all the properties and methods described earlier. Bias originates from the choice of diagonals. The 2DRR uses N diagonals for an $N \times N$ switch, although $N!$ possible diagonals exist. A different choice of diagonals leads to different service characteristics per input–output pair. To avoid this bias, one can extend the 2DRR to change the set of used diagonals occasionally. Enhanced 2DRR [95] is such an algorithm, which changes its set of diagonals every N cycles. Such algorithms provide more fairness on the average for service per input queue, but it results in relaxation of the service guarantee per input queue from N to $2N$ [95].

Distributed scheduling

An alternative way to model the scheduling problem is with a bipartite graph, where one part corresponds to inputs and the other to outputs while edges correspond to service requests, as shown in Figure 4-7. This model makes clear that the scheduling problem is a graph matching problem; a matching in a graph is a subset of its edges that have no common nodes. The graph matching problem has drawn attention for a long time for general or bipartite graphs, weighted or not, in efforts to calculate maximum size matchings or maximum weight matchings [176].

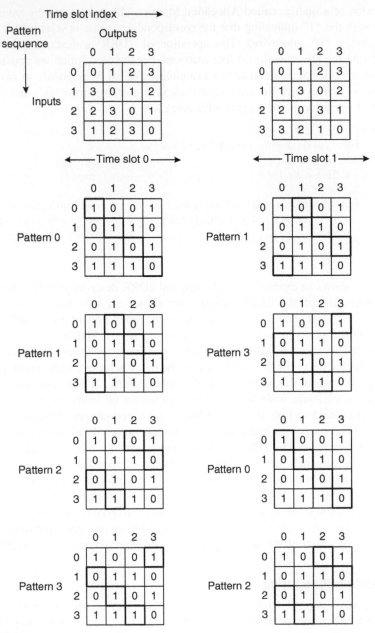

FIGURE 4-9

The 2DRR example.

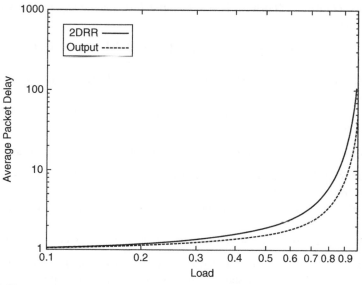

FIGURE 4-10

Performance of the 2DRR.

Because sequential algorithms that calculate maximum size matchings are expensive, that is, slow, considering the need to meet performance requirements of continuously increasing link speeds, which increase much faster than the speed of the electronics that perform algorithmic operations, efforts have been made to achieve higher scheduler speed through parallelized matching algorithms. These algorithms consider switch ports as independent and capable to operate in parallel.

The first parallelized matching algorithm that appeared was PIM [3], which introduces the main algorithmic method of a class of developed algorithms that calculate effective schedules efficiently. PIM is an iterative algorithm that calculates a good matching in an incremental fashion through iterations: the first iteration calculates a matching, the second one adds edges to it, and so on. This approach is followed by most existing distributed scheduling algorithms, which are iterative, and in every step (iteration) they use a handshake protocol between inputs and outputs to choose requests to serve. The generalized handshake protocol used in every iteration was first introduced by PIM and performs the following operations:

1. Inputs broadcast their requests to the outputs,
2. Each output selects one request independently and issues a Grant to it, and
3. Each input chooses one Grant to accept, as it may receive several Grant signals.

In order to provide a basis for describing the algorithms, we use the following notation. We consider an $N \times N$ switch with N inputs, $In[0] \ldots In[N-1]$, and

N outputs, $Out[0] \ldots Out[N - 1]$. Every input $In[i]$ maintains the following state information:

1. Table $R_i[0] \ldots R_i[N - 1]$, where $R_i[k] = 1$, if $In[i]$ has a request for $Out[k]$ (0, otherwise)
2. Table $Gd_i[0] \ldots Gd_i[N - 1]$, where $Gd_i[k] = 1$, if $In[i]$ receives a Grant from $Out[k]$, (0, otherwise)
3. Variable A_i, where $A_i = k$, if $In[i]$ accepts the Grant from $Out[k]$, (-1, if no output is accepted)

Analogously, each output $Out[k]$ maintains the following state information:

1. Table $Rd_k[0] \ldots Rd_k[N - 1]$, where $Rd_k[i] = 1$, if $Out[k]$ receives a request from $In[i]$ (0, otherwise)
2. Variable G_k, where $G_k = i$, if $Out[k]$ sends a Grant to $In[i]$ (-1, if no input is granted)
3. Variable Ad_k, where $Ad_k = 1$, if the Grant from $Out[k]$ is accepted (0, otherwise)

Functional differences among the various algorithms exist only in the way that outputs choose which input to issue the Grant to and in the way inputs choose which Grant to accept. Because every choice to issue a Grant is made with a process that examines candidate inputs in some fashion, we describe this process using two variables per output: g_k is a variable that shows which input will be examined first (to issue a Grant) during a step, while g'_k shows the input to be examined first in the consecutive step. Similarly, the choice of which Grant to accept at an input is made with an analogous process, which is described with the variables a_i and a'_i.

Functional differences in choosing which Grant to issue at outputs and which Grant to accept at inputs result in significant performance differences. PIM uses randomness, choosing among candidates with a uniform distribution. This decision for PIM led to the use of $\log(N)$ iterations, as it was proven that $\log(N)$ iterations with random decisions lead to the calculation of a maximal matching [3]. So, using the introduced notation, in every step PIM executes the following operations for all $Out[k]$ and $In[i]$:

```
Rd_k[i] = R_i[k]
g_k = random(among Requests)
G_k = g_k
Gd_i[k] = 1, if G_k = i
a_i = random(among Grant's)
A_k = a_i
```

Figure 4-11 shows the performance of PIM, plotting the average packet delay achievable for variable switch load for a 16×16 switch, with the scheduler performing 4 (=$\log(N)$) iterations. As the plot shows, PIM performs well but cannot serve high loads, as the average packet delay becomes unbounded well before load 1. In addition to this limitation, PIM is expensive to implement for two main reasons: (i) good random number generators are hard, and thus expensive, to

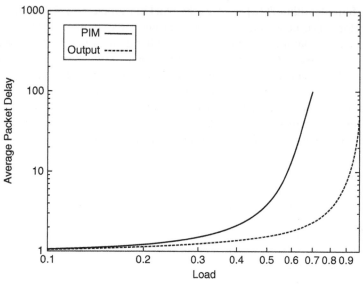

FIGURE 4-11

Performance of PIM.

implement in either hardware or software and (ii) the clock cycle of the switch needs to accommodate for 2·log(N) random number generations, which result in a long cycle and, thus, limit the link speed supported by the switch.

An alternative to the high cost of PIM and its inability to serve high loads is to replace the random decisions of PIM with deterministic ones, such as round-robin. Employment of round-robin can be made in various ways, as shown later, and was evaluated, leading to a class of algorithms, each providing a different contribution and resulting in different performance characteristics. Round-Robin Matching (RRM) [116], the first effort to replace random decisions with round-robin, leads to blocking and does not achieve switch operation under high load [116]. RRM calculates a matching with the same method as PIM, differing only in the way Grants and Accepts are issued. Specifically, each iteration of RRM is as follows:

```
Rd_k[i] = R_i[k]
g_k = g'_k
a_i = a'_i
G_k = i, if (Rd_k[i] = 1 AND g_k = i) OR (Rd_k[i] = 1 AND Rd_k[j] = 0, where
    g_k ≤ j < i (mod N))
Gd_i[k] = 1, if G_k = i
A_i = k, if (Gd_i[k] = 1 AND a_i = k) OR (Gd_i[k] = 1 AND Gd_i[j] = 0, where
    a_i ≤ j < k (mod N))
G'_k = G_k + 1 (mod N)
A'_i = A_i + 1 (mod N)
```

The iSlip algorithm [116] resolves the blocking problem of RRM and achieves good performance under high load. iSlip changes the simple, direct round-robin employment, so that it takes into account whether a Grant has been accepted. Specifically, if an issued Grant does not get accepted, iSlip moves the round-robin pointer of the output that issued the Grant to its prior position, that is, it behaves as if the Grant was never issued. This simple change alleviates RRM's blocking problem and leads to high performance, providing bounded average packet delay at all loads, as Figure 4-12 shows for a 16×16 switch. Considering the introduced notation, iSlip operates as follows, during every iteration:

$Rd_k[i] = R_i[k]$
$g_k = g'_k$
$a_i = a'_i$
$G_k = i$, if $(Rd_k[i] = 1$ AND $g_k = i)$ OR $(Rd_k[i] = 1$ AND $Rd_k[j] = 0$, where
    $g_k \leq j < i \pmod{N})$
$Gd_i[k] = 1$, if $G_k = i$
$A_i = k$, if $(Gd_i[k] = 1$ AND $a_i = k)$ OR $(Gd_i[k] = 1$ AND $Gd_i[j] = 0$, where
    $a_i \leq j < k \pmod{N})$
if $(Ad_k = 1)$ $g'_k = G_k + 1 \pmod{N}$
else $g'_k = g_k$
$a'_i = A_i + 1 \pmod{N}$

The FIRM algorithm [156] changes the way round-robin is implemented by iSlip and leads to even higher performance, up to 50% at high load, as Figure 4-12 depicts. FIRM handles the case differently when a Grant is not accepted. Specifically, when a

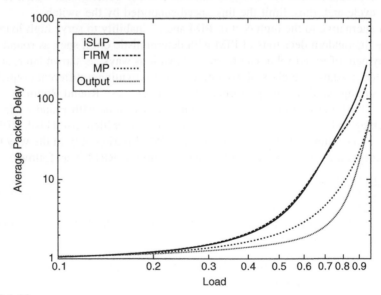

FIGURE 4-12

Performance of iSlip, FIRM, and MP.

Grant is not accepted, FIRM leaves the round-robin pointer at the position of the Granted input so that the same Grant is issued again during the next switch cycle. This change over iSlip leads to improved fairness, as this "persistent" Grant mechanism leads to service closer to first-come first-serve. In detail, each iteration of the FIRM algorithm operates as follows:

$Rd_k[i] = R_i[k]$
$g_k = g'_k$
$a_i = a'_i$
$G_k = i$, if $(Rd_k[i] = 1$ AND $g_k = i)$ OR $(Rd_k[i] = 1$ AND $Rd_k[j] = 0$, where $g_k \le j < i \pmod{N})$
$Gd_i[k] = 1$, if $G_k = i$
$A_i = k$, if $(Gd_i[k] = 1$ AND $a_i = k)$ OR $(Gd_i[k] = 1$ AND $Gd_i[j] = 0$, where $a_i \le j < k \pmod{N})$
if $(Ad_k = 1)$ $g'_k = G_k + 1 \pmod{N}$
else $g'_k = G_k$
$a'_i = A_i + 1 \pmod{N}$

Based on calculations of the algorithms, one can easily observe that after any number of iterations the algorithms have calculated a (correct) matching. Thus, one can employ any number of iterations in order to serve requests. This ability enables the design of schedulers with a small number of iterations so that scheduler implementation meets the requirements of high-speed links, that is, short switch cycles. However, a smaller number of iterations results in matchings with fewer edges, leading to lower performance. Figure 4-13 shows the packet delay achieved by iSlip and FIRM with different numbers of iterations per switch cycle, specifically with 1, 2, 3, or 4 iterations for a 16×16 switch. Results show switch performance for up to 4 ($=\log(N)$) iterations, similarly to PIM, although theoretical results do not exist that prove any specific property of the resulting matchings, for example, achievement of a maximal matching or similar; however, simulations and experiments show that a number of iterations beyond $\log(N)$ provides little improvement.

Algorithms also exist that combine characteristics of centralized algorithms, such as the 2DRR, and distributed ones. The class of Mutual Priority (MP) algorithms [192] combines the PIM-based iterative approach with diagonals, sending Grants to calculated inputs using the concept of diagonals, as introduced by the 2DRR. The concept introduced by MP algorithms, the mutual priority concept, creates "pairings" of inputs and outputs that have priority in each cycle; to avoid conflicts, these pairings are made using diagonal information. In this fashion, these algorithms reduce conflicts for the Grant and Accept phases significantly. The implementation of pairings is straightforward when implemented through the calculation of a new location to start each round-robin cycle, accordingly. The basic MP algorithm, for example, sends Grant signals using the following calculation:

$Rd_k[i] = R_i[k]$
$g_k = g'_k$
$a_i = a'_i$

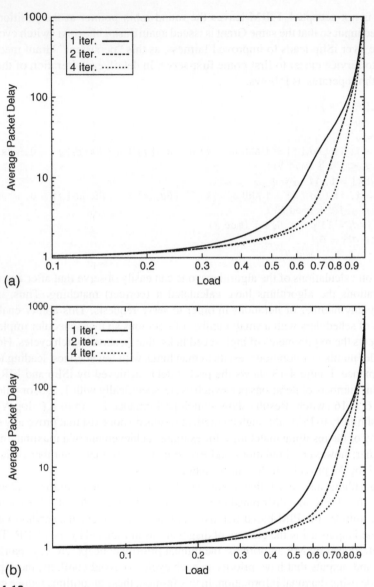

FIGURE 4-13

iSlip and FIRM performance with a variable number of iterations.

$G_k = i$; if ($Rd_k[i] = 1$ AND $g_k = i$) OR ($Rd_k[i] = 1$ AND $Rd_k[j] = 0$, where
  $g_k \leq j < i \pmod N$))
$Gd_i[k] = 1$; if $G_k = i$
$A_i = k$; if ($Gd_i[k] = 1$ AND $a_i = k$) OR ($Gd_i[k] = 1$ AND $Gd_i[j] = 0$, where
  $a_i \leq j < i \pmod N$))

$cyc = m \pmod{N}$
$g'_k = cyc + k \pmod{N}$
$a'_i = -cyc + i \pmod{N}$

In the aforementioned calculation, variable cyc enables the change of pairings between consecutive cycles. In general, the mutual priority concept leads to scheduling algorithms that have two benefits: (i) matchings are denser and (ii) large size matchings are achieved with a small number of iterations, even with one. This approach improves performance significantly, as shown in Figure 4-12.

Although results in the previous figures are all for 16×16 switches, in order to enable a direct comparison of schedulers for the same switch size, it is important to emphasize that the results are analogous for all switch sizes. Furthermore, the qualitative characteristics of the behavior of algorithms are the same, independently of the switch size. This is depicted in Figure 4-14, which plots the average delay achievable with algorithms 2DRR and iSlip for various switch sizes. As Figure 4-14 shows, the plots are similar for all switch sizes, although performance improves as the switch size increases.

An important difference in the performance of these algorithms is their service guarantee: the time between the arrival of a packet at the head of its queue—and the resulting posting of the request—and the time it is served. Interestingly, all aforementioned deterministic algorithms have different service guarantees and, as the service guarantee becomes tighter (i.e., the time is reduced), the average packet delay is reduced as well, leading to improved switch performance. Specifically, iSlip has a service guarantee of $N^2 + (N - 1)^2$ clock cycles, while FIRM provides a service guarantee of N^2 clock cycles and MP a service guarantee of N clock cycles, which is the optimal, considering an $N \times N$ switch and high load.

Use of randomization

Deterministic scheduling algorithms are widespread in all problems where conflict resolution is required because they achieve predictable behavior and lead to low-cost implementations. However, the use of randomness provides advantages as well. It enables mathematical analysis of several systems, whereas deterministic algorithms often do not. In scheduling algorithms for virtual output queuing switches, PIM introduced the use of randomness, but was soon replaced by deterministic alternatives due to its resulting performance limitations and high cost. Importantly, there are alternative ways to introduce and exploit randomness [55, 99, 157]. RRPM [99] is an iterative algorithm that calculates a matching using a step where inputs forward one request per iteration—using round robin—and each output chooses one request at random. LAURA [55] uses randomness to choose which previously matched requests should participate in a consecutive matching. Their adoption of randomness, though, is limited in that it complements deterministic methods. In contrast to these algorithms, Randomized On-Line Matching (ROLM) uses randomness as its basis for the calculation of matchings [157].

Randomized On-Line Matching, a representative of a class of algorithms, is a sequential algorithm that exploits a randomized efficient on-line matching algorithm

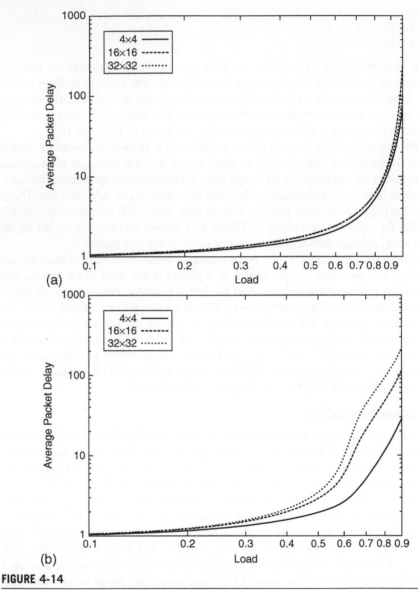

FIGURE 4-14

Performance of 2DRR and iSlip for variable switch sizes.

that calculates maximal matchings in bipartite graphs, named the Ranking algorithm [86], as its basis. The Ranking algorithm considers that the nodes of one part of the bipartite graph arrive on-line, that is, one after the other, and calculates a matching in an on-line fashion. Specifically, the algorithm calculates a random permutation of the nodes in one part of the graph and then considers on-line arrival of the nodes in the other part; each incoming node of the second graph part is matched with the first appropriate node in the permutation of the first graph part. Ranking calculates a maximal matching, as has been proved [86].

When applied to switching, the Ranking algorithm makes a matching decision considering one output after the other. Specifically, during every switch cycle, the Ranking algorithm calculates the (maximal) matching, incrementally with the following steps:

S1: Calculate a random permutation $\pi(In)$ (ordering) of inputs, which is the same for all outputs

S2: Consider output $Out[0]$ and identify the requests to it (i.e., the first input in $\pi(In)$ that has a request for $Out[0]$; the requests of the selected input are deleted from the graph)

S3: Match $Out[0]$ to the eligible input (if any) of highest rank

S4: Repeat Steps S2 and S3 for all remaining outputs

The Ranking algorithm is effective because of its first step, in which a random permutation of inputs is performed. If a random selection were made in Step S3, as for the PIM algorithm, and not a selection within the random permutation, the algorithm would not calculate a maximal matching.

Although the Ranking algorithm is sequential, because of the sequential on-line consideration of the outputs, a hardware implementation of the algorithm could exploit parallelism: outputs can issue a Grant in parallel, but they can make their final decision after receiving the match of the preceding output(s), using a method analogous to the carry calculation of a carry-look-ahead adder. Thus, ROLM can be considered a hybrid of centralized and distributed algorithms.

The Ranking algorithm solves the switch scheduling problem presented in each switch cycle. Its adoption and employment in subsequent switch cycles enable development of a class of switch scheduling algorithms, which prove to have different characteristics in terms of performance and implementation cost. These scheduling algorithms are differentiated by two parameters of the Ranking algorithm, as implemented in each cycle: (i) the *random permutation* of inputs (step S1) and (ii) the *online consideration* of outputs. In regard to random permutation, because the scheduler calculates a match in every cycle, one could change the frequency with which step S1 is executed. One could calculate more often or more sparsely the random permutation of inputs through switch cycles. Additionally, one could calculate a different input ordering for each output. In regard to the online sequence of outputs, one could change the order of outputs in every switch cycle. This approach to employing randomness in scheduling algorithms is effective, in contrast to the PIM approach. PIM is not suitable for analogous variations, because, if random selections are done more rarely during execution cycles, probable conflicts of Grant signals would hold until a new selection is calculated, leading to lower performance.

The basic algorithm of this class, the ROLM algorithm, calculates a matching with the following steps, where the first step, S1, is executed once every R switch cycle ($1 \leq R < \infty$):

S1: If (i (mod R) = 0), then calculate a random permutation $\pi(In)$ of inputs
S2: Inputs broadcast their requests to outputs
S3: Output $Out[0]$ issues a Grant to the eligible input (if any) of highest priority (based on random ordering)
S4: Step S3 is repeated for all remaining outputs

The performance of the ROLM algorithm is presented in Figure 4-15 where the average packet delay is plotted as a function of load for various values of R. As the plots indicate, ROLM performs significantly better than PIM, FIRM, and MP, achieving even 10-fold improvement in average delay over FIRM (with log(N) iterations) for high loads.

Variations of ROLM based on the parameters mentioned previously are the Dynamic Randomized On-Line Matching (DyROLM) algorithm and the Distributed Dynamic Randomized On-Line Matching (D-DyROLM) algorithm [157]. In DyROLM, the sequence with which the outputs calculate their match changes in a round-robin fashion, that is, in every switch cycle the first considered output is the one following the output that was considered first in the previous switch cycle. In D-DyROLM, each output calculates its own random permutation $\pi(In)$ once every R cycles. Simulations of switches operating with these algorithms demonstrate different behavior of the switches for variable R and, in general, comparable performance with ROLM and improved performance over PIM and switches with deterministic schedulers [157]. Importantly, ROLM algorithms target to reduce the latency introduced in hardware implementations by calculation of the random

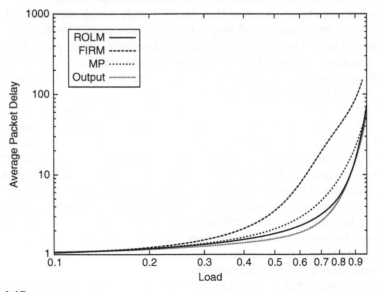

FIGURE 4-15

Performance of ROLM.

permutation. DyROLM algorithms provide improved fairness characteristics, in terms of equal service time for all outputs, whereas D-DyROLM algorithms increase the use of randomness further by making a different random ordering of inputs for every output, without increasing the complexity of hardware implementations, because random permutations can be calculated in parallel.

In regard to fairness, ROLM and all randomized algorithms do not provide a service guarantee because of randomization. However, one can calculate the average waiting time of a packet at the head of a queue, under conditions of high load, that is, when the requests are N^2, which is N, indicating that the average waiting time is equal to the optimal guarantee of deterministic scheduling algorithms.

Real-time traffic

The presented scheduling algorithms address requirements of nonreal-time data traffic. Their bounded service guarantee—for the deterministic algorithms—enables the provision of real-time characteristics, but additional mechanisms are necessary in order to enable strict real-time guarantees required by various types of traffic, such as multimedia. Such mechanisms, already used in real-time network protocols, include:

1. Reservations: the ability to reserve a clock cycle to serve a pending request
2. Priorities/urgency: the ability to differentiate classes of traffic to express urgency for the service of a specific pending request
3. Phases: the ability to serve a set of requests before examining newly posted requests.

Importantly, several of the described algorithms can be extended to include such mechanisms, enabling accommodation of real-time traffic. A characteristic example is FIRM, which can be extended easily to accommodate reservations and phases [159].

SUMMARY

This chapter presented the main issues of switches used as backplanes for network systems and of switches in switched networks. We described the main characteristics of switches and interconnection networks, as well as the main organizations of switches. Considering the effectiveness of switches with multiple input queues in the application area of interest, that is, networks and network systems, we described the related scheduling problem and presented a historical sequence of practical scheduling algorithms that achieve high performance and can be implemented efficiently. Furthermore, we evaluated the use of randomness in switch schedulers in efforts to identify effective ways for its employment. The effectiveness of all algorithms stems from their high performance, as well as their low-cost implementation, which can be achieved in either hardware or software [159].

Network adapters

INTRODUCTION

Network adapters are used to enable connectivity on a single network link and typically implement a single protocol stack. Network adapters provide the system implementation where that protocol stack is executed. The dependency of the adapter on the physical medium of the attached network usually influences the specification and naming of the adapter in the market. For example, off-the-shelf adapters are known as Ethernet adapters, Wi-Fi adapters, etc. Importantly, because adapters implement single protocol stacks, they are often considered and used as building blocks for multistack systems, such as bridges, routers, and gateways, implementing stacks of appropriate sizes, as described in Chapter 2. Despite the use of adapters in both end systems and network systems, we focus on adapters for end systems in this chapter, as typical end system adapters often implement stacks with more layers. Thus, the architecture of end system adapters presents more challenges and requires addressing of more issues than that of network system adapters.

An end system, as the one shown in Figure 5-1, is a computational system with a network attachment for a specific network technology. Thus, the end system implements a full protocol stack, typically as part of its operating system. The protocol stack interacts with one or more applications, exchanging data between the applications and the protocol stack. Considering the structure of typical end systems, network adapters constitute input/output (I/O) systems that deliver data between the end system and the network. Clearly, the mapping of the end system's functionality, including the protocol stack, onto the end system structure can be implemented in several ways, mapping one portion of the protocol stack on the network adapter and another one on the remainder of the end system. The lower layers of the stack, including the physical layer, which requires specialized hardware, constitute the portion mapped on the adapter, while the higher layers may be mapped on the end system. Consider, for example, the configuration of a typical personal computer (PC) with an Ethernet adapter. In the general case, the PC with the adapter implements at least a four-layer protocol stack with Ethernet physical and Media Access Control (MAC) protocols as well as Logical Link Control (LLC), Internet Protocol (IP), and Transmission Control Protocol (TCP), from lower to higher layers. However, the protocol stack is implemented partly on the

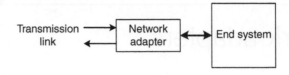

FIGURE 5-1

End system with network adapter.

adapter (e.g., the Ethernet physical and MAC) and partly on the PC (e.g., LLC, IP, and TCP as part of the PC's operating system). Clearly, partitioning of protocol stack implementation between the adapter and the end system is influenced by several factors, such as the support of several physical protocols in the same end system, the availability of low-cost network adapters, etc. This partitioning influences the architecture of network adapters significantly, as it sets the specifications of adapter development.

Independently of the partitioning of protocol stacks at end systems, network adapters need to address specified performance requirements. The basic problem that needs to be resolved is that of throughput preservation, that is, the problem of preserving the link throughput through all layers of the protocol stack. In addition, other requirements may exist, such as real-time requirements, as described in Chapter 3. This chapter focuses on the throughput preservation problem as the basic problem, with the goal of developing architectures that achieve link throughput preservation through protocol stacks. To achieve this goal, we follow a typical approach: we start with a basic network adapter and analyze its operation, identifying bottlenecks and proposing solutions that alleviate these bottlenecks and achieve improved performance.

BASIC NETWORK ADAPTER

A simple, typical network adapter is an I/O subsystem of an end system. Thus, its architecture is influenced by the typical decisions made for I/O subsystems, such as the use of DMA, etc. The structure of such an adapter, for a local area network, is shown in Figure 5-2 and is composed of five main components [118]:

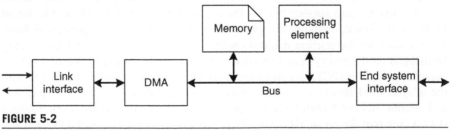

FIGURE 5-2

Typical adapter structure.

1. Link Interface: the subsystem that implements the physical layer and MAC sublayer of the data link layer
2. Processing Element (PE): the processing subsystem responsible for data management, data movement, and protocol processing
3. DMA unit: the component that handles fast data movement between the link interface and the memory
4. Memory: the data storage unit of the adapter
5. End system interface: the interface between the adapter and the end system

The structure of the adapter in Figure 5-2 indicates that it attaches to a local area network, considering the partitioning of the data link layer into its typical LAN sublayers: MAC and LLC. We use the model of a LAN adapter as an example because these adapters represent a significant base of adapters in the market and are fairly well known to network users. Importantly, the structure and the operation of this adapter are typical, being analogous to most existing architectures and designs for end system adapters [18, 168], including adapters employing special-purpose network processors, such as the Intel IXP1200 [110].

Before analyzing the operation of the adapter in detail, we need to clarify two important issues in the model adapter. First, we consider that the PE is assigned with protocol processing according to the partitioning of the protocol stack between the end system and the adapter; that is, the PE may be assigned with protocols ranging from none to the full stack above the MAC sublayer. Second, we need to specify how the memory is organized and managed. Clearly, an adapter needs a memory component, which stores packets for two reasons: (i) for temporary storage of packets as they arrive from the network or from the end system, before they are forwarded further to the end system or network, respectively, and (ii) for processing by the PE, as the PE requires memory for storing its code as well as its data. In some older adapters with simple PEs that do not execute any protocols, most of the memory component is composed of physical FIFOs, each one directed to a different system resource (i.e., link, end system, or PE). However, this approach has proven to have several disadvantages that have led to the use of random access memory (RAM) as the main technology for the memory component. Disadvantages of physical FIFOs originate from their limited accessibility, which does not allow them to be used efficiently by processing elements, and the partitioning of the memory capacity to several modules, which may lead to poor utilization of the overall capacity. For example, consider the case where one FIFO fills and starts dropping data, while another FIFO still has available space. Nevertheless, FIFOs are useful in network systems, as data packets arrive with their bits and bytes in FIFO order and packets are sequenced in a FIFO order before they are delivered to a protocol or to an adapter component. For this reason, most adapters employ a memory organization and management where the physical memory is a RAM and where stored data are organized in multiple logical queues, according to the system's requirements. The use of RAM not only enables use of the memory by the PE as well as all the other components, but also the use of large-capacity, low-cost memories.

For purposes of analysis, we consider a simple but effective memory management scheme that enables the organization of packet data in memory so that packets are assembled correctly and logical queues are organized efficiently and effectively. We consider that the adapter has a RAM memory, which is logically partitioned in fixed-size buffers. Considering variable-size packets, a packet is stored in a set of buffers, as its length may exceed the size of a buffer; these buffers are logically linked together in a queue, which establishes the correct ordering of packet data. Packets can be linked together in queues as well, forming queues of packets for various purposes. For example, one may want to organize a queue of packets that are ready to be delivered to the end system or the link; in general, queues are used to organize packets destined to a system resource, such as the link, the end system, or the PE.

ADAPTER OPERATION ANALYSIS

A network adapter, as the one shown in Figure 5-2, is a special-purpose computing system with a structure similar to the one of conventional computing systems. A network adapter includes its own processing element, memory, and I/O subsystems (i.e., the link attachment and the end system interface component). Its operation consists of receiving, processing, and transmitting packets in two directions, toward and from the network link. The overall operation of the adapter is a complex process, using all components, which influence performance in different ways. In order to evaluate the effect of the different components on system performance and to address the throughput preservation problem, we need to analyze the operation of the adapter in detail. Considering that the adapter's operation is packet reception from and transmission to the network and taking into account that reception and transmission are analogous, we will analyze the reception process in detail. Specifically, we present the reception process of a packet by the adapter in order to identify the delays involved and evaluate the adapter's ability to process packets in addition to receiving them. Transmission can be included easily in the analysis with a simple extension of the approach. This analysis follows the one presented elsewhere [118].

Figure 5-3 illustrates delays involved in the reception of a packet by the adapter shown in Figure 5-2. The axis of Figure 5-3 is time, showing two consecutive packets' arrivals at times t_1 and t_2. Clearly, reception of the packet arriving at t_1 must finish

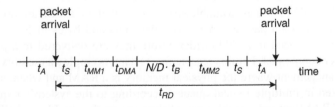

FIGURE 5-3

Packet reception process.

before t_2 in order for the adapter to sustain the stream of arriving packets and avoid loss of packet data. In a typical adapter reception process, the following operations occur. When the packet arrives at the link interface, an interrupt is issued to the processor to initiate the reception process. Responding to the interrupt, the processor performs a task switch, saving the state of its current process and loading the interrupt handler for reception; the delay for the task switch is denoted t_{TS}. Then, the interrupt handler performs the DMA setup to move incoming data to memory. In order to set up the DMA successfully, the processor needs to know the address in memory where data must be stored. Considering that memory is organized as described in the previous section, this implies that the processor needs to identify the address of an empty buffer in memory. Thus, the overall delay to set up the DMA with the appropriate memory address is composed of two delays: (i) t_{MM1} to find the address of a free memory buffer and (ii) t_{DMA} to set up the DMA controller itself. Because these delays are not insignificant, there is need for elastic buffers at the link interface to store incoming data temporarily until the delivery to memory starts.

When data start flowing over the adapter bus from the link interface toward the memory, the delay to store data in memory is influenced by several factors. Specifically, the parameters of interest are the byte length of the packet, denoted N, the width of the data bus in bytes, denoted D, and the clock cycle of the bus, denoted t_B. Assuming that the bus does not starve for data, the delay to move packet data to the memory is $\frac{N}{D}t_B$.

Assuming that the packet fits in one buffer, after storing all packet data in memory, the processor reads the packet header in order to identify the logical queue where the packet needs to be appended and then appends it appropriately. This delay is denoted as t_{MM2}. After packet data are stored and linked in the logical queue, execution of the interrupt handler is complete and the processor performs another task switch in order to return to its state before packet arrival; this task switch again has a delay t_{TS}.

We note that subscripts of the delays t_{MM1} and t_{MM2} originate from the fact that these delays constitute delays of memory management. Because these delays are relevant to the same general process, that is, memory management, we often group them and refer to them as t_{MM}. In the case mentioned earlier, $t_{MM} = t_{MM1} + t_{MM2}$.

Considering all the aforementioned, the packet reception delay, denoted t_{RD}, that is, the delay to receive the packet from time t_1, when its first bit arrives, until it is fully stored in memory and linked appropriately, is:

$$t_{RD} = 2 \times t_{TS} + t_{DMA} + t_{MM} + \frac{N}{D}t_B.$$

Clearly, this calculation holds even for packets that are longer than a single buffer, assuming the t_{DMA} and t_{MM} include all relevant delays. When an arriving packet needs more than one buffer to store its data in memory, the reception process differs from the one described earlier only in that the DMA setup and the memory management operations need to be repeated. Specifically, when a packet needs more than one buffer, the memory management operation that identifies a free buffer must be repeated for every allocated buffer, the filled buffers need to be linked together to form a packet, and the DMA setup has to be performed for every buffer. Assuming t_{DMA} includes the DMA setup for all used buffers and t_{MM} includes delays for identifying free buffers, linking them to form a packet and linking the packet to the appropriate queue, the aforementioned calculation of t_{RD} holds for any packet size and any number of buffers used.

The packet reception process of the adapter is only part of the packet processing in the adapter. Assuming that the PE executes at least one protocol above the MAC layer, the next step in packet processing is protocol execution. In order to execute the protocol(s), the PE needs to dequeue the packet from the logical packet queue where it is linked, execute the protocol code, and then enqueue the packet to an appropriate logical packet queue again. Thus, it requires memory management operations, enqueue, and dequeue, as well as code execution. Importantly, the delay for code execution has to account for several delays, depending on the type of processor used. For example, assuming that the PE is a reduced instruction set computer (RISC) processor and considering the lack of locality in header processing (among headers), one has to account for cache misses, as well as for the delay to move data between memory and the register files. In the following, we denote as t_P the delay for packet header processing, including the delay for enqueueing and dequeueing the packet.

The time available for packet processing by the PE is the time between the end of a packet's reception by the adapter and the time of arrival of the next packet. This available time, denoted t_A, is illustrated in Figure 5-3. Apparently, $t_A \geq t_P$ must hold in order to have the adapter preserve the reception throughput of the network link. If the relation does not hold, the adapter is not able to receive and process a packet before the next packet arrives, leading to loss of packet data if the packet arrival rate is constant.

Considering everything just mentioned, we can calculate the effective throughput T_E of the adapter in packets per second as

$$T_E = \min\left(P, \frac{1}{t_{RD} + t_P}\right),$$

where P is the packet arrival rate on the network link, in packets per second.

It is important to note that this last equation takes into account that the PE cannot perform any protocol processing during packet reception because it executes the reception interrupt handler and it remains idle during data transfer over the bus, because it does not have access to memory.

We evaluate the performance of the adapter architecture as well as the configurations introduced later in the chapter with a simulator of the adapter [38]. The simulator implements a model for the adapter shown in Figure 5-2 using CSIM19 [121] and is programmable to employ different processor technologies. This programmability enables analysis of different generations of adapters that employ different processors, which, in turn, influence system performance significantly overall, as all adapter components are designed based on the processor characteristics (bus cycle, DMA setup, etc.). Such analysis illustrates the significant performance improvement achievable with modern processors in over a decade. This chapter analyzes two different generations of processors, one similar to an Intel 80386 operating at 20 MHz and one for an ARM11 (ARM1136J-S) processor operating at 660 MHz; we refer to the corresponding adapters as the x86-based adapter and the ARM-based adapter.

Figure 5-4 plots simulation results for T_E for the two different generations of processors. For the x86-based processor configuration, we used data found

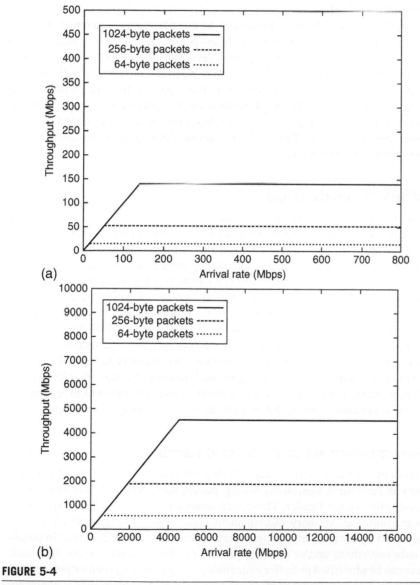

(a)

(b)

FIGURE 5-4

Effective adapter throughput (a) x86 based and (b) ARM based.

elsewhere [118]; simulation results are the same as in Meleis and Serpanos [118]. For ARM processor configuration, we consider use of the 64-bit AMBA High-performance Bus (AHB), operating at 133 MHz [7]. Importantly, ARM11 has a processing power of 660 MIPS [6] and a task-switching delay equal to 30 instructions [98], achieving low interrupt latency for interrupt-driven applications. In regard to protocol processing at the PE, we assume that the PE executes the LLC protocol with a critical path of 351 instructions as used elsewhere [118], based on data provided in [174].

Figure 5-4 shows effective throughput of the adapter as a function of packet arrival rate. Throughput is expressed in bytes per second, while the packet arrival rate is expressed in packets per second. Every plot shows three curves, one for a different scenario where fixed-size-length packets—different length for each scenario—arrive at the adapter link. The three packet lengths considered are 64, 256, and 1024 bytes. As the plots illustrate, the adapter throughput increases as packet arrival rate increases until it reaches a threshold value, after which performance remains steady. This is the maximum throughput achievable with the present adapter configuration.

MEMORY ORGANIZATION

Analysis of the reception process enables an architect to identify several limitations that can be addressed. In the basic adapter, shown in Figure 5-2, the processor executes all memory management operations in addition to protocol code execution. Furthermore, the processor remains idle during packet data movement on the bus because it cannot access memory and thus it can neither access data nor code, which is also stored in the same memory used by the DMA. Architectural enhancements are necessary to enable higher utilization of the processor, as well as off-loading of memory management operations, so that the processor can be dedicated to protocol execution. Taking into account architectural concepts from general-purpose processors, one can employ a specialized memory management unit (MMU) for the management of memory as well as a partitioned memory structure in order to enable parallelism among data transfer, memory management, and protocol execution. The following discussions describe and evaluate these architectural enhancements.

Memory management unit with local memory

Operation of the basic adapter requires that the processor performs at least four memory management operations during packet reception and two more during processing the packet header. These operations can be assigned to a specialized hardware unit, the Memory Management Unit, which implements all memory management operations. In principle, these operations can be executed in parallel with data movement and/or protocol processing. For example, a new free buffer address can be identified or buffer enqueueing (or dequeueing) can be performed in parallel with data movement to memory. However, such concurrency is achievable only if the MMU has its own local memory that holds the necessary data structure information. Specifically, the MMU needs to maintain pointers to memory buffers, link information for the packets and the queues, etc. When the MMU performs memory management operations, it needs to access and manipulate this data structure information. An MMU with its own local memory executes its operations without interfering with the bus and the remaining packet memory. Thus, a partitioned memory configuration is necessary for parallelism of memory management and the remaining adapter operations.

Figure 5-5 shows an adapter configuration, based on the basic adapter, with a specialized MMU and its own local memory. The specialized MMU can be implemented either in hardware, as an ASIC, or in software using a separate general-purpose processor, as described elsewhere [158]. Independently of its exact implementation, the MMU presents a coprocessor instruction set to the remainder of the system, which is specialized for the necessary memory management operations. This instruction set includes operations such as GetFree() and RetFree (buffer) where a buffer is obtained from a Free List or is returned to Enqueue (buffer, queue) and Dequeue(queue) where a buffer is enqueued to or dequeued from a queue, ReadTop(queue) where the address of a queue is read, etc. The cost of these operations is small, when using a specialized MMU, as Table 5-1 demonstrates. Table 5-1 shows the cost of these operations for an ASIC implementation,

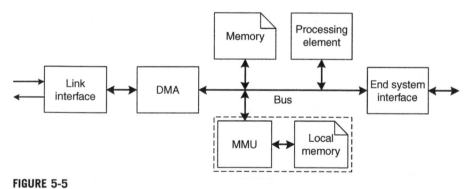

FIGURE 5-5

Adapter configuration with memory management unit.

Table 5-1 MMU Instruction Delays		
Instruction	**ASIC implementation**	**Software implementation**
Get free	Four cycles	34 assembly instructions
Return free	Three cycles	28 assembly instructions
Enqueue	Six cycles	29 assembly instructions
Dequeue	Eight cycles	33 assembly instructions
Read top	Five cycles	33 assembly instructions

as well as for a software one [158]. In the former case, the cost is expressed in clock cycles, while in the latter case it is expressed in assembly instructions per operation.

The effect of inclusion of a specialized MMU with its own local memory is illustrated in Figure 5-6, which plots the effective throughput of the two adapter configurations. As the plots illustrate, in the adapter configuration with the ARM

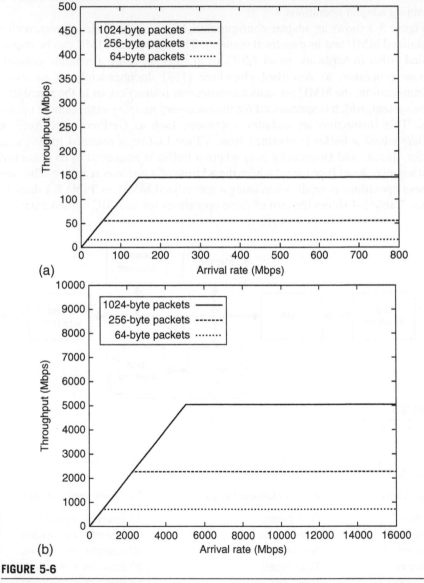

(a)

(b)

FIGURE 5-6

Effective throughput of adapter configuration with MMU (a) x86 based and (b) ARM based.

processor as PE, there is a 20% throughput improvement for short packets and a 10% improvement for long packets. In the case of the x86-based adapter, the corresponding improvements are 7.5 and 4.25%, respectively. The higher than double improvement of the adapter with the newer, faster processor is mainly due to improvement of the data bus performance: AHB has double the width of that used in the x86 processor [118] and a clock cycle that is 10 times shorter. The improvement in processing power of the attached PE is not a key factor for the performance improvement, considering that the packet transfer delay from the incoming link to the memory is not dependent on the speed of the processor but on the performance of the bus.

Memory management unit and processor with local memory

In the previous analysis of the reception process, we considered that the processor does not have any attached local memory. This results in the processor being idle during packet data movement between the network link and the adapter memory. However, the processor can execute instructions and process packets if one attaches a local memory to it containing protocol processing instructions and providing working memory space. This occurs because the processor can store necessary data in its own local memory and does not have to compete with other components for memory access during protocol code execution.

The inclusion of local memory to the processor can lead to significant improvement in performance due to the overlapping of protocol code execution with packet data transfer. As calculated earlier, the data movement delay over the bus is $\frac{N}{D} t_B$, that is, it is proportional to the received packet length and thus significant for long packets. For example, the delay to transfer a 1024-byte packet to memory is at least 128 bus cycles, that is, at least 628 idle CPU cycles in the case of the ARM processor and AHB bus, where one AHB bus cycle equals 4.9 CPU cycles.

Figure 5-7 illustrates the structure of the adapter adopting this partitioning of the memory, splitting physical memory into three partitions: one local to the

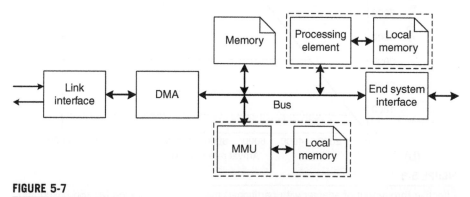

FIGURE 5-7

Adapter configuration with MMU and processor local memory.

MMU, one local to the processor, and one for packet storage. The effective throughput for the system for the two analyzed adapters, with the two different processors, is measured through simulation and is plotted in Figure 5-8.

As expected from the previous analysis, the throughput of this adapter configuration is significantly improved over the adapter configuration without the

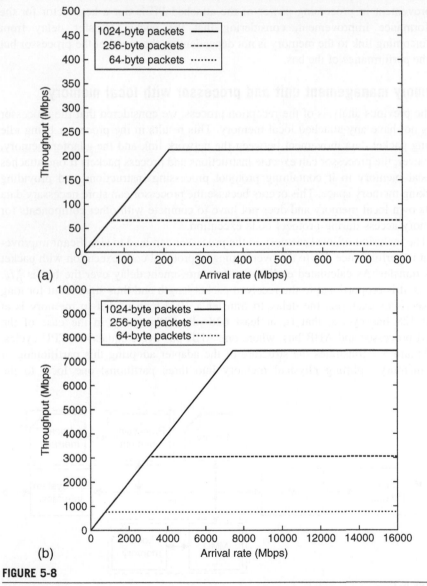

(a)

(b)

FIGURE 5-8

Effective throughput of adapter with partitioned memory configuration (a) x86 based and (b) ARM based.

processor local memory. In the case of long packets, the throughput increase is 45%. The origin of this improvement is the higher processor utilization due to overlapping header processing and data movement during packet reception. Improvement for the case of short packets is smaller, specifically 10%, because, in this traffic scenario, the throughput is dominated mostly by the protocol processing delay t_P rather than the shorter data movement delay $\frac{N}{D}t_B$. When the packet is long enough, the data movement delay becomes the dominant factor of system throughput.

In addition to throughput results, simulation data confirm that adapter components are utilized more efficiently in the case of partitioned adapter memory. Table 5-2 summarizes the peak processor utilization, for the case of the ARM processor, for various packet length traffic scenarios. Results show clearly that, for longer packets (256 and 1024 bytes), processor utilization improves significantly relative to the adapter configuration without the partitioned memory.

INTELLIGENT DMA

The effort to utilize the PE only for protocol code execution and offloading all other common operations to other components in the adapter also requires reengineering of the DMA component. A classical DMA controller requires that the system processor initializes it before data transfer and terminates the data transfer, as the DMA informs the processor upon completion of the data transfer. Adoption of an *intelligent DMA unit* enables transfer of packets between link and memory without the processor's intervention. This leads to significant delay savings, not only due to the relief of the processor from setting up the DMA transfer, but due to the avoidance of task switching due to interrupts as well; this is a significant saving, considering the high cost of context switching required for interrupt handling.

Figure 5-9 shows the effect of the inclusion of intelligent DMA in the adapter with the partitioned memory organization analyzed in the previous section. As Figure 5-9 illustrates, adoption of intelligent DMA provides significant further improvement, which reaches 20% for short packets and 10% for longer ones in the case of ARM-based adapter configuration. This improvement originates mainly from the elimination of processor context switching due to interrupts. In

Table 5-2 ARM11 Processor Utilization for Different Adapter Configurations

MMU local memory		MMU and processor local memories	
Packet length	*Processor utilization*	*Packet length*	*Processor utilization*
64	0.738	64	0.794
256	0.590	256	0.784
1024	0.328	1024	0.483

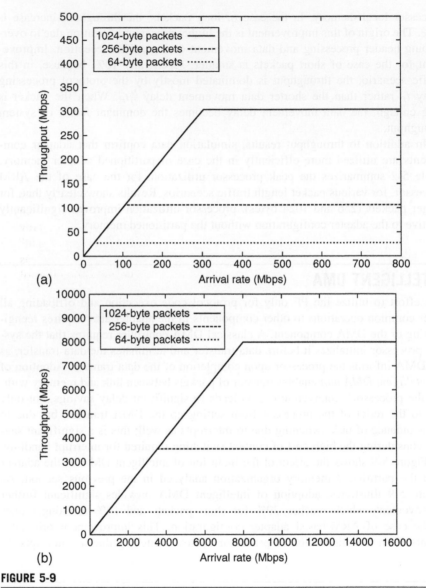

FIGURE 5-9

Effective throughput of adapter with partitioned memory and intelligent DMA (a) x86 based and (b) ARM based.

the case of the older processor, the improvement is 50 and 30% for short and long packets, respectively. The elimination of processor context switching delays is more beneficial for older processor generations because of their high interrupt cost. Specifically, one context switch on the x86-based adapter has a cost equal to 50 instructions [118, 155] (14% of the protocol processing delay), while the corresponding

Table 5-3 Protocol Processor Utilization

Packet length	Processor utilization
1024	0.519
256	0.921
64	0.968

cost is equal to 30 instructions [98] for the ARM-based adapter (8.5% of the protocol processing delay).

Considering all the previous architectural enhancements of the adapter, the PE is left only with the task of protocol processing, enabling it to be renamed as *protocol processor*. Peak utilization of the protocol processor for the analyzed packet lengths is shown in Table 5-3. Utilizations in the table, higher than those of the previous adapter configurations, show that for short packets, the protocol processor's utilization reaches almost 100%. However, utilization is relatively low for the case of long packets. This is due to several parameters, including the contention of the protocol processor with the MMU and, most importantly, with the intelligent DMA whose transfers occupy the bus for long intervals as the packet length increases.

Considering all of the aforementioned, an adapter employing a specialized MMU, a distributed memory organization, and an intelligent DMA unit is clearly the best solution in terms of throughput preservation. As simulation results indicate, an ARM-based adapter preserves the bandwidth of an 8-Gbps link delivering packets of 1024 bytes up to higher layers of the network protocol stack.

MULTIPROCESSOR PROCESSING ELEMENT

Adapter configuration analyzed up to this point attempts to achieve a balanced design among data movement, memory management, and protocol processing, demonstrating that a balanced design can exploit parallelism among operations and improve performance significantly. Importantly, the final configuration discussed earlier indicates that the protocol processor (the PE) becomes the system bottleneck with its utilization reaching 100% as packet sizes become smaller. Up to this point, we have considered a single processor for protocol processing, focusing on a modern RISC-type architecture, the ARM processor. The following evaluates use of a multiprocessor architecture for the protocol processor. Specifically, we evaluate a network adapter with a Cell Broadband Engine (Cell BE) [27, 57]. The Cell BE is an effective multiprocessor architecture suitable for high-performance network adapters due to its multiple high-performance processing elements and fast internal interconnection. Considering the hardware resources of the Cell BE, we analyze the effect of parallelizing protocol execution on its eight processing elements, as well as the configuration where multiple packets are processed in parallel, each by a different processing element.

The Cell BE is a product of collaboration among three major companies: IBM, Sony, and Toshiba. Its architecture, shown in Figure 5-10, is heterogeneous and includes several processing elements, specifically one Power processor and eight synergistic processor elements (SPE), all operating at 3.2 GHz. The Power processor element (PPE) employs a 64-bit, multithreaded Power processor with two concurrent hardware threads, each running as a separate core that executes a thread [57]. The PPE has a local memory subsystem composed of a two-level cache. Each of the eight synergistic processor elements (SPE) employs processor architecture with a local store unit and a local memory controller. Additionally, the Cell BE is equipped with a memory interface controller and an I/O interface controller.

All the components of the Cell BE are interconnected through an internal interconnection called the Element Interconnect Bus (EIB), which operates at 1.6 GHz. The EIB separates bus commands from data transfers; specifically, it employs a star network for commands and four 16-byte-wide data rings for data transfers, two of which run clockwise and the other two counterclockwise. Each ring allows up to three parallel data transfers, when their paths do not overlap. Each component attached to the EIB is enabled to send and receive 16 bytes of data simultaneously during every bus cycle; thus, the maximum data bandwidth of the EIB reaches 96 bytes per clock cycle [27].

Adoption of the Cell BE, or any similar architecture, in an adapter provides several degrees of freedom for the mapping of functions on multiple processing

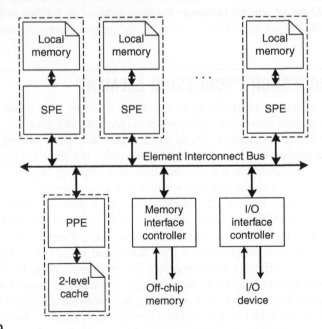

FIGURE 5-10

The Cell BE structure.

elements of the multiprocessor. For the remainder of the chapter, we use the most advanced adapter architecture as a basis, the one with partitioned memory, MMU, and intelligent DMA and map its components to processing elements in various configurations.

Single SPE configuration

Considering the organization of the Cell BE with heterogeneous elements, we employ the Cell BE elements as shown in Figure 5-11. The Cell BE is used for both the protocol processor and MMU functionalities. Specifically, the PPE is assigned with the MMU functionality, while a single SPE is assigned with protocol processing. The off-chip (off-Cell BE) packet memory is connected to the Cell BE memory interface, while the Cell BE I/O interface is attached to the intelligent DMA unit. Thus, the EIB interconnects all adapter components.

The case of the Cell BE offers significantly more advantages than just a set of powerful processing elements. These advantages originate from the EIB and its multiple data rings. The advantage of multiple data rings becomes apparent when considering the contention on the single bus of the adapter analyzed earlier. In the single bus adapter, it is often the case that two different resources compete for the bus for two different operations; for example, consider the scenario where the protocol processor requests the bus for an MMU operation while the intelligent DMA requests the bus for a data transfer. In the single bus adapter, these two requests are serialized, whereas in a system such as the Cell BE this scenario leads to parallel execution of the two requests. This parallelism is possible because the processor and the intelligent DMA can use different rings to complete their operations without conflict and thus conflict delays. The effect of multiple data rings of the EIB can be observed in data of Table 5-4 where utilization of the SPE protocol processing element, as measured with the simulator, for the packet lengths analyzed is presented A comparison with Table 5-3, which presents protocol processor utilization for the single bus adapter, demonstrates significant improvement for long packets (the utilization was approximately 52%), reaching almost the same utilization as for the traffic of short packets, about 98%.

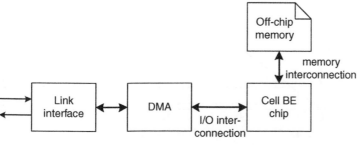

FIGURE 5-11

Adapter configuration with Cell BE.

Table 5-4 Protocol Processor Utilization in Cell BE

Packet length	Processor utilization
1024	0.979
256	0.983
64	0.983

The overall throughput of the on-chip Cell BE adapter configuration, as provided by the simulator, is shown in Figure 5-12. As plots indicate, results are improved significantly. Comparing the throughput with that of a conventional processor, such as ARM11, there is an improvement of 400% in the case of short packets; this improvement is analogous to the processing power increase. In the case of long packets, the improvement is double, reaching 800%, as a result of better processor utilization due to the faster and conflict-free element interconnection, as mentioned earlier.

Multi-SPE configuration—protocol multiprocessing

Cell BE offers eight SPEs in the system, enabling parallelism in protocol execution. In an effort to use additional SPEs, one can assign them to packet processing, exploiting parallelism in different ways. There are two main methods to exploit

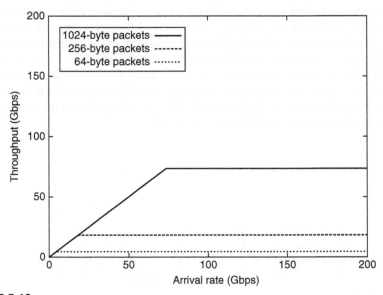

FIGURE 5-12

Adapter throughput in single-SPE configuration.

parallelism at this level. The first is to parallelize the execution of the protocol code to multiple SPEs, and the second is to have all SPEs execute protocol code on different packets in parallel.

This subsection analyzes the first case. We parallelize protocol execution by partitioning it into simpler functions [174] and assigning them to SPEs, retaining the dependencies between these functions through appropriate synchronization. In this case, protocol processing of a packet header is distributed to the eight SPEs of the Cell BE. Functional decomposition of protocol processing and mapping to eight execution elements results in a reduction of the critical path of LLC from 351 instructions to 208, according to the analysis of [174].

The performance of this adapter configuration is shown in Figure 5-13. As results show, there is an overall improvement of 40% for all packet lengths, which is in line with the reduction of the LLC critical path.

Multi-SPE configuration—spatial parallelism

An alternative approach for multi-SPE configuration is one exploiting spatial parallelism, where each SPE executes protocol processing on a different packet header. In the Cell BE system, where there are eight SPEs, eight different packets can be processed simultaneously. However, special attention must be paid to packet sequencing after processing. In a multiprocessor environment, if packets are placed immediately in an output queue after processing, they may be forwarded in a different order than they are received. This occurs for two reasons: (i) the processing

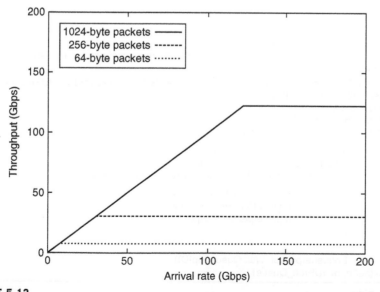

FIGURE 5-13

Adapter throughput in multi-SPE configuration exploiting spatial parallelism.

time of headers may differ, even if the same protocol code is executed on all headers, and (ii) there may be postprocessing resource contention, which may lead to a different order of packet header operation completion. Thus, a resequencing process is necessary in an adapter that exploits spatial parallelism.

The problem of resequencing packets is a known problem, as it appears in many protocols [140] and in multiprocessing environments [117]. The following describes an effective resequencing algorithm, the Priority-Coupled resequencing algorithm [13], which is executed by the processing elements rather than any other adapter component, such as the memory management unit. Using this approach, resequencing requires the use and management of two additional types of queues. Although the algorithm has been developed to accommodate multiple packet priorities, we consider only one priority for simplicity in the description.

The resequencing algorithm maintains the following queues: one input queue (Input_Queue) where incoming packets are enqueued, one output queue (Output_Queue) where processed packets are enqueued in the right order, one wait queue (Wait_Queue) per processing element where processed but out-of-sequence packets are enqueued, and, finally, one processor ID queue (IDProc_Queue), which stores the order in which the processors fetch packet headers from the Input_Queue. The concept of the resequencing algorithm is to have processors (SPEs) process headers, when idle, and sequence outgoing packets to the Output_Queue using the IDProc_Queue as the synchronizing, resequencing information.

An idle processor executes the algorithm shown in Figure 5-14, when the Input_Queue is unlocked and nonempty. In that case, the processor locks and

```
Lock(head_of_Input_Queue)
Dequeue(Input_Queue)                      // dequeues packet header and removes packet
from Input_Queue
Enqueue(MpID, IDProc_Queue)               // appends the Processor ID to IDProc_Queue
Unlock(head_of_Input_Queue)
Process_header()
Lock(head_of_IDProc_Queue)
if (MpID == first_ID_in_IDProc_Queue) {
              Dequeue(ID, IDProc_Queue)
              Enqueue(packet, Output_Queue)
              While (Wait_Queue(first_ID_in_IDProc_Queue != empty) {
                      Dequeue(ID, IDProc_Queue)
                      Dequeue(packet, Wait_Queue)
                      Enqueue(packet, Output_Queue)
              }
}
else      Enqueue(packet, Wait Queue(MpID))
Unlock(head_of_IDProc_Queue)
```

FIGURE 5-14

Resequencing algorithm.

accesses the head of the Input_Queue, obstructing any other processor from accessing the Input_Queue at this time. Then, the processor fetches the header of the packet at the head of the Input_Queue and removes the packet from the Input_Queue. Subsequently, the processor enqueues its own ID to the tail of the IDProc_Queue and unlocks the head of the Input_Queue; this enables the next packet of the Input_Queue to become available for processing. The processor executes the protocol code on the header and, when it completes processing, locks the head of the IDProc_Queue and checks if the head ID in that queue matches its own ID. If the IDs do not match, the processor enqueues the packet to its Wait_Queue, unlocks the head of the IDProc_Queue, and becomes idle. If the IDs match, the processor removes the ID from the IDProc_Queue, enqueues the packet in the Output_Queue, and checks the Wait_Queue of the next processor ID in the IDProc_Queue; this Wait_Queue is checked because already processed out-of-sequence packets may be waiting for the packet that was just enqueued in an Output_Queue. If this Wait_Queue is empty, the head of the IDProc_Queue is unlocked and the processor becomes idle. Otherwise, the processor dequeues the ID from the IDProc_Queue and transfers a packet from that Wait_Queue to the Output_Queue. It repeats this process until it finds the IDProc_ Queue empty or it encounters an empty Wait_Queue. When one of these conditions is satisfied, the processor unlocks the head of the IDProc_Queue and becomes idle.

Adoption of this resequencing method enables dynamic assignment of incoming packets to available processors, leading to high processor utilization and load balancing among the SPEs. The cost of resequencing is due to two sources of delay: (i) the execution of 64 instructions, inserted to the critical path of the protocol processing process [13], and (ii) additional memory management requests to the MMU.

The throughput of the Cell BE-based adapter exploiting spatial parallelism is shown in Figure 5-15. In order to evaluate the effect of resequencing, the processing delay follows an exponential distribution with mean value equal to 351 instructions so that outgoing packets are delivered out of sequence and thus invoke the resequencing overhead. In case of short packets, the adapter throughput is 5.5 times higher than that of the single SPE case. Considering the use of eight SPEs, the maximum speedup would be eight. The inability to achieve this speedup is due to resequencing, which places additional load to the SPEs as well as to the MMU. In the case of long packets, throughput is only 2.5 times higher than that of the single SPE case. This occurs because the memory controller becomes a bottleneck. As mentioned earlier, because each unit is connected to the EIB, the memory controller can send and receive up to 16 bytes per bus cycle, that is, 204 Gbps; the maximum throughput of the adapter is 180 Gbps in this case, a number that approximates the limit of data that can be transferred by the memory controller. This demonstrates clearly that the addition of multiple processing elements is not beneficial unless it is accompanied by a sufficiently high-performance memory system.

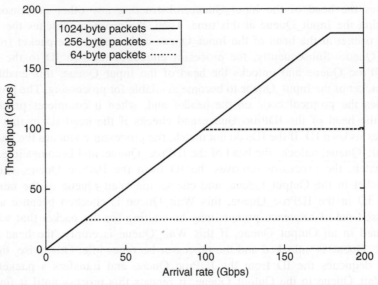

FIGURE 5-15

Adapter throughput in multi-SPE configuration—spatial parallelism.

MEMORY MANAGEMENT SCHEMES

The effective throughput of a network adapter is affected by the performance of all its components. Based on analyses given earlier and considering the simplicity of designing intelligent DMAs, critical components in the adapter architecture are the protocol processing element and the memory management unit. After analyzing the effect of protocol processing on overall performance in the previous section, we focus on the effect of the memory management unit in this section. We investigate alternative configurations of the basic, single bus adapter to overcome the bottlenecks introduced by it.

The MMU affects adapter performance significantly. Consider, for example, the reception process of a packet in the adapter shown in Figure 5-7. The packet is moved to the packet memory and then it is enqueued to a queue. When a new packet arrives, a free buffer pointer must be provided, but it may be unavailable before the enqueueing process of the previous packet is finished by the MMU. Although caching and pointer pre-fetching techniques can overcome such conflicts as the above, the delay to obtain the necessary memory management information is unavoidable in several traffic scenarios, such as short packets arriving in long bursts.

The problem becomes clear when we consider an adapter where packets arriving at the network interface are transferred directly to the end system without any protocol processing. Assuming a packet interarrival delay equal to zero, the only delays in the system are those of data transferring to/from packet memory and those of memory management operations. This enables us to focus on the effect of the memory management unit on adapter performance, as both link and end system interfaces use MMU services to perform reception and transmission to the end system. Simulation results for system throughput of the attached MMU, in packets per second, are plotted in Figure 5-16 as a function of packet length along with other adapter configurations described later.

As Figure 5-16 indicates, system throughput decreases as packet length increases. This occurs because the delay of data movement increases and becomes dominant as packet length increases. In the case of short packets, the limit on system throughput is posed by the MMU performance limitation, originating from the contention of all link interfaces on the MMU and because all MMU communication takes place over the bus. Figure 5-17, which plots MMU utilization as a function of packet length, shows that attached MMU reaches 80%, its maximum

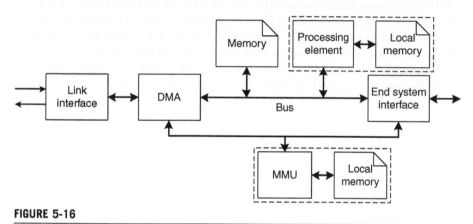

FIGURE 5-16

Adapter throughput for various memory management schemes.

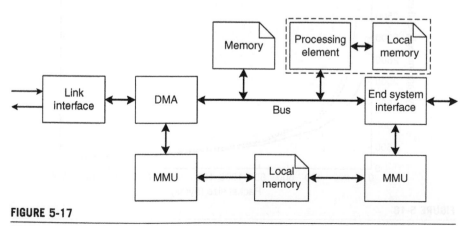

FIGURE 5-17

Memory management unit utilization for various memory management schemes.

value, in the case of short packet traffic and decreases as packet length increases. MMU utilization never reaches 100% due to contention on the adapter bus.

Detached MMU

Considering the limitations of the MMU and its conflicts on the single bus of the adapter with the intelligent DMA and the resulting data transfers, an architectural enhancement toward a better MMU performance is to detach the MMU from the bus and provide an alternative path to it, as shown in Figure 5-18. This allows interaction with the MMU to take place separately, without interference from packet data movement. The overall system performance of the detached MMU is plotted in Figure 5-16. The detachment of the MMU and the resulting reduction of conflicts on the bus result in a throughput improvement, which reaches 31% in the case of short packets. The improvement is due to better MMU utilization, which reaches 90% for 128-byte packets and 100% for packets up to 96 bytes long. Such utilization is significantly higher than that of previous configuration, even for longer packets. As Figure 5-17 illustrates, utilization of the detached MMU is higher than that of the attached MMU. The MMU utilization of both configurations decreases as the packet length increases and, when packet length equals to 1024 bytes, the two utilizations are approximately the same.

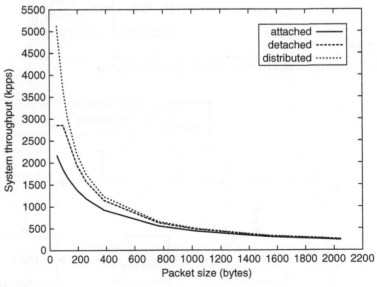

FIGURE 5-18

Detached MMU adapter configuration.

Distributed MMUs

Although detachment of the MMU from the adapter bus improves performance, MMU utilization reaches 100% fairly quickly, at packet lengths over 128 bytes, indicating that the MMU becomes the bottleneck of the system. One method to alleviate this bottleneck is the use of a parallel or distributed MMU scheme. Figure 5-19 shows the design of the adapter with the distributed MMU approach, employing two separate memory management units. The concept is to have the first MMU serve the intelligent DMA unit and the second serve the end system interface, while the processor can be served from either of the MMUs. For consistency and correct operation, MMUs share memory, which stores the MMU data structure information. The distributed MMU approach can be used efficiently because the need for synchronization among the MMU units, when accessing the shared memory, is limited. Such an approach increases performance dramatically, as Figure 5-16 demonstrates. The figure shows that the throughput is almost doubled for short packets. Performance improvement is due to alleviation of the MMU bottleneck, as Figure 5-17 illustrates with plots of the aggregate utilization of the distributed MMU scheme.

SUMMARY

This chapter introduced the basic operation and architecture of network adapters. We analyzed the operation of the adapter in a systematic way and identified bottlenecks of the system. Starting with the structure of the memory subsystem of the

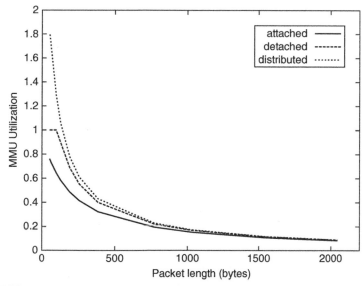

FIGURE 5-19

Distributed MMU configuration.

adapter, we introduced a partitioned memory configuration that improves adapter performance significantly. We considered the effect of adoption of intelligent DMA techniques, which prove to be beneficial. We also analyzed the effect of processor structure and performance, exploring multiprocessor structures for the processing element and their effect on the performance of the adapter. Importantly, we analyzed the resequencing problem that emerges when spatial parallelism is exploited at the protocol processing level. Finally, we identified the memory management bottleneck of the adapter and evaluated alternative architectures for further performance improvement. The presented analyses indicate that a well-balanced design that balances the load of operation among all adapter components leads to high component utilization, achieving the maximum achievable performance for the network adapter.

Bridges and layer 2 switches

INTRODUCTION

Bridges and layer 2 switches are network systems that interconnect networks at the Data Link layer of the OSI Reference Model. Considering the classification of network systems presented in Chapter 2, bridges and layer 2 switches implement a two-layer protocol stack for each network attachment, as shown in Figure 6-1, and switch frames among these stacks.

Layer 2 switches can be considered a special implementation of bridges and thus can be viewed as a subset of bridging systems. The following discussion uses the term *bridge* to refer to all data link layer internetworking systems and describes the specifics of layer 2 switches at the end of the chapter.

Figure 6-1 shows the route of a frame traversing two networks attached to the bridge. In general, a data link layer frame arriving at the bridge is received and examined to identify whether it should be forwarded to another network or not. This examination is necessary considering the broadcasting nature of several common local area network (LAN) technologies (e.g., Ethernet or Token Ring). When using broadcasts, a bridge commonly receives frames that are targeted for end systems on the same LAN segment as the transmitting end system. If a frame is targeted for an end system on the same LAN segment, then the bridge does not forward it, but rejects it; this process is commonly called *filtering*. If the frame is targeted to an end system attached to another network, then the bridge identifies the appropriate output port for the frame and transmits the frame accordingly.

The operation and the structure of bridges are influenced by organization of the data link protocol layer as defined by the IEEE standardization effort. As discussed in Chapter 2, the evolution of local area networks has led to a standardization that divides the data link layer in two sublayers: the Media Access Control (MAC) and the Logical Link Control (LLC). IEEE has been leading a systematic standardization of local area networks, and some networks classified as Metropolitan Area Networks (MANs), in the following fashion: All standards are defined as part of the 802 standard family, where 802.2 defines a standard LLC protocol operating on top of all 802.x ($x > 2$) network standards. Each 802.x standard defines a corresponding pair of protocols for the physical layer and MAC layer (i.e., lower data link sublayer). This standardization approach is shown in Figure 6-2.

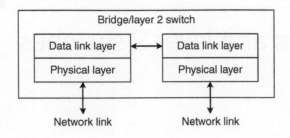

FIGURE 6-1

Bridge and layer 2 switch operation.

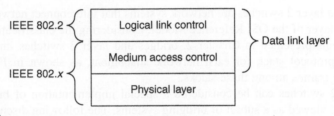

FIGURE 6-2

IEEE 802.x standardization.

Considering the IEEE standardization effort, network systems operating at the data link layer can switch frames at two levels: (i) MAC or (ii) LLC. The ability to switch at the MAC level seems like a natural choice, as all MAC protocols of the IEEE 802.x family—the predominant family of bridged networks—operate under the same standard 802.2 protocol. However, standardized protocols of the 802.x family present significant differences between them in many parameters, such as frame length, priorities, routing methods, etc. As a characteristic example, Figure 6-3 illustrates the frame format of Ethernet (IEEE 802.3) and Token Ring (IEEE 802.5) protocols. The structure and fields of the corresponding headers indicate significant differences in the operation of the two networks, which make the

Ethernet frame

Preamble	Start delimiter	Destination address	Source address	Length	Data	Frame check sequence

Token Ring frame

Preamble	Start delimiter	Frame control	Destination address	Source address	Data	Frame check sequence

FIGURE 6-3

Ethernet and Token Ring frame format.

ability to switch frames directly at the MAC sublayer a challenging task. However, if one assumes that the bridged networks are all the same, for example, Ethernet, then frames can be switched at the MAC sublayer in a straightforward fashion. Thus, data link layer network systems may switch frames at two different levels, depending on the environment and the requirements.

Bridges are used as building blocks for large networks, interconnecting large numbers of local area networks. Bridges enable network connectivity at a low level and with less processing requirements per frame than other network systems, such as routers.

TYPES OF BRIDGES

While the conceptual operation of bridges is simple, there are many specific issues relating to the types of local area networks connected, as well as the methods used to establish routing function between end systems. These details lead to complex operation requirements, especially for bridges that interconnect heterogeneous local area networks with significant differences in their protocols. Different types of bridges have emerged based on bridge operation, associated link layer protocols, and implementation parameters.

Various parameters are used to classify bridges. One parameter is the exact protocol sublayer used for frame switching, that is, MAC or LLC. Although an LLC-level bridge appears as a generic solution to bridge between heterogeneous networks, significant differences between associated MAC protocols do not allow for a generic solution. For example, a bridge between an Ethernet and a Token Ring network is unable to translate priorities of Token Ring frames, simply because Ethernet does not support priorities; this is independent of the fact that both Ethernet and Token Ring networks operate under the IEEE 802.2 LLC protocol. In contrast, MAC bridges, which interconnect network segments of the same type (i.e., link layer protocol), can easily switch MAC frames between networks. However, it is clear that MAC bridges are protocol dependent. For this reason, several MAC bridges include LLC level switching, that is, LLC frame handling consistent with the standards.

A second classification of bridges is based on their location relatively to network segments, as depicted in Figure 6-4. In some network configurations, bridged networks are separated geographically, with local area networks interconnecting end systems in each location and a wide area network (WAN) interconnecting bridges of the different locations. A local bridge is one that interconnects networks at one location, while a remote bridge is one that interconnects one location with another one, thus providing bridging services at the remote location [70, 71]. An alternative view is to consider the two interconnected bridges of the locations as a *split* bridge interconnecting the two locations, where the two portions of the split bridge are separated geographically and interconnected through a wide area network. This classification is interesting from an architectural point of view due

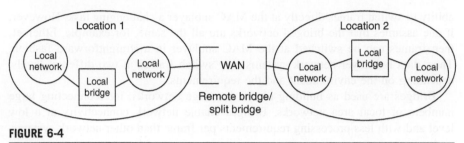

FIGURE 6-4

Local and remote bridge.

to the need for managing heterogeneous ports (LAN and WAN), which typically have different requirements for performance and functionality.

The third and most widely used classification for bridges is the one based on the routing method used by the bridges. The two routing methods used are transparent bridging and source routing bridging. In transparent bridging, routing of frames is performed using a routing table in every bridge, as shown in Figure 6-5(a). The routing tables in interconnected bridges are populated using a learning method, as is described in the following section; for this, transparent bridges are often called *learning bridges*. In contrast, source routing bridges forward frames based on a route specification that is included in the frames. Assume, for example, that end system ES_1, shown in Figure 6-5(b), transmits a frame to end system ES_2, which resides in a different network. Using source routing, ES_1 attaches to the frame the specific route that has to be followed in order to reach ES_2. End systems, like ES_1, calculate the specific route for a target system by discovering available routes; this discovery operation requires that origin systems transmit special frames, called *explorer packets*, to discover routes and then choose among the candidate routes using various criteria, such as first discovered route, shortest route, etc. Transparent bridging and source routing bridging have been combined in source-route transparent bridging (SRT), a methodology that has been included in the IEEE 802.1 standard, in addition to transparent bridging. The goal of SRT is to provide a standardized solution that accommodates transparent bridges, as well as source-route bridges.

TRANSPARENT BRIDGING AND SPECIAL-PURPOSE SUBSYSTEMS

Transparent bridging is a popular bridging method that enables efficient routing and management, as well as mobility of end systems. The term "transparent" originates from the fact that, with this method, end systems are oblivious to the existence and configuration of bridges inserted in the network. Transparent bridges operate transparently, performing the necessary routing and management functions without the involvement of end stations. The effectiveness of transparent bridging led to its inclusion in the IEEE 802.x standard suite as part of standard IEEE 802.1.

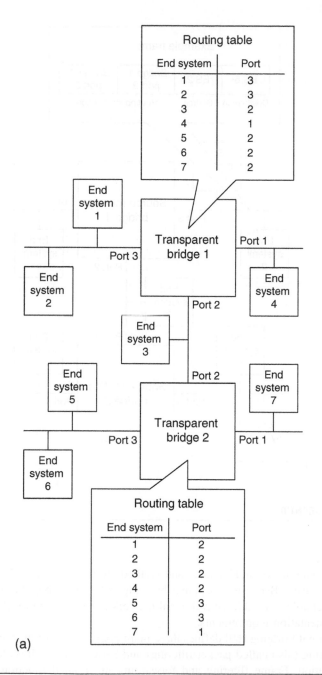

(a)

FIGURE 6-5

Transparent and source routing bridges.

(Continued)

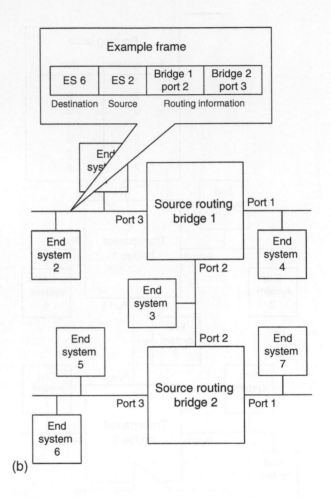

FIGURE 6-5—CONT'D

There exist alternative architectures and methods to transparent bridging, as mentioned previously. Because transparent bridging is the most popular and common bridging technology used in conventional networks, we focus on its characteristics and implementation requirements.

Transparent bridging [69] defines three main operations for transparent bridges: frame filtering (also called packet filtering) and forwarding, address learning, and loop resolution. Frame filtering and forwarding are related functions in that an incoming frame has to be examined by the bridge in order to decide whether the frame is filtered by the bridge (i.e., dropped) or forwarded (i.e., routed toward the receiving end system). The bridge drops frames for which the transmitting and receiving end systems are connected to the network segment(s) that are reachable through the receiving port of the bridge; otherwise, the bridge forwards the receiving frame accordingly. The decision about whether to filter or forward, and through which outgoing port, is made using a filtering database (FDB), which is maintained by the transparent bridge and constitutes one of its main components.

Address learning is the process through which a transparent bridge inserts and manages the filtering database in order to include current information about the network and end systems. The goal of the address learning process is to enable transparent bridges to be autonomous and learn routes to end systems without explicit intervention of end systems or other bridges. The learning process is straightforward: when a frame arrives at a port, the bridge extracts its source address and then inserts in the filtering database an entry with the source address and the bridge port at which the frame arrived; if an entry already exists, it is updated accordingly; the port listed in the filtering database can be used to route frames to this end system. Thus, a transparent bridge learns the ports through which each end system is reachable by monitoring the source address of each frame received by every bridge port. If the bridge needs to forward a frame for which there is no entry in the filtering database, the frame is broadcast on all ports (except the receiving port). Because there must be support for end system mobility and network reconfiguration, learned routes to end systems are valid only for limited amounts of time. A set of timers, for example hello timer, topology change notification timer, and aging timer, are employed by the transparent bridging standard. Among them, aging timers are the most important ones from the bridge design point of view because an aging timer is associated with each entry of the filtering database and needs to be reset every time the entry is accessed due to frame forwarding; when an aging timer expires, the corresponding entry of the filtering database becomes invalid.

Frame forwarding and address learning processes are effective and lead to correct operation of the transparent bridging architecture as long as the overall network does not contain any loops. However, this assumption is unrealistic for real-world networks. For this reason, the transparent bridging standard includes a loop resolution process. The concept of the loop resolution process is simple: modeling the network as a graph with nodes being the bridges and the end systems and with edges being the corresponding links; the transparent bridges calculate a spanning tree of the network. A spanning tree, by definition, is a subset of the graph that maintains connectivity of all nodes and does not contain loops. All frame forwarding is performed over links that are part of the spanning tree. The spanning tree is calculated using a spanning tree algorithm, implemented through a bridge protocol running over the LLC-1 protocol [74], which is used to exchange bridge control information. The spanning tree algorithm is described in detail elsewhere [69, 139].

Transparent bridging places significant requirements on the architecture of the bridge because of the functionality required and the operations performed on a per-frame basis. The bridge has to perform several operations per frame, which include forwarding the frame and managing the filtering database, as required for the learning process. In contrast, source-routing bridges do not require such significant number of operations per frames because the complexity of identifying routes and routing frames across networks is placed at the end systems, which perform all needed operations.

To identify the functional and performance requirements of transparent bridges, we analyze the route of a frame through the bridge, focusing on operations required for the filtering database. When a transparent bridge receives a frame, the bridge examines the header to perform filtering and forwarding based on the filtering database information. Specifically, the FDB is accessed twice per frame: (i) the destination address is used to decide whether the frame is forwarded through another bridge port or filtered (if it is targeted for a system on the same side of the port through which it is received) and (ii) the source address is used to update the location information of the transmitting system (the learning process is implemented with the transparent bridge learning the ports through which a certain system is reachable by monitoring the source addresses of incoming frames). In addition to the aforementioned FDB accesses, the bridge needs to perform timer operations on a per-frame basis. For example, the aging timer of an address needs to be reset every time an incoming frame is received from a specific address. In this way, if a system becomes silent for a long time, its associated FDB entry becomes invalid after a certain interval; this is necessary in order to delete old FDB entries, which may be wrong in case a system is moved to a different location in the network. If no FDB entry exists for a destination address, then the corresponding system is unknown to the network, that is, it has not transmitted anything yet. In this case, the transparent bridging protocol requires that the bridge broadcasts the frame to all ports except the source port, in expectation that the destination system will respond and a route will be identified eventually.

Considering the operations performed in a transparent bridge during a frame's processing, it becomes clear that special attention has to be paid to implementation of the subsystems that manage the filtering database and the timers. Management of the database is critical to performance, as incoming frames, which may arrive in parallel on different ports, may trigger multiple access requests. Because the database is read and may be updated during frame processing, special attention has to be paid to data consistency. Accommodation of parallel operations requires the use of parallel/distributed processing methods, as well as database consistency techniques. Importantly, the strict timing requirements of high-speed networks lead to additional, important issues that need to be addressed (e.g., the use of hashing mechanisms for the indexing of MAC addresses, determining appropriate data structures for the database that enable real-time processing of frames).

In addition to management of the filtering database, critical operations include management of the timers related to the database entries. Although the transparent bridging standard employs several timers, the most critical one is the aging timer: for every incoming frame, the corresponding timer associated with the source address of the frame needs to be reset. If the timer is not reset, the corresponding entry expires at some point in time and the entry needs to be erased from the filtering database. Thus, management of the aging timers requires fast operations for timer reset as well as entry deletion. These operations require special data structure designs so that they can be performed efficiently, that is, in constant time independently of the size of the database, and meet the performance requirements of the attached networks. For example, the *timing wheel* data structure, a data structure used commonly for timer management, helps achieve constant time deletion of several expiring timers. However, it does not enable timer reset in constant time, considering that several timers may have the same time value; a different data structure (e.g., a table) can be employed to provide efficient reset. Thus, the nontrivial problem of achieving several efficient operations requires development of complex combined data structures. An example of this approach is described in detail in the following section.

HIGH-PERFORMANCE TRANSPARENT BRIDGE ARCHITECTURE

High-Performance Transparent Bridge (HPTB) is an architecture of a transparent bridge targeted to achieve scalability and connectivity of packet networks up to 800 Mbps and cell-based (ATM) networks up to 622 Mbps [9, 53]. This section presents HPTB architecture in detail as an example of a sophisticated layer 2 network system.

Figure 6-6 illustrates the structure of HPTB, which is analogous to the structure of network systems, as presented in Chapter 2. HPTB includes four main subsystems: (i) network attachment units, (ii) memory (buffering), (iii) internal interconnect, and (iv) a protocol processing subsystem. The goal of network attachment units is to enable network connectivity to the attached networks, executing physical and MAC layer protocols. Incoming frames are processed and buffered. Buffering is necessary, as there is no guarantee that a frame is forwarded to the outgoing port immediately due to conflicts with other frames targeted to the same outgoing port. The internal switching component provides connectivity among network attachment units and the memory subsystem. The decision to use a switch as the internal interconnection is due to the need to exploit parallelism in data frame processing, transfer, and storage in order to meet the high-performance requirements of the attached networks. In addition, one needs to accommodate processing of frames that do not require forwarding (or filtering), but are destined to the bridge itself. A protocol processing subsystem processes these frames. Because these frames do not need to be forwarded to a network, but are absorbed by the bridge, the protocol processing subsystem can be viewed as analogous to the network attachment units: it constitutes the final destination of these frames within the bridge.

The main subsystems and their interaction are described in more detail here.

1. Internal Switching Component (ISC): The ISC implements data paths necessary in HPTB for delivering frames (or cells) between the memory and the network attachment units and the protocol processing subsystem. The ISC operates in a synchronous fashion, using a system clock with two phases, each phase

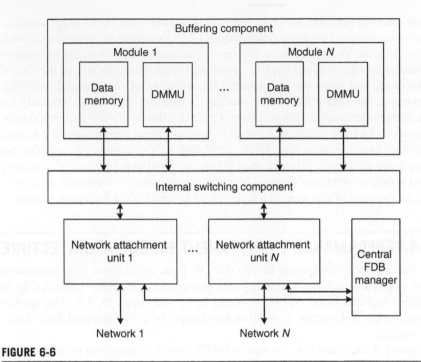

FIGURE 6-6

Structure of the High-Performance Transparent Bridge.

employing 50% of the clock cycle. During the first phase, called *receiving phase*, data are transferred from the network attachment units (and the protocol processing unit) to the buffering subsystem, while during the second phase, called *transmitting phase*, data are transferred from the buffering subsystem to the network attachment units (and the protocol processing unit). Data transfers over the ISC are implemented using internal, fixed-size packets that contain 64 bytes of data and 8 bytes of control information, denoted as the *control word*. The control word includes information necessary for memory management. The ISC is implemented using a crossbar fabric and a scheduler, which schedules data transfers based on status information of data in the buffering subsystem and the status of the network attachment units.

2. Network Attachment Unit (NAU): Network attachment units provide connectivity to the attached networks, one unit per network. Each NAU implements the corresponding protocol stack of the attached network, that is, physical and MAC protocol. In addition, each NAU contains the necessary components to perform the bridging functions necessary for every frame, that is, filtering and forwarding, as well as learning. Thus, each NAU contains a copy of the filtering database and the data structures necessary for management of the corresponding timers. Inclusion of the local FDB copy and timer management

is necessary to enable parallel processing of frames and to meet the high-performance requirements placed by the attached network speeds.

3. Buffering Component: The buffering subsystem provides the necessary storage area for frames that need to be queued in the bridge. Considering the scaling goals of HPTB, the buffering component is structured as a set of parallel memory modules, each managed by a corresponding memory management unit, called *Data Memory Management Unit* (DMMU). The number of memory modules is equal to the number of NAUs plus one for the protocol processing subsystem; as noted previously, the protocol processing subsystem is analogous to the NAUs. The equal number of NAUs and memory modules enables the parallel storing of frames in memories during the reception phase of the internal switching components, thus enabling conflict-free operation of the frame reception by all active NAUs. Clearly, this modular approach to the design of the buffering component may lead to low or unbalanced memory utilization, as each memory module is used for storage by its corresponding NAU. However, the parallel memory modules enable very high aggregate data transfer rates, avoiding memory contention that would appear if the buffering component was designed with a centralized single-port memory unit. Each memory module is managed in a similar fashion as the adapter described in Chapter 5. The memory is logically divided in fixed-size blocks, which are used to store frame data. Blocks that store data of the same frame are linked together in a logical queue, and frames directed to the same outgoing NAU are also linked together in a logical queue. The DMMU is the subsystem that implements all enqueue and dequeue operations for the logical queues and maintains all the necessary control information for implementation of the queues. In the HPTB design, each DMMU is implemented in hardware to meet the performance requirements placed by the attached networks. The adoption of parallel DMMUs, one per memory module, enables exploitation of parallelism in frame data transfers, as well as in queue maintenance operations, such as parallel enqueue and dequeue operations.

4. Protocol Processing Component: This component is responsible for the execution of all bridge operations that relate to the bridge protocol itself, network management, monitoring, etc. The transparent bridging standard requires that each bridge executes certain protocols, such as the bridge protocol and the bridge management protocol, for example, the loop resolution process. Furthermore, network management requires that specific information is maintained and managed by each network system. Finally, from an architectural point of view, it is necessary that a subsystem exists that monitors the system's operation and performs maintenance, checking, and reconfiguration operations occasionally. The protocol processing components implements all these processes. Although these operations do not place hard real-time performance requirements as frame forwarding operations do, they still generate a processing load that should not interfere with the strict, real-time processing of frame forwarding. The need to provide additional processing power for these operations, as well as the structure

of the HPTB, enables the development of a special-purpose protocol processing component (subsystem) with a dedicated memory unit (and corresponding DMMU) similar to the NAUs. Inclusion of a specialized protocol processing component creates an appropriate architecture that meets the performance requirements of the overall bridge. The protocol processing component can be based on a general-purpose processor, a parallel processing system with processors [200], or even special-purpose protocol processors.

Operation of the HPTB and its components can be explained when considering the route of a frame through the system. An incoming frame arrives at the NAU attached to its network. On arrival, it is stored in a small buffer within the NAU and all time-critical operations are performed in the receiving NAU in real time; these operations include accesses to the filtering database and a reset of the corresponding aging timer. After this real-time processing of the frame, the frame is forwarded to the corresponding memory module through the internal switching component (ISC). The frame remains in this memory module until it is transferred to the appropriate outgoing NAU. During its storage in the memory, the frame is linked by the corresponding DMMU to the appropriate logical queue; typically, there is one logical queue organized and maintained per outgoing NAU. As frames are transmitted by the outgoing NAU, the frame eventually reaches the head of the logical queue and then is forwarded through the ISC to the outgoing NAU. As the frame is transmitted, it is stored only temporarily in a cut-through mode in a buffer on the outgoing NAU. Thus, each incoming frame is stored only once in data memory and traverses the internal switching component twice, once to be written into memory and once to be read.

In addition to frames being switched by the bridge, frames exist that are received and processed by the bridge, such as Bridge PDUs, as well as frames created and transmitted by the bridge. Incoming frames destined to the bridge are stored to the memory module that corresponds to the receiving NAU in exactly the same way as incoming frames destined for transmission. The only difference to regular frames is that these bridge frames are transmitted to the protocol processing component instead of an outgoing NAU. Similarly, frames that the bridge needs to create and transmit are generated by the protocol processing component. When the protocol processing unit creates a frame, it stores it to its corresponding memory module and the corresponding DMMU links it to the queue of the appropriate outgoing NAU where the frame needs to be transmitted. Typically, a bridge generates or receives frames for the protocol processing unit only infrequently. Thus, low-speed protocol processing components can meet the requirements of current networks easily. However, the scalability of the HPTB enables it to adopt any technology for the protocol processing component, employing high-speed processors and memories meeting the requirements of any attached network suite.

High-Performance Transparent Bridge Architecture constitutes a generic, scalable architecture, which can employ different technologies and accommodate different parameters, such as network speeds, memory sizes, etc. The design presented elsewhere [202] targets accommodation of network speeds up to 800 Mbps for variable size packet networks and 622 Mbps for cell-based ones. Using this structure, employing the internal switching interconnect, modular buffering, and independent network attachment units for the attached networks, the HPTB architecture is modular, scalable, and provides a high degree of parallelism in its operation.

Transparent bridging support unit

Management of the filtering database is one of the critical functions of a transparent bridge, as mentioned previously. Processing of an incoming frame to the bridge requires two FDB lookup operations (one with the source address as key and one with the destination address) and one timer operation. Assuming a continuous stream of incoming frames, it becomes clear that it is necessary to perform lookups and timer operations during a time interval equal to the duration of a frame transmission. For example, a sequence of short 30-byte frames arriving at an NAU over an 800-Mbps link leads to the requirement that all the aforementioned operations be executed within 300 ns (i.e., the transmission time of one frame on the link). The strict real-time requirements placed by high-speed networks lead to strong performance requirements on all operations, which, in turn, lead to the adoption of sophisticated architectures that exploit parallelism in order to meet the targeted performance. This is manifested in the HPTB through the use of replication for the FDB and the segmentation of the timer database, in addition to the maintenance of a dual data structure for the timers, in order to provide low complexity operations for all operations required on the timer data structure. The details of these techniques, employed by HPTB, are presented next.

Replicated filtering database

In a bridge like HPTB, many frames may be arriving simultaneously through different ports, all requiring access to the FDB in order to identify the port of exit and to implement the learning process. Thus, several FDB accesses may be required simultaneously, resulting in the FDB being a potential performance bottleneck. HPTB replicates the FDB to each network attachment unit, as shown in Figure 6-6, in order to enable parallel FDB accesses from the different network attachments. With a complete FDB copy, each NAU can perform fast read accesses, as required, in parallel with any other NAU that can access its own local copy in parallel. This concurrency is feasible and beneficial because the common case of an NAU access is that it is a read access. However, write operations on the FDB are also necessary and need to be accommodated appropriately so that consistency is guaranteed. For this purpose, write operations are implemented through a centralized FDB manager, considering that write operations are infrequent and thus noncritical in terms of performance.

The *central FDB manager* is responsible for management of the FDB overall, controlling and synchronizing all operations on the FDB, that is, read, write, and delete operations, which are performed by all NAUs. The main goals of the central

FDB manager are coordination and synchronization of the update operations (write and delete), which change the contents of the FDB. To achieve this, HPTB adopts a master/slave scheme, where the central FDB manager maintains a local copy of the FDB that serves as the reference copy of all FDB copies at the NAUs. The operation is simple: all NAUs, including the protocol processing unit, maintain their FDB copy and synchronize it with the central FDB manager's copy as necessary. For this purpose, HPTB implements one point-to-point connection per NAU between the NAU and the central FDB manager, which serves as the data path over which the NAU transmits to the manager requests for FDB update operations; these requests are sent through special commands, which include several parameters, such as the corresponding MAC address, port id, etc. Furthermore, a broadcast bus transmits data from the central FDB manager to all NAU-local FDB copies for synchronized updates. In this fashion, the update information is transmitted for all NAU-local FDB copies simultaneously. Each NAU receives information over the broadcast bus and updates its local FDB copy concurrently. The only consideration in this process is synchronization of an update at a local NAU FDB copy with any local read operation that may be in progress at the time of the update. As database operations are atomic, a NAU may need to store the update operation temporarily until a progressing read operation finishes first and then perform the update subsequently. If the central FDB manager receives two or more update operations from NAUs simultaneously, these operations are serialized by the manager. Importantly, the protocol processing unit acts equivalent to a NAU because the bridge protocols may also need to change FDB entries (e.g., set maximum value of the aging timer or include some static entries in the database).

Indexing of the FDB is an important issue since it affects system performance. In the case of HPTB, identification of an FDB entry is implemented through use of a simple hashing mechanism, taking advantage of the structure of IEEE universal 48-bit MAC addresses [184]. Considering that the 24 low-order bits of the MAC address are likely different among nodes, as manufacturers are provided with consecutive MAC address blocks, and the lack of structure in these 24 bits, HPTB uses these 24 low-order bits as the basis for a key for the identification of an FDB entry. In this hashing approach, the probability of a hashing conflict is low [83]. More specifically, HPTB uses the N low-order bits for the key when the FDB has a maximum size 2^N. Such a hashing mechanism enables the use of low-cost RAM memory for the storage of an FDB entry identifier rather than the use of high-speed CAM memories, which are typically used for lookup operations [47, 199]. Despite the low probability of hashing conflict, the mechanism has to be prepared for the case of conflicts as well. In that case, new entries are written in a hashing conflict area of the memory and are linked to the basic entry corresponding to the hashing key. In the HPTB implementation presented in [202], the architecture of HPTB can perform a conflict-free FDB operation in 90 ns. The hashing scheme, as well as details about the FDB data structure and the fields of each FDB entry, is described in more detail elsewhere [202].

Distributed aging timer

Transparent bridging employs several timers for the management of FDB data, such as the hello timer, the topology change notification timer, and the aging timer. Most of the timers are related to (re)configuration operations, which seldom occur. However, aging timers are used continuously during normal operation and constitute a critical set of variables in the system, influencing performance significantly.

Every entry of the FDB is associated with a specific aging timer. When an incoming frame arrives at the bridge, the source address is used for an FDB access and the corresponding FDB entry is reset to a maximum value; the recommendation of the transparent bridging standard is that this maximum value is 300 s [69]. Furthermore, every aging timer is decremented every second; if an entry is not reset within the 300 s from the last time it was reset, the value of the aging timer expires, that is, it becomes zero, and the entry is deleted from the FDB. Thus, two operations need to be implemented efficiently with aging timers: (i) a reset (or restart) operation (to the maximum value) that is used every time an entry is accessed and (ii) a delete operation that is used once a second to remove all expired aging timers. Both operations are critical to system performance: high-speed links with high frame arrival rates require one reset operation per frame arrival; delete operations may happen to a variable number of expired timers per second. Thus, an efficient data structure for maintaining aging timers and their operations is necessary.

High-Performance Transparent Bridge architecture addresses the issue of efficient aging timer management through partitioning of aging timer entries and the adoption of two data structures, each achieving close to linear complexity for each of the restart and delete operations. HPTB partitions aging timers for FDB entries according to NAUs, as a restart operation to a specific timer is performed by a specific NAU. Specifically, because frames from a specific MAC address will always arrive at the specific NAU through which the MAC address is reachable, this NAU is the only one that performs reset operations on the aging timer of the entry for this MAC address. Thus, the sets of aging timers reset by NAUs are disjoint, enabling partitioning of the aging timer set among all NAUs.

The concept of aging data structure management is the following. Each NAU implements a timing wheel and a timer table that enables direct access to a timer entry in the timing wheel [183], as shown in Figure 6-7. The timing wheel, with perimeter size equal to the maximum value of the aging timer, enables the organization of aging timers according to their value. This organization is achieved through a doubly linked list, which links all timers with the same value. This structure is useful for the deletion of expired entries from the FDB, as all expired aging timers at every second are included in a single doubly linked list of the timing wheel— the one that corresponds to timer value zero. When deletion of expired timers is required, the double-linked list of expired timers is extracted from the timing wheel, the list is traversed, and the corresponding FDB entries are deleted linearly.

At the same time, the timer table enables identification of a specific timer based on the hashing method used for FDB entry identification. When an incoming frame leads to the restart operation of an aging timer, the timer table leads to

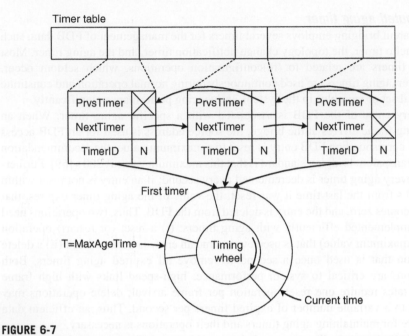

FIGURE 6-7

Aging timer data structures.

identification of the appropriate timer, with near-linear complexity, and then the aging timer is deleted from the double-linked list where it belongs in the timing wheel and appended to the double-linked list that corresponds to the new timer value (300 s). Considering identification of the timer, deletion from the double-linked list and insertion to the other double-linked list of the timing wheel are operations that have linear complexity.

The data structure organization in HPTB enables efficient operations on aging timers overall. The combination of the timer table with timing wheels enables fast restart and expiration operations, avoiding highly complex algorithms, such as sorting ones [19]. In the case of the original HPTB, data structures enable the processing of only six pointers for the move of a timer entry during a restart operation, leading to 11 accesses in the timer memory employed for the design presented in Zitterbart and associates [202].

Network attachment unit design

Network attachment units implement all protocol functions required for filtering and forwarding operations, as well as the update of the filtering database and timers. Importantly, these units also support frame format conversion, as well as frame segmentation and reassembly, as HPTB enables the interconnection of heterogeneous networks, including cell-based and packet-based ones.

In order to perform operations that meet the strict performance requirements of high-speed attached networks, NAUs include specialized support for each necessary function. The core of bridging operations, that is, filtering and forwarding, requires the use of the filtering database and timers. Thus, each NAU includes a filtering database module as well as a timer management module, as described earlier. In addition, each NAU includes three additional components (units) for the remaining operations. These components are as follows.

1. **Frame conversion unit**: This unit implements the conversion of frames for packet-based networks so that heterogeneous networks can be accommodated. As mentioned in the beginning of the chapter, bridged networks, such as 802.x local area networks, have significant differences among them, leading to different frame formats, including different header syntax and maximum frame length allowed. In order to enable support of heterogeneous networks, HPTB uses a generic frame conversion method: every received and transmitted frame is converted to a predefined normalized data unit (NDU) format [175] within the bridge. Thus, all incoming frames are converted to the NDU format, and all outgoing frames are converted from the NDU format to the format of the corresponding network. This decision provides simplicity to the design of each NAU and scalability to the system, as each NAU needs to accommodate only two formats—the format of the attached network and the NDU format.

2. **Frame handling unit**: This unit is responsible for communication between the NAU and the corresponding data memory management unit of the memory unit that corresponds to the NAU. This communication is necessary for correct storage and management of each frame. Specifically, note that each NAU is responsible to perform all functions necessary for filtering and forwarding of frames. Thus, for every incoming frame, the NAU identifies the outgoing port out of which the frame must be transmitted. Considering that frames targeted to a specific outgoing port are linked in a logical queue, the NAU needs to provide the necessary information to the data memory management unit so that the memory management unit can enqueue the frame to the appropriate queue. The frame handling unit is responsible for managing this information and creating the necessary 8-byte word that is included in each 72-byte internal packet that is transferred between the NAU and the buffering component. Importantly, the frame handling unit needs to manage one such control word for every packet that is being received; this may mean more than one packet in the case of cell-based networks, which may be receiving several packets concurrently due to cell interleaving.

3. **Segment formatter**: The segment formatter is a unit required only when the attached network is cell based, for example, an ATM-based network. Its main goal is to implement segmentation of frames that are transmitted over the cell-based network. In order to achieve this goal, the segment formatter needs to format the cells, segmenting frames to the appropriate data units and calculating the appropriate header fields, which include channel and message identifiers.

Importantly, the segment formatter enables the avoidance of frame reassembly in the case when two homogeneous cell-based networks are bridged; in that case, the unit just translates the corresponding header fields appropriately. Importantly, the segment formatter supports interleaved reception and transmission of frames as required by existing cell-based networks.

The structure of the HPTB network attachment unit is shown in Figure 6-8. When an incoming frame arrives at an NAU, the frame is forwarded to the frame conversion unit and the necessary header information is delivered to the transparent bridging support unit; this information includes source and destination addresses, priority, etc. The addresses are used for accesses in the FDB, as described earlier. The resulting information about the outgoing NAU for the received frame is then forwarded together with the priority to the frame handling unit. In addition, the frame handling unit receives control information from the frame conversion unit about the beginning or end of a frame, etc. Based on all this information, the frame handling unit creates the necessary control words for the switch and the memory modules in order to enable the memory modules to store and manage the frame

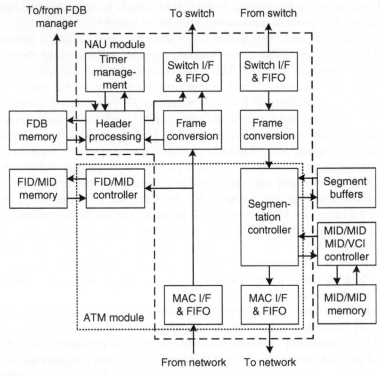

FIGURE 6-8

Structure of a network attachment unit.

data appropriately, organizing them in logical data structures. The NAUs of HPTB provide the necessary support for management of all types of frames and cells of the potential attached networks. For example, if two cell-based networks are attached to HPTB and traffic is bridged between them, then there is no need for frame conversion between the homogeneous cell-based networks. In contrast, when bridging occurs between heterogeneous networks such as a packet-based one and a cell-based one, the NAU is responsible for the segmentation of the outgoing frame to cells. Because not all NAUs in a bridge need to be identical, the generic structure of the NAUs (Figure 6-8) accommodates all cases. Once a bridge is implemented and the attached network technologies are known, the corresponding NAUs include only the necessary modules for the handling of the related frames or cells. A detailed description of all cases appears elsewhere [202].

Internal switching component operation

The internal interconnect of HPTB is a crossbar switch interconnecting network attachment units and memory modules, including memory management units. The switch operates in a synchronous fashion with a global clock. The clock has two phases, one per transfer direction: during the reception phase, data flow from NAUs to the memory, while, during the transmission phase, data flow from the memory to NAUs. The switch transfers fixed-size packets, called *bursts*, of 72 bytes composed of 64 data (packet) bytes and 8 bytes of control information (a control word).

The 64-byte payload of the switch's burst may contain up to 64 bytes of frame data, depending on the size of the incoming/outgoing frame or cell. The control word delivers information necessary for the memory management unit in order to handle the corresponding packet data appropriately. There are several types of control words that define the enqueuing requirements of a packet [201]. Specifically, as shown in Figure 6-9, the first byte of the control word contains a control code and the number of queues where the corresponding packet needs to be enqueued. A packet may need to be enqueued to one, multiple, or all queues, depending on whether the frame is a unicast, multicast, or broadcast one. The second byte specifies the length of data within the burst. The third byte specifies the frame to which the cell belongs, in case of a cell-based (e.g., ATM) network NAU, while the fourth one specifies the source port from which the frame has been

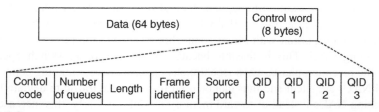

FIGURE 6-9

Format of the internal switch burst.

received; this last information is necessary for the protocol processing unit, which may need to send a response to the receiving NAU.

The last four bytes of the control word are queue identifiers with values that depend on operation of the control word. Special consideration is given to the size of the incoming frame. If the frame fits in a burst, that is, it is up to 64 bytes, then the burst delivers a frame that needs to be enqueued to a logical queue of the system directly. In contrast, if the incoming frame is longer than 64 bytes, then each burst delivers a portion of a frame to memory and the enqueuing process of the frame must be performed when the last portion of a frame is written to memory. Thus, the control word needs to indicate whether a complete frame or a portion of a frame is transferred over the switch in order to initiate the appropriate enqueuing operation at the right time. Furthermore, as the bridge supports multicasting, in this case, the control word indicates the group of queues where the packet must be enqueued to. Considering that four words are available in the control word for the specification of multiple queues in case of a multicast transmission, there are two different multicast words defined: positive and negative. The positive multicasting ones include in the control word the queues where the packet should be enqueued to, while the negative multicasting ones include the queues where the packet should not be enqueued to. For example, consider the case where the protocol processing unit as a result of a received frame prepares a packet to broadcast to all NAUs except the one where the frame was received through. In this case, the control word may specify a negative multicast indicating the ID of the source NAU as the queue information where the packet should not be enqueued; this also illustrates the usefulness of keeping source port information in the control word and subsequently in memory.

The HPTB switching fabric provides multicast support as well. Transmission of multicast packets in HPTB occurs in a single cycle with parallel transmissions to all appropriate NAUs. When the appropriate cycle is identified, the multicast packet is delivered to all outgoing NAUs in a single cycle, avoiding bandwidth waste that would occur if a multicast packet was allowed to be transmitted as a sequence of unicast packets, one per outgoing NAU. Although the decision for a single cycle multicast transmission saves bandwidth, it requires more sophisticated scheduling decisions, increasing the complexity of the switch's scheduler, which needs not only to schedule outgoing packets appropriately, but take into account multicast cases as well.

Importantly, the switching component of HPTB supports the transmission of real-time traffic in addition to regular nonreal-time unicast and multicast traffic. For the case of real-time traffic, HPTB does not store the frames, but schedules them directly for transmission with direct connections between the incoming NAU and the outgoing NAU. This is feasible because of the two-phase switch operation: during the reception phase, when isochronous packets arrive, outgoing connections toward NAUs are silent and thus can be used for real-time traffic to deviate frames to outgoing NAUs instead of toward memory modules. Clearly, this increases fabric complexity significantly, but enables handling of an important class of traffic, especially in the emerging multimedia world.

Considering the switch operation, it is clear that incoming frames, in general, are delivered from incoming NAUs to the corresponding memory modules and then are transferred to the appropriate outgoing NAUs. Frames in memory are organized in logical queues, which may indicate different priorities among stored frames. During every transmission phase, every memory module presents one high-priority queue per outgoing NAU for service. This is the virtual output queuing model, described in Chapter 4. A switch scheduler is used to schedule traffic [96], taking into account parameters such as multicasting requests, outgoing NAU availability, etc.

Performance requirements on the switch, fabric, and scheduler depend on the attached networks. For example, in the case of HPTB, which was designed to sustain full wire traffic up to 800 Mbps, the fabric needs to provide throughput of 1.8 Gbps [202].

Partitioned data memory organization

The data memory modules store frames, which are managed by the data memory management units, with one DMMU per memory module. Each DMM is organized logically with a three-level hierarchy: blocks, frames, and queues. Memory is organized as a sequence of fixed size blocks, which store frame data. Because a frame may need more than one block to be stored, several blocks are used for a frame and are organized logically with a linked list that indicates the sequence of data bytes within the frame. Frames are organized in logical queues, depending on several of their parameters, such as priority, multicast or unicast requirements, outgoing NAU, etc.

Information required for management of linked lists constituting frames and the queues is kept in tables in the DMMU. These tables hold information about each block, frame, and queue, identifying the sequence of linked blocks, constituting frames, and the sequence of linked frames, constituting queues. Unused blocks are also organized in a linked list of empty blocks.

Each DMMU not only contains management information for the memory hierarchy, but also manages the logical queues and provides the interface to the switch scheduler, which, in turn, schedules the frames for transmission. The DMMU operates as a special-purpose slave processor, implementing operations and providing responses to instructions delivered by the control words of bursts. As a control word is delivered over the switch, it is decoded and processed by the DMMU, which identifies an empty buffer for the incoming burst data. The DMMU enqueues the block to the appropriate frame and queue, in the case of a cell or the case of the last burst of a variable size frame, etc. Furthermore, the DMMU dequeues frames and blocks for transmission during transmission phases appropriately. DMMUs also perform the necessary bookkeeping for multicast frames in order to avoid dropping them from memory in case a multicast frame has not been transmitted fully; this occurs only when some NAUs are not ready for transmission when a multicast frame is selected—the frame is transmitted in a single cycle only through the ready NAUs. Importantly, DMMUs are prepared for management of cell networks, whose frames may arrive interleaved; special attention is paid to the reassembly process of frames, as frames need to be fully reassembled before being transmitted to heterogeneous, variable-size packet networks.

Based on the aforementioned components and operations, the HPTA presents an effective network system for implementing a data link layer bridge.

Layer 2 switches

Layer 2 switches are similar to bridges. They interconnect networks at layer 2, most commonly at the MAC sublayer, and operate as bridges, building tables for the transfer of frames among networks.

Historically, layer 2 switches emerged to alleviate the contention problem of shared media LANs. As structured cabling emerged and star-based connectivity to network centers was adopted, the exploitation of existing cabling and existing network adapters led to the continuation of using typical LANs, such as Ethernet and Token Ring, but enabled the development of layer 2 switches. The original goal of these switches was to enable use of a single LAN segment, if feasible, per attached end system, minimizing contention delays that existed in the older shared segments. For example, with an Ethernet switch and a dedicated Ethernet segment per attached system, collisions are avoided and delay is minimized.

Considering the need for autonomous operation and high performance, layer 2 switches perform all operations that typical bridges do. However, due to their focus on performance for dedicated segments, they employ specialized hardware for frame forwarding, and some of them even employ cut-through routing techniques instead of the typical store-and-forward technique used in common bridges. Thus, their main difference from bridges is typically the technology used to implement frame forwarding, which is mostly hardware-based, in contrast to typical bridges, which generally are more programmable and accommodate a wider range of heterogeneous LANs.

SUMMARY

This chapter introduced the concepts of bridges and layer 2 switches and presented the various types of bridges. We described the operation of bridges, focusing on transparent bridging, which is the latest bridging architecture that has been standardized. We identified the technical challenges of transparent bridges that need to be addressed to achieve high performance. Finally, we described in detail the architecture of HPTB, a specific high-performance transparent bridge architecture, which achieves high-speed processing of frames in order to support high bandwidth networks. Importantly, the scalability and modularity of the architecture enable the adoption of its modules in a wide range of conventional bridges and layer 2 switches.

Routers

NETWORK LAYER

As discussed in the previous chapter, link layer systems can interconnect end systems at the scale of a local area network. However, scaling a network built of bridges and switches to global scale is not feasible. The filtering database would be very large, broadcast storms would limit the operation efficiency, and routing would be inefficient due to the spanning tree algorithm. Therefore, it is necessary to use systems that are specifically designed to achieve global connectivity. These network layers systems (or "routers") overcome the limitations of link layer systems. Routers interconnect local area networks, and the resulting network of networks is an Internet that spans the globe. Due to the size of the resulting network, it is important to consider scalability as one of the key aspects of router design.

This chapter discusses the design and operation of routers. Specifically, we address these questions:

- Functionality of the network layer: What functions need to be implemented in the network layer? What are the performance requirements? What are the main components of a router?
- Design of data plane: What operations are performed on every packet that is forwarded? What data structures and algorithms are used to ensure correct packet forwarding?
- Design of control plane: What control operations are necessary to ensure correct operation? What routing algorithms are used to determine least-cost paths? What types of error handling are necessary?
- Example systems: What does a typical commercial router system look like? What are the differences between low-performance edge routers and high-performance network core routers?

Functionality of the network layer

The main functionality of the network layer is to provide end-to-end connectivity. An end-system network interface should be able to reach another end-system network interface by sending a network layer packet. This simple functionality is the basis of the Internet design. As discussed in the Appendix, the Internet Protocol

Architecture of Network Systems.

(IP) is the one common protocol among all systems connected to the Internet. Lower layers use different link and physical protocols; higher layers use different transport and application protocols. The IP is the single common protocol of hourglass architecture and ensures that all systems can communicate with each other.

To achieve end-to-end connectivity, several important protocol features need to be implemented in the network layer.

- Addressing: In order to reach a particular end-system interface, it needs to be possible to uniquely identify it. Thus, global addressing is necessary. In IP, all interfaces have a globally unique IP address. (With the deployment of Network Address Translation (NAT), load-balancing switches, and so on, global uniqueness is not true anymore for all systems. For the purpose of our discussion, we can assume global uniqueness.) The way IP address assignments are structured is important to simplify routing and forwarding as discussed later.
- Routing: This is the process of determining how to reach a particular network interface. Any router in the Internet needs to determine which of its output interfaces to use when directing traffic toward a particular destination. To do that, routing protocols exchange information about destinations and how to reach them. When doing a routing computation, a router determines the best routes from its local perspective. We discuss different routing protocols and their interactions later.
- Forwarding: There is an important distinction between routing and forwarding. Routing determines the best path for a packet to take. Forwarding is the actual process of receiving a packet on a router system and determining to which output port to send it to achieve the path determined by routing. Additionally, there are several processing steps that ensure the correct operation of the IP (e.g., checksum check, time-to-live decrement).

The following sections discuss in more detail what the requirements of these systems are and how they are implemented.

Systems requirements

We distinguish between two types of requirements: the functional requirements that dictate how the system operates and the performance requirements that state quantitative goals for the system.

Functional requirements

Functional requirements for an IP router are determined by a standards document. The Request for Comments (RFC) 1812 is the de-facto standard for network layer systems in an IP network [10]. RFC 1812 lists a number of functions that the system must perform, as well as suggestions of how it should operate to support other optional features. The RFC contains many detailed (and carefully worded) statements on functional requirements. Instead of repeating all of them here, we focus on the most important ones.

- Internet Protocol header checksum validation: The IP header contains a checksum that covers the header fields (including any options). To ensure that these important fields have not been corrupted, a checksum is used. When receiving a packet, any network layer system must verify that this checksum is still correct.
- Time-to-live (TTL) decrement: The TTL field in the IP header maintains a counter that is decremented on every hop in the network. When a packet has been forwarded so many times that this counter reaches zero, then it is discarded (assuming that there is a routing loop). This feature ensures that packets that cannot reach their destination do not travel through the network forever. Thus, a network layer system must decrement the counter in the IP header accordingly. Because the TTL field is covered by the IP header checksum, it is necessary to recompute the checksum.
- Destination address interpretation: A network layer system must determine how to forward a packet based on the destination address in the header. There are different types of addresses (unicast, broadcast, multicast), as well as a set of reserved addresses (e.g., loopback). Also, strict or loose source routing needs to be considered. In the most common case, a packet is simply forwarded to a destination interface. A network system typically performs a destination address lookup to determine which of its output interfaces leads toward that destination. We discuss algorithms for this lookup process later.
- Other operations: A number of other operations may need to be performed. These are not standard for all packets (unlike the ones listed earlier), but constitute special cases. Examples of such operations are IP fragmentation, IP options processing, and error conditions (e.g., TTL expiration). In practice, they may occur never or only rarely. Network layer systems are usually not optimized to handle these cases very efficiently.

To accomplish this type of processing, a typical router system (software based or hardware based) implements three steps: input processing (handling of link layer processing to receive IP packet), forwarding (implementation of RFC 1812 functions including forwarding lookup), and output processing (queuing and scheduling of packet and link layer processing for transmission). We discuss these data plane functions in more detail later. In particular, we focus on lookup in this chapter and on scheduling in Chapter 10.

Note that forwarding requirements do not specify anything about routing. What specific routing algorithm is implemented does not matter to the forwarding process. As long as packets get forwarded to the correct output ports, any possible routing algorithm (including a statically configured table) is acceptable.

Performance requirements

The performance of network layer systems often determines the performance of the overall network. Network layer functionality must be implemented by all systems connected in the network. Therefore, it is crucial that these functions can be performed efficiently. Lower layer functions also need to be implemented, but they are typically comparably simple and can operate at high speeds.

The performance of a router can be expressed in many dimensions. Typical performance metrics include:

- Link speed: The maximum data rate of a link that can be connected to a router port determines an upper bound of how much data can be forwarded through the system.
- Aggregate throughput: The aggregate data rate is the amount of data that can be forwarded through the system when considering all ports. In some systems the aggregate throughput is less than the number of ports times the link speed. In such cases, the system cannot forward all packets under full load.
- Packet rate: The size of packets that need to be forwarded by the router has an impact on the performance limits. Because most operations have to be performed for each packet (e.g., lookup), small packets cause a higher workload for the router for a given data rate. Therefore, packet rate is often used to express router performance independent of packet size.
- Power consumption: The power consumption of the router system under load (as well as during standby) is an important operational metric.

Examples of performance requirements for typical link speeds and packet sizes are shown in Table 7-1, which shows packet rates for packet sizes of 64, 576, and 1514 bytes. These sizes represent the smallest typical packet (i.e., minimum Ethernet packet size), the IP minimum maximum transfer unit, and the largest typical packet (i.e., maximum Ethernet packet size including Ethernet header). For the lowest data rate of 10 Mbps, a router system needs to forward between around 800 packets per second if packets are large and 20,000 packets per second if packets are small. As the data rate increases, the performance requirements for a network system can become as large as 77 million packets per second for 40-Gbps links and small packets. In a practical network, packet sizes vary due to the mix of applications

Table 7-1 Performance Requirements for Network Systems[a]

Link speed		Packet rate		
Data rate	Standard	64-Byte packets	576-Byte packets	1514-Byte packets
10 Mbps	10Base-T	19.5 kpps	2.17 kpps	0.82 kpps
51.84 Mbps	OC-1	101 kpps	113 kpps	4.28 kpps
100 Mbps	100Base-T	195 kpps	21.7 kpps	8.26 kpps
622 Mbps	OC-12	1.21 Mpps	135 kpps	51.3 kpps
1 Gbps	1000Base-T	1.95 Mpps	217 kpps	82.6 kpps
2.488 Gbps	OC-48	4.86 Mpps	540 kpps	205 kpps
10 Gbps	10GBase-T	19.5 Mpps	2.17 Mpps	826 kpps
39.81 Gbps	OC-768	77.8 Mpps	8.64 Mpps	3.29 Mpps

[a]Packets per second (pps) shown for different link rates and packet sizes.

using the network. Thus, average packet rate demands are somewhere between those for minimum and maximum packet sizes. However, to ensure stable performance under load, network systems are often designed to handle the packet rate for the worst case scenario, which is traffic only containing minimum size packets.

Generic router design

The functional and performance requirements determine the demands on router designs. First, the router needs to perform packet forwarding correctly. Second, packet forwarding needs to be done efficiently. Even under full load, where each link receives short packets at the maximum data rate, the router should still be able to handle all traffic. To achieve these goals, most typical router designs avoid centralized components that could become bottlenecks. Instead of having a single processing system to perform packet forwarding for packets received from all input ports, each input port could use its own processing system. Similarly, packet scheduling and other operations can be distributed.

An illustration of a generic router design is shown in Figure 7-1 where input ports are shown on the left and output ports on the right. In a real implementation, the left and right sides are folded together such that the input and output ports line up as shown in Figure 7-2. However, for our discussion, it is simpler to consider input and output separately and to assume traffic flows from left to right. Each port of the router system is equipped with the necessary physical and link layer

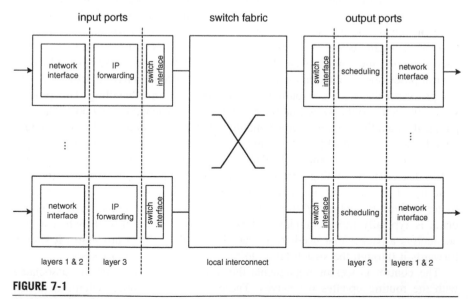

FIGURE 7-1

Generic router design. Traffic traverses router from left to right. Input ports forward packets to the output port determined during IP forwarding.

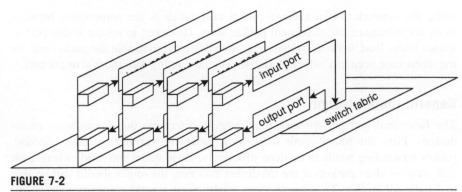

FIGURE 7-2

Physical router view. Input and output ports are combined on line cards. The switch fabric connects all line cards.

components. The main network layer function on the input port is IP forwarding. This step includes the destination address lookup. Without this information, it would not be possible to determine to which output port to send the packet. The main component that connects all router ports is the switch fabric. As discussed in Chapter 4, these switch fabrics can be scaled to a large number of ports and thus can support large amounts of bandwidth to interconnect numerous ports. The output port receives packets from all input ports and schedules them for transmission. Scheduling is part of network layer processing. However, we defer the discussion of scheduling to Chapter 10, where we discuss quality of service, which is based on different scheduling mechanisms used on the output ports of routers.

One important aspect of router systems is that there is a distinction between the data plane and the control plane. Figure 7-3 shows these two cases as well as the control processor involved in the control plane. Most routers have a dedicated control processor that manages routing computations and error handling. This processor is connected to the switch fabric and thus can be reached by any port. The data path is the data flow and the corresponding sequence of operations that are encountered by a "normal" packet that is simply forwarded from an input port to an output port. The control plane handles the data flow and operations that are performed for traffic that contains routing updates, triggers error handling, etc. Because the vast majority of packets encountered by the system are conventional data packets, router designs are optimized to handle these packets very efficiently. The control plane is typically more complex and not as performance critical. When a port encounters a packet that needs to be handled by the control processor, it simply forwards it through the switch fabric to the dedicated control processor.

The control processor implements the routing algorithms that are associated with the routing updates it receives. These routing algorithms determine which output port to use when forwarding packets that go to a particular destination. For packet forwarding, as it is implemented on the input ports of the router, it is

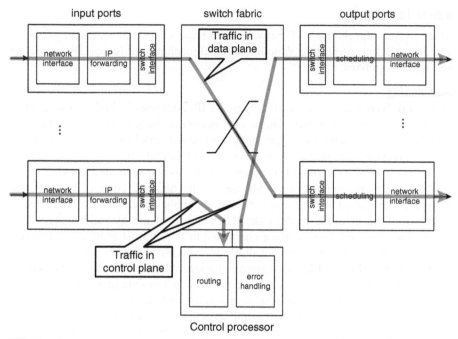

FIGURE 7-3

Data plane and control plane in routers. Data plane transmissions go directly from input to output ports. Control plane interactions involve the control processor.

not necessary to know all the details of various routing metrics that have led to particular forwarding paths. Instead, it is sufficient to know where packets with particular destination addresses need to be sent. Thus, the routing information can be condensed to a forwarding information base (FIB), which is distributed by the control processor to all router ports. The FIB is used to perform forwarding lookups as discussed later.

DATA PLANE

The data plane of a router implements a sequence of operations that are performed for typical network traffic. As discussed earlier, these steps include IP processing of the arriving packet, transmission through the switch fabric to the output port, and scheduling for outgoing transmission. One of the key operations in the data plane is to determine to which output port to send the packet. This process is known as route lookup, which is described in detail later. We also discuss how buffer management is handled on a router to ensure that packets can be stored effectively.

Route lookup

Route lookup algorithms in IP networks make use of the inherent structure of IP addresses. Before presenting various lookup algorithms, we review IP addressing and address prefixes.

Addressing

In network layer protocols, specifically in the IP, addresses identify network adapters. It is important to note that a single end system may have multiple network interfaces. For example, a typical laptop today has one network interface that uses wired Ethernet, one network interface that uses wireless Ethernet, and possibly another one that uses a cellular data connection. Each interface uses its own IP address.

One of the requirements for addresses in the network layer is that they are designed such that end-to-end connectivity—the main functionality of the network layer—becomes possible. In the case of IP, addresses are globally unique. That means that every network interface connected to the Internet must use a different IP address. This global uniqueness of all IP addresses is no longer true due to Network Address Translation, which is discussed in Chapter 8. However, for the purpose of our discussion in this chapter, we assume that IP addresses are indeed unique.

With a globally unique IP address, an end-system interface can be unambiguously identified. A sender who wants to transmit a packet to that interface can then simply put the corresponding IP address into the destination address field. The network uses this destination address then to determine how to forward the packet throughout the network such that it reaches the receiver's network interface in the end.

One important observation is that each router in the network needs to know where to send packets for every possible IP address. End systems may decide to send traffic to any possible destination at any time. A router needs to be able to forward any packet and thus needs to know on which of its links to forward a packet with any possible IP address. In the IP protocol, the address field is 32 bits long. Ignoring that some addresses are reserved and cannot be used, there are $2^{32} \approx 4 \times 10^9$ possible IP addresses. For each of these addresses the router needs to maintain information on where to send a packet that is destined for them.

If IP addressing was done the same way as addressing is done for Ethernet, where each interface gets an address assigned at manufacturing time, then there would be no structure to the IP address space. In such a case, routers would have to maintain a separate forwarding entry for each existing IP address. Such a forwarding table would require around four billion entries and consume a large amount of memory. To avoid this problem, IP uses structured address assignments that ensure that interfaces located on the same subnetwork have similar addresses. The similarity in addresses can be used to condense the information that needs to be stored on routers.

Internet Protocol addresses can be divided logically into a network portion and a host portion. The network portion identifies a network (i.e., a set of interconnected network interfaces that share the same network portion in their addresses). The host portion identifies a particular interface within a network. With this structure, a whole network of computers can be represented by a single network portion of an IP address. Because the network portion of the address is stored in the most significant bits of the address field, it is also called a prefix. Figure 7-4 shows an example of how addresses are allocated within a domain. The 128.119/16 prefix applies to all interfaces within that domain. Additional structure is achieved by assigning longer prefixes to subnetwork addresses (e.g., 128.119.91/24). End systems (as well as router interfaces) within a subnetwork use IP addresses that match the subnetwork's prefix.

When assigning IP addresses to interfaces, an address block (i.e., a set of addresses with the same prefix) needs to be obtained. The Internet Assigned Numbers Authority (IANA) is in charge of managing the IP address space. Address blocks can be assigned by IANA or by someone who already has a block of IP addresses. This allows for a hierarchical management of the address space.

Another benefit of the structure of IP address allocation is that it allows simplification in the routing table: instead of having to keep track of all possible addresses, it is only necessary to keep track of all address prefixes. Once a packet has reached the local network, where all machines have the same prefix, link layer methods for local area networks can be used to determine the path to the final destination (e.g., address resolution protocol (ARP)). As of May 2009, the number of active prefixes in the Internet was around 240,000, which is nearly 18,000 times less than the number of possible IP addresses.

One of the challenges with hierarchical address allocation is that it is difficult to maintain an address assignment that ensures that all address prefixes are colocated with all their neighboring prefixes. In the scenario shown in Figure 7-5, the 128.119.13/24 prefix is not located within 128.119/16. This configuration can

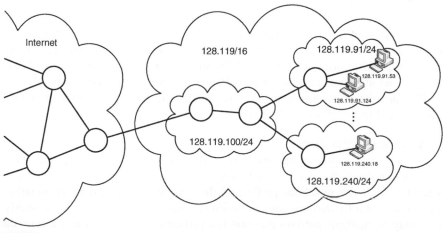

FIGURE 7-4

Network addressing. The 128.119/16 prefix applies to all subnetworks in the shown domain. Longer prefixes are used within each subnetwork and apply to the end systems within that network.

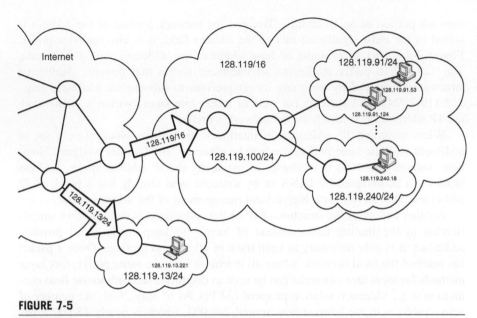

FIGURE 7-5

Prefix advertisements. The longest prefix takes precedence in case of overlapping prefixes.

occur when subnets are moved (either physically or logically). The problem is that traffic destined for 128.119.13/24 matches the 128.119/16 prefix and may be directed incorrectly. To avoid this problem, each network advertises its prefix independently. Advertising of overlapping prefixes leads to ambiguity when forwarding packets, as a destination address may match multiple prefixes. To resolve this ambiguity, an order of precedence is defined, where longer prefixes take priority over shorter prefixes. Thus, network traffic is always directed toward the longest advertised prefix. In Figure 7-5, where the advertised prefixes are shown as arrows, traffic for the 128.119.13/24 subnetwork is directed to the lower network and all other traffic for 128.119/16 is directed to the upper network.

This process of determining where to send traffic is the route lookup process implemented in the IP forwarding step on routers.

Route lookup algorithms

One of the most important operations in a router system is the lookup that determines where the packet needs to be forwarded. The packet's IP destination address is used to find the matching prefix and the associated forwarding information. An example of a forwarding table is shown in Table 7-2. As discussed previously, there may be multiple prefixes that match a particular address; in such a case, the longest matching prefix needs to be found.

Prefix matching algorithms have been developed to pursue two goals: performing the lookup quickly and requiring only a small amount of storage space to keep the forwarding table. The metric used commonly to determine lookup speed is the (peak or

Table 7-2 Example Routing Table[a]

Prefix	Output port
0/0	3
92.134.59.128/25	2
128.119/16	1
128.119.13/24	2
129.119.13.44/32	4
129.64/14	3
150.140.18/24	3

[a]*The output port specified for each prefix indicates where matching packets should be forwarded.*

average) number of memory accesses necessary for one packet. Memory is often the bottleneck in a lookup engine, as computations related to lookups are often very simple and thus do not cause as much delay as a memory access. The metric for storage space is the size of the total data structure. If different types of memory are used, distinctions are made between expensive and fast memory (e.g., SRAM, TCAM) and inexpensive and slow memory (e.g., DRAM). Note that all algorithms are designed to always perform a correct lookup (i.e., they do not employ heuristics that may yield incorrect forwarding information for some lookups).

We look at a few examples of prefix lookup algorithms, which range from a straightforward, unoptimized approach to a solution that is tuned for very high performance. An excellent review of many other algorithms is provided elsewhere [151]. For our discussion, we use the example prefixes shown in Table 7-3. Each prefix is named with a letter and noted in binary to simplify discussion. Further, the prefixes used in our example are considerably shorter than the average prefix encountered in real forwarding tables. Finally, output port information is omitted because it has no impact on the lookup data structures. In practice, each prefix in a data structure has a pointer to the associated port information.

Table 7-3 Prefixes Used for Route Lookup Examples[a]

Prefix name	Prefix
A	0/1
B	0000/4
C	01/2
D	0101/4
E	11/2
F	011/3

[a]*Prefixes are named with letters to identify them in data structures and are noted in binary.*

Binary trees

Using a binary tree to represent the prefix information in the forwarding table is the classic, straightforward solution to the prefix matching problem. The prefix is represented in binary, and each bit is represented as an edge that connects nodes in a tree. Starting from the root node, the first bit of any prefix is either a zero or a one. Therefore, there are up to two edges from the root node connection to the next level of the tree. This process continues until all prefixes are represented in the tree as shown in Figure 7-6. Any node can only have between zero and two nodes. By convention, edges that represent a 0 bit are drawn to the left and edges that represent a 1 bit are drawn to the right. The actual prefixes are noted within the nodes. Note that in this (or any other lookup algorithm), it is implied that finding the prefix implies that the remaining information from the forwarding table (e.g., output port) can be found.

When looking up which prefix matches a destination address, the binary tree is traversed starting from the root node. Based on the bit in the destination address, the edge to the left or to the right is taken. Any prefix encountered while traversing the binary tree matches the destination address. Because the longest matching prefix needs to be found, the search process does not terminate when a prefix is found, but continues until the end of the binary tree is reached. Because the last node on the tree may not actually contain a prefix, it is important that the search procedure remembers the last encountered prefix. This prefix is the longest match and is used to forward the packet.

Figure 7-7 shows an example of the lookup process. Assume a packet has a destination address of 01001111 (for simplicity, addresses are 8 bits long in our example). Starting at the top node, the lookup traverses down the tree until the data structure ends, which ensures that no matching prefix exists that is longer than any that has already been encountered. In the fourth step, the search process "falls off the tree" and cannot continue. At this point, the prefix corresponding to the

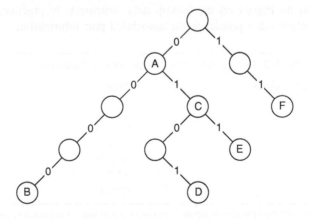

FIGURE 7-6

Binary tree data structure for prefixes from Table 7-3.

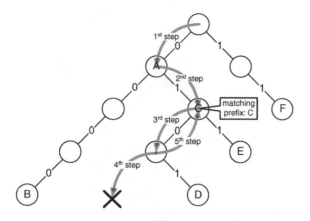

FIGURE 7-7

Lookup example in binary tree data structure. The sequence is shown for lookup of 01001111.

local node is the best match. However, that node does not have any prefix associated with itself. Therefore the search backtracks to the last found prefix. This backtracking can be done by returning on the path of the search or by remembering the last prefix encountered in the lookup process in a temporary variable.

While this algorithm clearly performs correctly, it exhibits poor performance when implemented on a router system. In a typical implementation, a node is a data structure stored in memory and an edge is a pointer to the corresponding node data structure. When traversing the tree, each encountered node needs to be fetched from memory to retrieve prefix information and the pointers to its children. Each memory access is independent of the previous one, which incurs the full memory access delay for each bit in the destination address. The total lookup time is therefore roughly the number of bits in the longest matching prefix times the access delay. With a maximum of 32 bits in the prefix, the total lookup time can be in the low microseconds, which is too much for most high-performance routers.

Several optimizations have been proposed to speed up the lookup process. For example, to avoid backtracking, prefixes located inside the tree can be duplicated and pushed into leaf nodes. This "leaf pushing" is shown in Figure 7-8, where all prefixes are located on leaf nodes. During a search, the disjoint prefix tree is simply traversed until a leaf node is found. The prefix at that node corresponds to the longest matching prefix. Another optimization is "path compression." In this case, long paths that contain no branches are compressed into a single edge. The example path-compressed tree is shown in Figure 7-9. The long sequence of nodes to reach prefix B (0000/4) is reduced to a single edge beyond prefix A. Note that internal nodes now require an annotation on which bit needs to be compared (as long paths of internal nodes without branches would be compressed into a single edge). When performing the lookup, the prefix in the final matching node needs to be compared to the address that is searched. If there is no match, backtracking

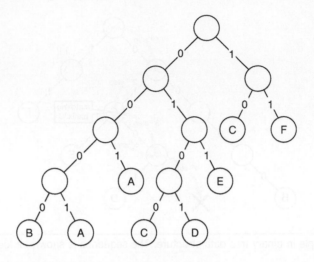

FIGURE 7-8

Disjoint prefix binary tree. All prefix matches are pushed to leaf nodes.

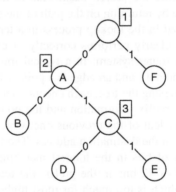

FIGURE 7-9

Path-compressed binary tree. Paths without branches are compressed into a single edge.

is necessary. This scenario occurs when looking up the previous example address of 01001111. These optimizations improve the lookup performance over the straightforward binary tree for sparse trees. However, they do not reduce the lookup time in case of a dense tree created from a large number of prefixes. For such cases, other data structures may be necessary.

Tries

A data structure that addresses the memory access problems of a binary tree is a trie (pronounced "try"). In an n-bit trie, each node has either zero or 2^n children. An example trie with a stride length of $n = 2$ is shown in Figure 7-10. Prefixes may need

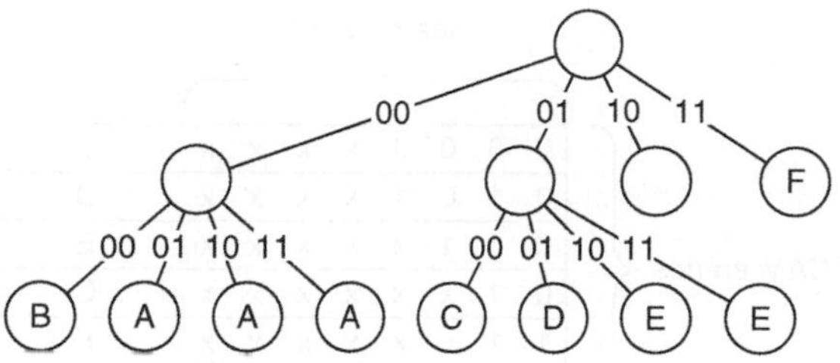

FIGURE 7-10

Trie data structure with a stride length of 2.

to be expanded such that their length is a multiple of n bits. Also, all internal prefixes are pushed to leaves. When traversing the trie, conceptually the same process is used as for the binary tree. The only difference is that each step covers n bits at a time. Thus, the longest matching prefix can be found in fewer steps. A lookup in a trie requires factor n fewer memory accesses than a lookup in a tree. However, each node needs to store 2^n pointers to children and is thus bigger than a node in a tree.

This data structure is an illustrative example of how system characteristics (i.e., memory access delay) are taken into consideration when designing an algorithm and its associated data structure. A trie requires more space than a binary tree, but significantly reduces the number of memory accesses required to find a matching prefix.

Ternary content-addressable memory

A completely different way of implementing prefix lookups is with the use of a ternary content-addressable memory (TCAM). In a conventional memory, data are accessed by providing the memory address that should be read. In a content-addressable memory, a portion of data values are provided for memory accesses. The memory then "searches" through all stored entries and returns one where this data matches. This search process is implemented in hardware and can be performed in parallel. The read time is comparable to that of normal memory, but the power consumption is much higher, as all memory rows are activated in parallel. In a TCAM, some bits of the search index can be set to "x" (don't care).

To store a prefix in a TCAM, the bits of the prefix are stored as the search word. Because the search word is typically of fixed length, but prefixes are not, the unused bits are set to "x." The remainder of the memory line contains forwarding information (or a pointer to it). When performing a lookup, the destination address is provided as the word for which to search. The TCAM inspects all stored prefixes and returns one. To ensure that the longest prefix is returned, TCAM-specific priority rules need to be considered. Typically, the match with the lowest physical address is returned. Thus, prefixes need to be stored in order of decreasing length to ensure that the longest prefix match is returned. An example of a TCAM system is shown in Figure 7-11.

The example of a TCAM shows that specialized hardware solutions can be used to overcome performance bottlenecks that are difficult to solve in software. Prefix

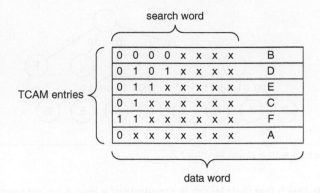

FIGURE 7-11

Ternary content-addressable memory.

lookups in particular lend themselves to such solutions, as they are necessary for every packet and one of the more time-consuming operations.

Queuing and buffering management

Another important operation in the data plane of routers is the buffering of packets. Due to statistical multiplexing, it is possible (and quite likely) that a router receives packets on two different ports destined to the same output port. The outgoing link limits the speed at which any of these packets can be transmitted. Therefore, it is necessary to temporarily store packet while the other is transmitted. This queuing step is often done with a single first-in-first-out (FIFO) queue. Chapter 10 shows more complex scheduling disciplines that require multiple queues in the context of quality of service.

To implement a FIFO queue, convenient data structures have been developed. We discuss briefly a solution that is used commonly in operating systems. We also discuss how heterogeneous memory systems can be used to handle packet queues most efficiently.

Single memory

There are a number of different ways of implementing a queue using a conventional random access memory. The principal operation is to store packets in dedicated memory spaces (e.g., buffer pool). The FIFO behavior can be emulated by maintaining a logical order of the packets that are stored in memory. Two typical approaches are a ring buffer and buffer chain.

Ring buffer

In a ring buffer, a fixed number of buffer slots are available (i.e., the size of the queue). Two pointers (or indices) are used to indicate which slot in the ring represents the head of the queue and which slot represents the tail of the queue. When

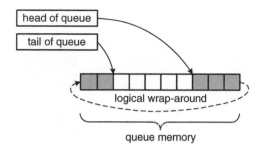

FIGURE 7-12

Queue implementation using a ring buffer.

the ring buffer is empty, the head and tail pointers are the same. When a packet is added to the queue, then the head pointer advances by one slot. The increment of the head pointer occurs modulo the ring size. That is, when the end of the physical buffer space is reached, the initial ring slots are reused. Removal of a packet advances the tail pointer with the same modulo constraint. A ring buffer is illustrated in Figure 7-12.

Buffer chain

A more flexible approach to implementing queues, especially when using queues with changing sizes, is a buffer chain. In a buffer chain, packets are stored in data structures that contain control information on the logical chaining of buffers. Each buffer points to the next buffer in the queue (or to *nil* at the end of the queue). Packets are added at the end of the queue by chaining the newest buffer to the tail of the queue. Packets are removed from the head of the queue.

A commonly used buffer chain data structure from the BSD operating system is an *mbuf*. This data structure can implement the buffer chain as described earlier. Several additional features are also useful for packet queues.

- Data offset within *mbuf*: The location of where packet data is stored within a data structure can be shifted by an internal offset. This shift permits memory space to be left available at the head and the tail of the packet data structure. As packets traverse multiple protocol layers within a system, headers and trailers (e.g., link layer header and CRC) can be added without copying the packet content to another memory location. Such zero-copy operations improve system performance significantly.
- Multiple buffers for single packet: As a packet is processed, it is possible to change its size significantly. Therefore, multiple *mbuf* structures can be used to store the packet. Thus, there is not only a chain of buffers among packets, but also within a packet.
- Buffers of different size: There are different sizes of buffers. Small buffers can be used to store packet headers and short control packets. Large buffers can be used to store the packet payload (while keeping the packet header in a separate,

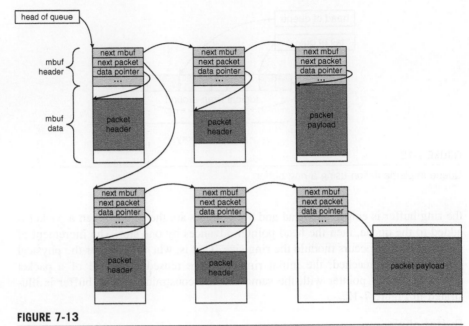

FIGURE 7-13

Buffer chain using *mbuf* data structures.

small buffer). Providing buffers of different sizes improves the memory utilization efficiency. Limiting the number of different sizes avoids the fragmentation problem that can occur when arbitrary size buffers can be allocated.

Figure 7-13 shows an example of a buffer chain using *mbuf* data structures. The first packet stores its headers in two *mbuf* data structures (which may have been added before the payload as the packet traverses the protocol stack downward from network layer to link layer). For larger packets, as shown in the second packet in Figure 7-13, the packet payload can be stored in a cluster *mbuf*. More details on the detailed implementation of these buffers can be found in [189].

Multiple memories

Router system design exhibits an interesting design problem related to memories used for queuing. On one hand, routers need large memories to avoid link underflow during Transmission Control Protocol oscillations. On the other hand, memories need to be fast and inexpensive to meet performance and cost constraints. Dynamic Random Access Memory (DRAM) provides large memory space inexpensively, but performs less well when performing random memory accesses. Static Random Access Memory (SRAM) is more expensive than DRAM and thus is only affordable in smaller sizes, but performs much faster than DRAM. The difference in density (i.e., memory size per cost) and speed (i.e., random access time) is about one order of magnitude.

Thus, the problem is to decide how to use these memories to obtain a large and inexpensive packet queue.

One solution is to use both types of memory in a router system. The memory is logically partitioned such that packet headers are stored in SRAM and packet payloads are stored in DRAM. The motivation for this allocation is that read-and-write accesses to packet headers are common during protocol processing. Accesses to packet payload are less common (single write and single read unless transport or application layer payload processing is performed as discussed in Chapters 8 and 9). Because packet payloads are typically much larger than packet headers, DRAM is the ideal memory type. Packet headers, which are smaller, are stored in SRAM to achieve the necessary performance.

When using buffer chaining with different buffers of different sizes, such a separation can be implemented in a straightforward manner. Large buffers for packet payloads are retrieved from the buffer pool in DRAM. Small buffers are kept in SRAM. On a real router system, the software needs to explicitly distinguish between the memory interfaces used for these memory accesses. Often, more than one memory interface for each type of memory is available.

CONTROL PLANE

The control plane of a router handles functions that are not directly related to traffic forwarding, but that are necessary to ensure correct operation. Typical control plane operations include:

- Exchange of routing messages and routing algorithms
- Handling of error conditions

We discuss these topics in more detail.

Routing algorithms

Routing algorithms ensure that a router system can determine where to forward traffic to reach a particular destination. The information necessary for route computation is obtained by exchanging routing messages with other network systems. Computation of routing algorithms occurs occasionally (typically triggered by updates on the network state), but is much less frequent than forwarding lookups. As mentioned earlier, the data plane uses the forwarding information base, which contains the condensed routing information specific to a single port.

Routing metrics

When computing a path for traffic to a particular destination, a number of different criteria can be chosen to select from different available paths. Frequently, the "best path" is desired, but numerous different metrics can be used when optimizing the path. The only fundamental criterion that needs to be met by any routing algorithm is that some traffic eventually reaches the desired destination. This requirement is typically easy to meet (e.g., even when forwarding traffic to a random output port, there is a nonzero probability that some traffic reaches its destination). Note that it is not necessary (but desirable) that all traffic reaches the destination since the network layer is inherently unreliable. Of course, a good routing algorithm ensures that all traffic is directed along a path toward the destination.

When choosing between paths that traffic can take, a number of optimization metrics can be considered.

- Shortest path: This metric counts the number of hops between the source and the destination. The optimal path is the path with the least number of hops. This metric is easy to use in practice, as a hop is clearly defined and does not change unless the network is physically reconfigured. However, the hop count metric treats all hops equally, no matter if the hop is between two routers in the same machine room or if the hop is a transoceanic link.
- Lowest delay: One of the main limitations to achieve high throughput on long-distance connections is the propagation delay of signals. Therefore, delay is also a widely used metric for routing. Each link cost is proportional to the propagation delay on that link (which is related to the physical distance between the transmitting and receiving interface and the propagation speed in the transmission medium). The optimal path has the least end-to-end delay between the sending and the receiving end system.
- Highest available bandwidth: For some applications (e.g., remote backup, video transmission) the amount of bandwidth available along a path is an important metric. In such a case, the available bandwidth of each link can be considered. The optimal path has the maximum available bandwidth. Note that bandwidth is not added, but determined by the link with the least amount of bandwidth (i.e., the bottleneck link).
- Lowest packet loss: Some applications require low packet loss (e.g., voice over IP). For those applications, a good path metric is the overall packet loss probability. The optimal path has the highest probability for a successful transmission (i.e., the highest product of successful transmission probability of all links in the path).

A number of other metrics can be defined for routing in a network. The main criteria by which metrics differ in the context of routing are how metrics are aggregated and how dynamic they are. The aggregation is important, as many routing algorithms (including the ones discussed later) assume that metrics are additive (i.e., the cost of communication is added when adding a link to a path). However, some metrics do not follow this principle (e.g., available bandwidth, which is a minimum operation over all links). The dynamics of routing metrics are also important. Some metrics do not change under traffic conditions (e.g., hop count or delay if propagation delay dominates queuing delay). In these cases, routing results do not change under load. Other metrics change with the traffic conditions (e.g., available bandwidth) or environmental conditions (e.g., packet loss in wireless network). In such cases, the result of an optimal path computation may change as the metrics change. This can lead to instability and needs to be considered in practical routing protocols.

A number of other constraints may also be imposed on a route computation due to practical reasons. Examples of such constraints are as follows.

- Minimum bandwidth: A path may require a certain minimum available bandwidth. If bandwidth information is available for the links of the network, a routing algorithm may need to identify a path that meets a minimum bandwidth requirement.
- Load balancing: When using optimal paths for all network connections, certain links may become overloaded since they provide better connectivity than others. In some scenarios it may be desirable to intentionally direct some traffic over suboptimal paths to balance the load of the network. Finding such alternative paths is also important when trying to identify backup paths that have little or no overlap with another path.
- Policies: Some routing protocols consider policies, which may potentially be very complex (e.g., do not route traffic across nodes controlled by a competitor). Routing decisions may be constrained by such policies.

In all these cases, a routing solution can be found by (virtually) removing links and nodes that do not meet the requirements from the set of links and nodes considered by the routing algorithm. This process ensures that the algorithm does not consider them for optimal path computation and thus identifies a path that meets the constraints. Clearly, adhering to these constraints may lead to a path that is suboptimal compared to the path that considers the entire, unconstrained network. Also, constraints may cause the path computation to fail if no valid path can be found.

Routing metrics and constraints are independent of any particular routing algorithm. A variety of routing algorithms are now discussed. Each of them can be used with some of the metrics and constraints discussed here.

Routing information exchange and computation

Routing algorithms can be distinguished by the way their two main operations are performed: exchange of information on the state of the network and computation of the shortest path between two nodes.

To be able to exchange any information about the network, some entity needs to collect data related to the metrics used in the routing algorithm. This task is typically performed by routers because they can determine the local state of the network. For example, to find out which links exist in the network, each router determines which neighboring routers are connected to its ports. Most links inside networks (except in local area networks (LANs) on the network edge) are point-to-point links with only one router on each end, which allows for easy collection of this information. Similarly, a router can determine the round-trip delay to these neighboring systems or the available bandwidth on the link. Thus, a local view of the network can be obtained. The next step then is to exchange this information with neighbors so that it can propagate through the network and be used by all routers that implement routing algorithms.

Once the state of the network is available, route computation can be performed in a centralized or a distributed process. A centralized algorithm has complete knowledge of all links in the network and their routing metrics. Based on this global view, the algorithm can make a routing decision without a need for further interaction with other nodes. In a distributed algorithm, the route computation is performed jointly by all routers as no single node has a complete view of the network. However, each node can obtain enough information through information exchanges with its neighbors and by performing local computation to determine optimal routing. We consider examples of each type of algorithm.

Centralized routing algorithms

A centralized routing algorithm maintains a data structure that represents the network and its link information (i.e., "link state"). Based on this data structure, it can compute the shortest path between two nodes. One of the most well-known shortest path algorithms for this scenario is Dijkstra's algorithm [43]. We describe this algorithm in general and then show how it works on an example network.

Dijkstra's shortest path algorithm computes not only the shortest path between two specific nodes, but the shortest path between a source node and all other nodes in the network. This shortest path tree can then be used to determine the optimal path to any destination from the perspective of the source node. Dijkstra's algorithm computes this shortest path tree incrementally, adding one node per iteration. To do this, the algorithm maintains a set of nodes for which the shortest path has already been found and the complementary set, which contains nodes that still need to be added to the shortest path tree. In each iteration, the node that is not yet part of the shortest path tree and that is closest to the source is added. Once a node is added, distances to its neighboring nodes are recomputed to consider any newly discovered shorter paths.

To describe this algorithm, we use the following notation: $V = \{v_1, \ldots, v_n\}$ is the set of n nodes (vertices), v_1 is the source node, c_{ij} is the cost of communication between nodes v_i and v_j (i.e., link cost), d_i is the communication cost between the source and v_i, p_i is the previous node that is along the path from the source to v_i, and S is the set of all nodes for which the shortest path has not yet been found.

```
for i from 1 to n do:
    d_i: = ∞            // initialize distance of all nodes to infinity
    p_i: = null         // set previous node to undefined value
    d_1: = 0            // source node has zero distance to itself
    S: = V             // need to find shortest path for all nodes
while S is not empty:
    i = argmin_j {d_j|v_j in S}   // find index of node with least distance
    S: = S - v_i                  // remove node i from set S
```

```
for j in {k|c_ik < ∞}:      // iterate over all neighbors of i
   if (d_i + c_ij < d_j):   // check if path via i is lower cost than
                               existing path
   d_j = d_i + c_ij      // set distance to new lower distance via i
   p_j = v_i      // record new path by setting previous node to i
```

When the algorithm terminates, the set of previous nodes, $p_1,\ldots,p_n$, contains the information on the shortest path tree from node 1.

An example of Dijkstra's shortest path algorithm is illustrated in Figure 7-14. The graph figures on the left show the progression of the shortest path tree. The table on the right shows the distance and previous node for all nodes.

For this algorithm, it is necessary that the cost metric used for the path is additive (and nonnegative). This ensures that the triangle inequality can be applied. Thus, the algorithm can be used with hop counts, delay, and so on but not with the minimum operation used to determine maximum available bandwidth.

In practice, Dijkstra's shortest path algorithm is used in the Open Shortest Path First protocol (see later).

Distributed routing algorithms

Distributed routing algorithms involve computations performed on all participating nodes to obtain optimal path information. One of the most well-known distributed routing algorithms is based on the Bellman–Ford algorithm [15]. Note that this distributed shortest-path algorithm can also be implemented as a centralized algorithm. However, using multiple distributed nodes for processing reduces the overall data exchange and reduces the overhead on the network.

The core of the algorithm is the observation that to find the shortest path, a node can take the shortest path information from its neighbors, add its cost to reach those neighbors, and choose the least cost sum as its solution. This process can be expressed as a dynamic programming problem. We denote d_{ij} as the shortest-path cost between node i and node j and c_{ik} as the link cost between i and k (assuming that a direct link exists). Then the Bellman–Ford equation can be expressed as

$$d_{ij} = \min_k \{c_{ik} + d_{kj}\},$$

where k is taken from the set of all neighbors of i.

In a distributed implementation of this algorithm, each node (asynchronously) advertises its knowledge about shortest paths to all its neighbors. The advertisement is also called the distance vector, as it includes all d_{ij} values of a node. Initially, only information about destinations connected directly to a router is known by observing link costs c_{ik} (similar to how link states are obtained in centralized routing). As information exchanges occur, more information becomes available to routers in the network. Once all information has propagated through the network once, the shortest path information is stable and the shortest paths are known to all routers.

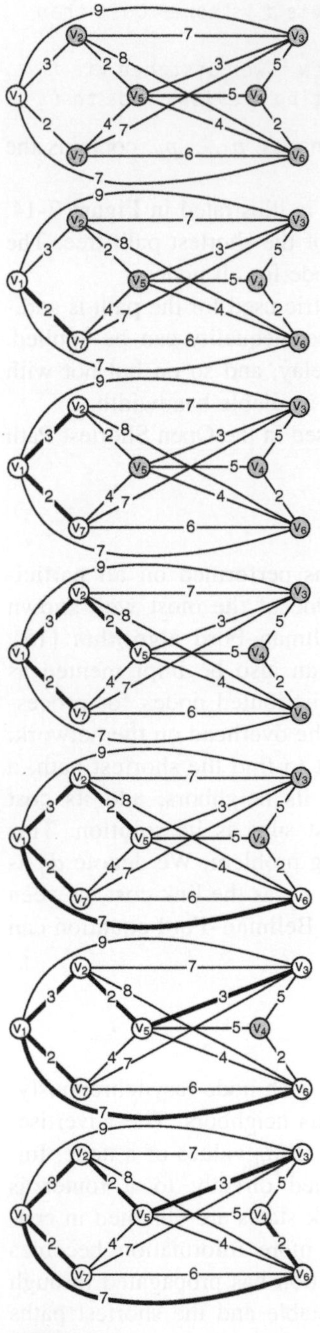

	d_1,p_1	d_2,p_2	d_3,p_3	d_4,p_4	d_5,p_5	d_6,p_6	d_7,p_7
	0,-	∞,-	∞,-	∞,-	∞,-	∞,-	∞,-
		3,v_1	9,v_1	∞,-	∞,-	7,v_1	2,v_1
		3,v_1	9,v_1	∞,-	6,v_7	7,v_1	
			9,v_1	∞,-	5,v_2	7,v_1	
			8,v_5	10,v_5		7,v_1	
			8,v_5	9,v_6			
				9,v_6			

FIGURE 7-14

Example of Dijkstra's shortest path algorithm. The set of nodes, S, that has not been added to the shortest path tree is shown shaded. The node that is added to the tree in each iteration is marked in the table.

Figure 7-15 shows an example of the distance vector exchange among nodes. In the example, the initial state is shown as well as two updates by nodes. Fields that are changed due to a distance vector exchange are shaded.

In practice, the distance vector algorithm based on the Bellman–Ford equation is used in the Routing Information Protocol, which is discussed in more detail later.

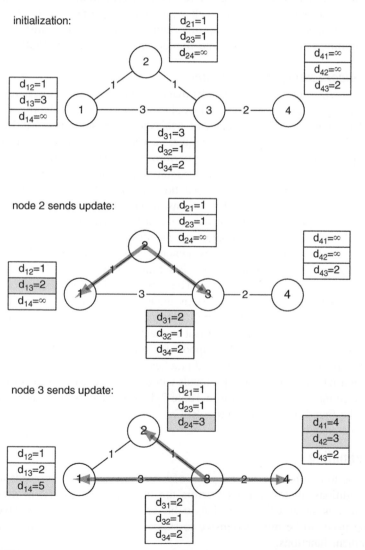

FIGURE 7-15

Distributed shortest-path algorithm based on distance vector. Distance vector fields affected by an update are shaded.

Another example of a distributed routing algorithm is path vector routing. In path vector routing, not only the distance to a destination is exchanged among nodes, but also a list of nodes along the path. Knowing the nodes that are involved in a path lets a node decide on the suitability of the advertised path using criteria other than simply least cost. When network policies need to be considered, a number of other concerns may arise (e.g., not to send traffic via a network that is not trusted). With the exchange of full path information, such policies can be implemented. However, because each node may implement different policies, it is not guaranteed that the routing algorithm converges. An example of a path vector algorithm in the Internet is the Border Gateway Protocol (BGP).

Hierarchical routing in the Internet

In the Internet, where millions of links make up the entire network, neither of the two routing approaches just described would work very well. Scalability to support such a large number of links cannot be achieved by these approaches for several reasons. The sheer number of links requires a very large data structure on which shortest-path computations need to be performed. In the centralized solution, updates to any link in the Internet would require an update to all data structures on all routers and trigger a routing computation. Clearly, it does not matter to most paths if a link fails on a continent far, far away. However, a straightforward implementation of Disjkstra's algorithm requires that the network graph is updated and that the shortest path is recomputed. In the distance vector algorithm, updates would propagate whenever a link cost change triggers a change in the vector.

The routing structure in the Internet is set up in a hierarchy of two layers. This hierarchy is illustrated in Figure 7-16. The network is divided in autonomous systems (AS). Within an autonomous system, the local administrator may use any type of routing algorithm (hence the name). Between autonomous systems, a common routing protocol is used to ensure global connectivity. In the Internet, BGP is used for this interdomain routing. The support for implementing policy-based routing makes this path vector protocol a good practical choice. Within domains, a number of different intradomain routing protocols can be used. A list of some of the protocols used in the Internet is shown in Table 7-4. More details on their implementation can be found in their respective RFCs.

Error handling

In addition to routing, the control plane of a network layer system needs to handle error conditions. In lower layers, errors are often handled by silent drops (e.g., when the link layer CRC fails due to bit errors). At the network layer, error handling needs to be more extensive to support based network-layer control and management functions.

The Internet Control Message Protocol (ICMP) defines how systems should handle and respond to unusual conditions [143]. Examples for such conditions include the following.

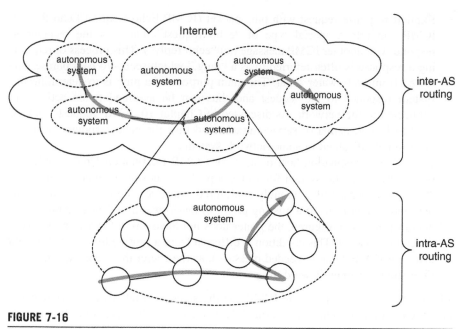

FIGURE 7-16

Hierarchical routing used in the Internet.

Table 7-4 Routing Protocols Used in the Internet			
Name	**Usage**	**Type**	**Details**
Open Shortest Path First (OSPF)	Intra-AS	Link state routing	RFC 2328 [128]
Routing Information Protocol (RIP)	Intra-AS	Distance vector routing	RFC 1058 [62], RFC 2453 [111]
Enhanced Interior Gateway Routing Protocol (EIGRP)	Intra-AS	Distance vector routing	Proprietary
Border Gateway Protocol (BGP)	Inter-AS	Path vector routing	RFC 4271 [148]

- Expiration of Time-to-Live field (ICMP Time Exceeded): When a packet has been forwarded too many times (e.g., due to a forwarding loop or a very low starting TTL value) and the TTL value in the packet header reaches zero, it must be dropped. Instead of dropping the packet silently, an ICMP response is generated to inform the sender of the dropped packet. The motivation behind this notification is that a sender may stop sending traffic that cannot reach its destination and (in cases of persistent route loops) that an administrator may be notified to remedy the problem.

- Explicit response request with ping packet (ICMP Echo Request/Echo Reply): ICMP supports a special type of "echo request" that asks the receiver to respond with another ICMP message (an "echo reply"). This process of requesting a response is often referred to as a "ping," which seems to be a phrase borrowed from underwater sonar. The main purpose of a ping is to determine if a system responds to the request and thus can be assumed to be active and connected to the network. As discussed in Chapter 10, ICMP requests may be used to launch denial of service attacks and thus the echo response feature is occasionally disabled in some network systems.
- Unreachable destination host or network (ICMP Destination Unreachable): In some cases, the end system for which a packet is destined cannot be reached. This can be caused by a wrongly configured router or an erroneous route computation, which leads to a missing prefix in the forwarding data structure. If no default route is configured, the router does not have any information on where to send the packet. This condition is different from a routing loop (which would cause an ICMP Time Exceeded message), as the router that generates the message simply cannot forward the packet.

All control messages involving ICMP use the same general structure. Depending on the condition or control operation, different header values are used. It is important to note that ICMP operates in conjunction with IP. ICMP messages are encapsulated within an IP header.

Using the ICMP control message protocol, a number of useful tools have been developed that are widely used in practice. Examples of these tools are:

- ping—the ping program is a utility that sends an ICMP Echo Request to a specified destination and waits for the ICMP Echo Reply. Using this process repeatedly, the tool reports if a destination is reachable and what the statistics of the measured round-trip time are.
- traceroute—the traceroute program is a utility that attempts to determine the path between a source and a destination. The key idea of traceroute is to intentionally send traffic that causes an error message along the path and thus to identify routers that respond with error messages. Using the time-to-live field in the IP header, IP packets can be crafted that expire before reaching the destination. The first packet uses a TTL value of 1 and thus expires on the first hop, generating an ICMP response from the router. Then the TTL value is incremented to identify the second router and so on until the destination is reached. The assumption is that the path does not change during the measurement and thus the results are consistent (even though different packets could take different paths).

Not all network systems implement all error-handling features. Also, in some cases, administrators decide to turn these features off because they may cause increased load on the system (e.g., to generate response messages) or because they may reveal information about the setup and policies used in a network (e.g., through traceroute).

EXAMPLE NETWORK LAYER SYSTEMS

All routers in the Internet need to implement routing and packet forwarding functionality. However, considerable differences exist in performance requirements depending on where a router is located. Routers in a home network need to handle much lower data rates than routers in the Internet core. Differences in requirements lead to differences in the way these systems are implemented. We describe three types of routers and discuss their implementation differences.

- Home router: Most home networks use a single (wired or wireless) LAN to connect all end systems in the home. All traffic that is sent to or received from the Internet traverses the home router. The router typically interfaces with a single Internet uplink (e.g., DSL or cable modem). Because the bandwidth of network access is often limited to a few megabits per second, the aggregate throughput requirement for the router is equally low. Note that some routers provide very high data rates on the LAN side (e.g., 100 Mbps or 1 Gbps). These data rates are achieved only on LAN-to-LAN connections switched at the data link layer. No network layer functions are performed on these connections. Packet forwarding for traffic that uses the Internet uplink is straightforward because there is only one link to choose from. Due to these low performance requirements for network layer functions, home routers can typically use simple shared memory switch architecture and a single processor core for data plane forwarding and control functions. The typical cost of such a system is less than one hundred dollars. Note that typical home routers are often combined with transport layer features (e.g., firewalls and NAT) as discussed in Chapter 8.
- Edge router: These routers typically aggregate traffic from numerous network access links (e.g., in an Internet service provider network) and connect to the network core. In this domain, the number of ports in such a router is typically in the order of tens (with each port supporting a large number of aggregated access links). Routers typically support aggregate bandwidths of tens to low hundreds of gigabits per second. To achieve the required data rates, routers use more advanced switch fabrics (e.g., crossbar) and packet processors that are replicated on each port. Dedicated control processors support routing as well as advanced functions (e.g., traffic engineering, access control). The cost of these systems is in the order of thousands to tens of thousands of dollars. This big increase in cost over home gateways is due to the significant increase in system performance, as well as the need for reliability and manageability.
- Core router: Routers in the core of the network need to support the highest data rates. Single links may carry as much as 40 gigabits of data per second and dozens to low hundreds of ports may be necessary. This leads to aggregate data rate requirements in the order of terabits per second for the highest end of core routers. These systems may use multistage switching fabrics to achieve the necessary scalability. Also, each port may use high-performance custom logic or dozens of embedded multicore processors to implement packet processing functions. Core routers are the size of several racks and require considerable

power and cooling. The cost of these systems is in the hundreds of thousands of dollars due to their performance requirements and the low number of units built.

These examples illustrate the range of router systems deployed in the Internet. With increases in network traffic, specific performance requirements increase. However, the relative gap in performance demands between these systems remains. Therefore, it can be expected that there is always a need for routers with widely varying cost/performance trade-offs.

SUMMARY

This chapter discussed the basic functionality of network layer systems. In the data plane of these routers, packets need to be forwarded at high data rates. The main operation in the forwarding process is to match the destination address against a set of prefixes, which contain routing information. The data structures for lookup algorithms can consist of simple binary trees and tries or can be implemented in hardware-supported TCAMs. In the control plane, routing information is exchanged to determine where packets should be forwarded. The control plane also handles error conditions.

Transport layer systems

8

TRANSPORT LAYER

The transport layer is responsible for providing connectivity between end-system applications. When looking at the transport layer, packets can be grouped into "connections" or "flows" that are used by end-system applications. This grouping is finer-grained than the grouping by IP prefixes that we have seen in the network layer, as each end system may have numerous active connections in parallel. Using this finer granularity, network systems can perform operations that are connection-specific. For example, network address translation translates the address information for a connection from a local network to the global Internet. In another example, packet schedulers can provide different levels of quality of service to packets that belong to different connections (as discussed in Chapter 10).

This chapter discusses design and implementation issues related to such transport layer systems. Specifically, it focuses on these questions:

- Functionality of the transport layer: What functions are provided by the transport layer? How do these functions affect the operation of transport layer systems?
- Packet classification: How can packets be associated with connections? How can packets be matched to policies?
- Example systems: How are transport layer systems used in practice?

Functionality of the transport layer

The main functionality of the transport layer is to provide a connection between processes on end hosts. Communication between processes is the basis of any distributed application.

Transport layer features

Unlike the Internet Protocol at the network layer, there is no single transport layer protocol. Instead, several different protocols have been developed to meet different application needs. The only functionality that is common among all protocols and that is a requirement for any transport layer protocol is the ability to identify the end-system process to which traffic is sent:

- Multiplexing/demultiplexing: When traffic is sent from different end-system processes, their packets are multiplexed onto a single network interface and network link. In the reverse direction, network packets for different processes arrive on a single network interface and need to be demultiplexed accordingly. To facilitate the demultiplexing process, typical transport layer protocol headers contain a field for an identifier representing the destination process (e.g., destination port number). Using this identifier, the operating system on the receiving host can distribute the packets. Typical protocols also contain a source process identifier (e.g., source port number) to allow bidirectional communication.

Numerous other functions can be implemented in transport layer protocols:

- Explicit connection setup: In many connection-oriented protocols, the transfer of data is initiated by an exchange of connection setup messages. This step informs the receiver (and the network) of the impending stat transfer. During the connection setup, system resources (e.g., packet buffers, link bandwidth) can be allocated to ensure that the data transfer can be handled.
- Reliability: One of the key functions of the widely used Transport Control Protocol (TCP) is to provide reliable data transfer over an unreliable network. As discussed briefly in the Appendix, reliable data transfer can be achieved by maintaining sequence numbers of packets and triggering retransmission on packet loss.
- Congestion control and flow control: Congestions and flow control provide feedback from the network and the receiver, respectively, on what data transmission rate is acceptable. This feedback allows the sender to adjust the transmission speed to ensure that the receiver can process the traffic. Similarly, congestion control information is used to limit transmission speed to avoid an overloaded network.

Transport layer protocols

Several different transport layer protocols exist to accommodate different application layer needs. By combining different features (e.g., the ones discussed previously), different types of transport layer protocols can be created. Despite the potential diversity in transport layer protocols, two protocols dominate in the Internet.

- User Datagram Protocol (UDP): This connection-less protocol uses datagrams to send messages from one end system to another. Because UDP operates in a connection-less mode, no prior connection setup is necessary to transmit data. UDP does not provide any services beyond multiplexing and demultiplexing. Datagrams may be delayed, lost, and reordered. In addition, use of the checksum field present in the UDP header is optional. Therefore, UDP is considered a "bare bones" transport layer protocol. UDP is often used for applications that tolerate packet loss but need low delay (e.g., real-time voice or video). The full details of UDP are specified in RFC 768 [142].

- Transmission Control Protocol: The transmission control protocol operates in connection-oriented mode. Data transmissions between end systems require a connection setup step. Once the connection is established, TCP provides a stream abstraction that provides reliable, in-order delivery of data. To implement this type of stream data transfer, TCP uses reliability, flow control, and congestion control. TCP is widely used in the Internet, as reliable data transfers are imperative for many applications. The initial ideas were published by Cerf and Kahn [25]. (The authors of this paper received the highest honor in computer science, the Turing Award, in 2004 in part for their work on TCP.) More details on TCP implementation are available in several RFCs, including RFC 793 [145].

An example of another, less commonly used transport layer protocol follows.

- Stream Control Transmission Protocol (SCTP): This transport layer protocol combines some aspects of UDP and TCP. SCTP provides reliability similar to TCP but maintains a separation between data transmissions (called "chunks") similar to datagrams in UDP. Further, SCTP supports multiple parallel streams of chunks (for both data and control information). More information on SCTP can be found in RFC 4960 [170].

Other transport layer protocols are used for media streaming, transport layer multicast, improved TCP congestion control, high-bandwidth transmissions, etc. Many of these protocols employ some variations of the basic functionalities of the transport layer discussed earlier.

Network flows

The transport layer focuses on traffic that belongs to a network connection or a "flow." A connection is a sequence of packets that originate from the same end-system process and are sent to the same receiving process. For some connections (e.g., those using TCP), a formal connection setup process is used to initialize the connection. When using UDP, packets are sent without a connection setup step. In this connection-less mode, datagrams are sent independently from each other with no implied relation among them. Nevertheless, both types of transport layer communication between end-system processes are considered a flow.

End-system sockets

Many end-system application processes need to establish communication to another end-system process. To hide the complexities of the transport layer, most operating systems provide functionality for handling communication at this protocol layer. The UNIX operating system provides an elegant network "socket" interface, which is an abstraction used to send and to receive network traffic. A socket provides an interface that is as simple as reading from and writing to files and thus can be used easily by applications.

Sockets come in two different flavors: connection-based for use with the TCP protocol and connection-less for use with UDP. Connection-less sockets do not establish explicit connections and all datagrams are sent independently. The typical set of functions used for connection-less sockets is the following:

- Socket() creates a new socket,
- Sendto() sends a datagram to the destination specified as an argument, and
- Recvfrom() receives a datagram (if available) from a sender specified in an argument.

When using TCP sockets, additional functions are used to establish the connection before sending traffic. Typical functions used for connection-based sockets are:

- Socket() creates a new socket,
- Bind() associates a socket with a particular address,
- Listen() makes the server socket wait for a connection setup request,
- Connect() allows the client to initiate a connection to the server,
- Write() transmits data from one side of the connection to the other, and
- Read() allows the caller to read available data from the socket.

To ensure correct operation, these functions need to be called in the correct order. For connection-based sockets, the following order is typically used:

1. Receiver establishes socket with socket(), binds the socket to the specified local port with bind(), and begins to wait for connection at port with listen().
2. Sender establishes socket with socket() and initiates connections with connect().
3. Once connection setup phase has finished successfully, the sending socket and the receiving socket can be used similarly to a file handle to read and write the data stream.
4. Sender uses write() to send data into the socket.
5. Receiver uses read() to receive data from the socket.

A connection-based socket automatically establishes bidirectional communication. Thus, it is also possible for the receiver to send data back to the sender (e.g., to respond to a request).

One key difference between the connection-less socket and the connection-based socket is how data are written to and read from the interface. In the connection-less socket, the application explicitly partitions data into datagrams, each of which is sent via an explicit sendto() command. On the receiver side, the packets are also received one by one. Thus, data partitioning used by the application layer is maintained. In connection-based sockets, these barriers between individual packets disappear and data are represented as a stream. The sender may write data at the end of the stream with write() calls that may be completely different from how the receiver uses the read() calls. For example, the sender may write data into the socket with a few large blocks, and the receiver may read from the socket one byte at a time.

Except for the explicit connection setup, the remaining functions of TCP (e.g., flow control and congestion control) remain hidden from the application that uses sockets. For example, if the receiving application is slow about reading data from the socket, the buffer in the receiver's operating system and then the buffer in the sender's operating system will fill up. Once they are full, the sender's socket can no longer accept any data and the write() call will block. This blocking will stall the sender application and thus achieve flow control. Similarly, congestion control may limit the rate at which data are transferred between the sockets. Additionally, the reliability feature of TCP, which ensures that lost packets are retransmitted, is not visible to the application that uses a connection-based socket.

Flow 5-tuple

When establishing a connection, the port number on the receiver side is of critical importance. The sender and the receiver need to agree upon which port number is used for their communication, as it is the identifier used to demultiplex data to the correct process. In case of a mismatch, the receiving operating system is not able to deliver data to the correct process.

Applications can therefore use either a previously agreed upon socket number or one that is "well known." Well-known port numbers are associated with commonly used applications. Servers that provide a commonly used service listen for connections at these port numbers to ensure that a client can connect. Examples of well-known port numbers and the associated applications are:

- Port 80: Hypertext Transfer Protocol (HTTP) (i.e., Web server)
- Port 22: Secure Shell (SSH) protocol
- Port 53: Domain Name Service (DNS) protocol

The source port of a connection is typically not a predefined value. Instead it is chosen randomly by the sender's operating system, and no two active connections use the same port. This selection process avoids problems when a connection setup fails and needs to be repeated or when two connections are active between the same hosts using the same destination port. Port numbers can typically be grouped into numbers that are used for well-known services (ports 0 through 1023) and numbers that are used for originating user connections (ports 1024 through 65535).

An example of IP addresses and port numbers used in a typical connection is shown in Figure 8-1. In this example, the sender attempts to connect to a Web server on the destination.

It is hypothetically possible that a connection-less socket uses the same IP address and port pairs as a connection-based socket. The operating systems can distinguish between these connections based on the layer 4 protocol used. Thus, to uniquely identify any connection in the Internet, the following 5-tuple is used:

- Source IP address
- Destination IP address
- Source port number
- Destination port number
- Transport layer protocol identifier

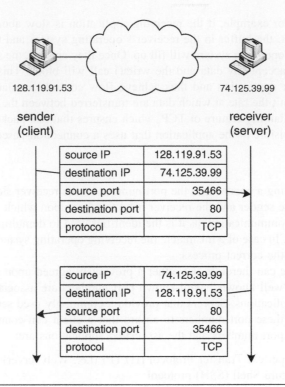

128.119.91.53   74.125.39.99

sender   receiver
(client)   (server)

source IP	128.119.91.53
destination IP	74.125.39.99
source port	35466
destination port	80
protocol	TCP

source IP	74.125.39.99
destination IP	128.119.91.53
source port	80
destination port	35466
protocol	TCP

FIGURE 8-1

Connection information in network and transport layer headers.

Note that the 5-tuple of a connection remains unchanged throughout the network and for the entire duration of the connection. It is possible that a particular 5-tuple can be reused. For example, the sender's operating system may choose the same source port number again when connecting to the same destination end system and port. However, if the operating system attempts to avoid reuse of recent port numbers, it takes thousands of connections before the same source port number is reused. Thus, for all practical purposes, a 5-tuple can be considered unique.

Aggregates

A flow 5-tuple specifies traffic from a single end-system process to another. In the core of the network, a link may carry traffic from tens to hundreds of thousands of active connections. When managing network traffic, it may be infeasible to consider each connection individually. In such cases, multiple individual connections may be combined into aggregates. For example, an aggregate may encompass all traffic that originates from one network as identified by an IP address prefix. To specify any aggregate, it is necessary to use one or more "wildcards" in the 5-tuple. Typical wildcards include:

- Arbitrary value: "*"
- IP address prefix: e.g., "128.252./16" or "128.252.*"
- Port number range: e.g., "[0-1023]"

The use of wildcards for specifying flow aggregates is also used when specifying matching rules as discussed later.

Packet classification

Any transport layer system needs to be able to identify which packets belong to a specific connection. Therefore, it is essential that packets can be classified by their packet header information. There are two ways of classifying packets:

- Flow classification: Flow classification uses complete network and transport layer information to determine to which connection a packet belongs. In particular, wildcards (i.e., undefined field values) or ranges are not allowed. Only packets belonging to the same connection are classified as belonging to the same flow.
- Matching: In matching, packets are matched up with a set of rules. These rules are given a priori (e.g., as policies) and may contain wildcards and ranges. Multiple flows may match a rule and a packet may match multiple rules.

We present commonly used flow classification and matching algorithms in more detail.

Flow classification

Flow classification is widely used in transport layer systems. In many systems, decisions are made based on individual flows. For example, the system may maintain state information specific to each flow (e.g., number of packets or bytes transmitted by a connection). In some other cases, forwarding decisions for packets depend on the flow to which the packet belongs. Therefore, it is important to have an efficient process for classifying packets into flows.

A flow is identified by its 5-tuple, which contains complete source and destination addresses, source and destination ports, and the transport layer protocol identifier. Because there can be a large number of possibly 5-tuples, it is not feasible to maintain a data structure that has an entry for every possible flow. It is also not possible to predict the 5-tuples that will be encountered in any particular system, as port numbers are often chosen at random and user decisions determine to which network interface a connection is directed. Instead, it is necessary to develop a data structure where flows can be added (and removed) dynamically.

Because the data structure for maintaining active flows is smaller than the set of all possibly 5-tuples, a many-to-one mapping of flows is necessary. For example, a hash table uses a hash function that maps the flow 5-tuple to a hash index. Multiple different flows may map to the same hash index. Therefore, conventional methods for resolving hash collisions need to be used (e.g., chaining or open addressing). An example of a flow classification data structure is shown in Figure 8-2.

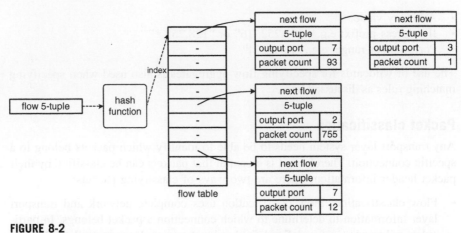

FIGURE 8-2

Flow classification with hash table and chaining for collision resolution. The flow record contains forwarding information and other flow-specific information.

The flow record, which is maintained for each active 5-tuple, can be used throughout the system to store flow-specific information. A challenging problem is to determine when a connection has terminated (and thus no longer requires the flow record). In TCP, FIN packets can indicate termination of a connection. However, they are not always used. In addition, some other protocols (e.g., UDP) do not provide any indication on when a connection has terminated. Thus, it is typically necessary to maintain a timeout for each connection. Flow records from expired connections can be removed and reused for other connections. The removal of these records can be done opportunistically, as there is no harm in keeping records beyond the timeout period.

General matching rules

When operating a network, it may be necessary to specify rules and policies about the traffic that is carried in the network. For example, traffic that comes from a particular IP prefix may be treated differently than other traffic. Thus, traffic rules can be specified using the 5-tuple for the packet classification process. However, the large number of possible 5-tuples makes it impractical to flow classification and fully specified 5-tuples. Instead, rules can be expressed using aggregates and wildcards in the 5-tuple specification.

An example of rules is shown in Table 8-1. For simplicity, we assume that simple deny/permit decisions are associated with each rule. In practice, more complex information may be stored with each rule (e.g., forwarding information, quality of service information).

Because a packet's specific 5-tuple may match multiple rules, there needs to be an ordering on rule priority. In general, rules higher in the list of rules take precedence over those lower in the list (i.e., a lower sequence number takes priority).

Table 8-1 Example Rule Set Requiring General Matching

Source IP	Destination IP	Source port	Destination port	Protocol	Action
128.252.*	*	*	*	TCP	Permit
*	128.252.*	*	80	TCP	Permit
128.252.*	129.69.8.*	*	554	UDP	Permit
150.140.129.*	128.252.*	[1024-65535]	*	*	Permit
*	*	*	*	*	Deny

The size of a rule set can vary drastically depending on the location in the network and how the rules are used. Small configurations may only have a few to a dozen rules. Large enterprise configuration may contain hundreds or thousands of rules.

Matching algorithms

A transport layer network system that implements this type of general matching needs to be able to determine to which rule(s) a packet belongs. A packet may match multiple rules, as these rules may overlap in the space of all possible 5-tuples. The resulting matching problem is difficult to solve efficiently and requires specialized matching algorithms. We discuss several of these algorithms later. For a more extensive review of matching algorithms, see [59, 177].

For a discussion of these algorithms, we assume a two-dimensional rule space and the example rules shown in Table 8-2. Figure 8-3 visualizes this rule set on a plane, where each rule covers some prefixes of each dimension. As shown in Figure 8-3, rules may overlap (e.g., B overlaps with D). When using an example packet, we assume it carries field values (1010/0111) for the two dimensions we consider. This example packet's location in Figure 8-3 is shown as a black dot.

When discussing the performance of different classification algorithms, we need to consider how they scale as the number of rules, dimensions, and field sizes increase. We use the Landau notation ("big-O" notation) to describe the upper

Table 8-2 Simplified Rule Set Used for Discussion of Matching Algorithms

Rule	1st field	2nd field
A	0*	00*
B	10*	00*
C	0*	01*
D	1*	0*
E	*	1*

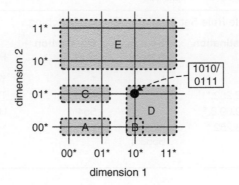

FIGURE 8-3

Visualization of rule set from Table 8-2.

bound on the growth of the metrics we consider. For notation, we assume there are n rules with d dimensions each. The length of each field in each dimension is assumed to be l bits.

Metrics

Similar to the performance requirements for prefix lookup algorithms in the network layer, matching algorithms are typically evaluated based on the following metrics.

- Classification complexity: This metric measures how computationally expensive the classification computation is based on the number of rules and their characteristics.
- Space requirement: This metric reflects the amount of memory necessary to store the data structure used in the classification process.
- Update complexity: Rules used for classification may change during operation of the system. As a result, the classification data structure may need to be updated. The update complexity characterizes the cost of modifying this data structure.

Classification complexity has a direct impact on the maximum packet rate that a transport layer system can sustain. Space requirements have implications on the maximum number of rules that can be supported. For highly dynamic systems, where rules get added and removed frequently, update complexity may have important implications. However, in systems where the rule set remains unchanged for longer periods of time, this metric can be ignored. In our discussion of classification algorithms, we focus on classification complexity and space requirements.

Linear search

Linear search is a straightforward algorithm for matching a packet to a set of rules. The classifier simply iterates over the set of rules and attempts to match each to the packet. If a match is not possible, the next rule is considered. Once the first match is found, the search is terminated and the matching rule is reported. Because rules are ordered by priority, there is no need to search beyond the first match.

The classification complexity of linear search scales linearly with the number of rules. It is also proportional to the number of dimensions of each rule (because each field needs to be checked) and the number of bits in each field (because prefixes need to be checked incrementally). The space requirement scales similarly. Thus, linear search requires:

- Classification complexity: $O(ndl)$ because each rule and field may need to be considered and each prefix match may require l steps.
- Space requirement: $O(ndl)$ because each rule and field are stored individually.

While linear search is very easy to implement, it is expensive for large numbers of rules. In practice, it is only used for very small classification databases (a few to a dozen rules).

Hierarchical trees

To avoid the cost of scanning each rule linearly, classification lookups can be structured into trees similar to how it was done for prefixes in the network layer (see Chapter 7). However, the challenge with such an approach is that longest prefix matches in one dimension may not lead to a valid solution in the other dimension. For example, when matching (1010/0111), the longest prefix match for 1010 in the first dimension yields rule B. However, rule B does not match in the second dimension. Similarly, the longest prefix match for 0111 in the second dimension results in rule C. Again, this rule does not match in the other dimension. Thus, it is necessary to use a matching approach that considers both dimensions in the process.

The hierarchical trees algorithm uses a prefix tree in each dimension as shown in Figure 8-4. The classification prefixes of the first dimension are represented in

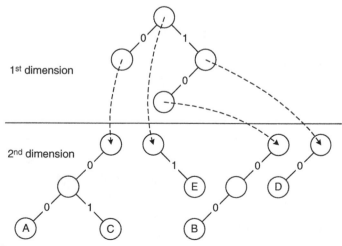

FIGURE 8-4

Hierarchical trees data structure for rule set from Table 8-2.

the top tree. Because classification decisions cannot be made based on a single dimension, there are no prefixes in the top tree. Instead, nodes in the top tree contain pointers to prefix trees in the second dimension. Trees in the second dimension contain prefixes from rules that match in the first dimension. For example, the second dimension tree that is connected to 0* in the first dimension contains rules A and C because these rules have 0* in their first field.

The lookup procedure for the hierarchical trees algorithm starts at the top node of the tree in the first dimension as shown in Figure 8-5. All prefixes that match the field in the first dimension need to be matched. The first possible match is the root node. From there, the search transitions into the second dimension, where a match for 0111 is attempted. However, the search "falls off the tree" before reaching a node that has an entry for a matching rule. Thus, no match is found, and the search transitions back into the first dimension. From the root node in the first dimension, the search continues to match 1010 (step 3). On each node along the way, the search in the second dimension is repeated. In step 4, the search matches rule D. At this point, a valid match has been found. However, the search cannot stop yet because there could be multiple rules that match the packet. Because rules are no longer ordered (as they were in linear search), it cannot be guaranteed that this match is the rule with highest priority. Therefore, the search continues. In steps 5 and 6, no further matches are found. The result of the classification process is rule D.

One problem with this algorithm is that it requires multiple prefix matches in each dimension. For long prefixes, the number of steps necessary to find all matching rules can become very time-consuming. The computational complexity and space requirement of this algorithm is:

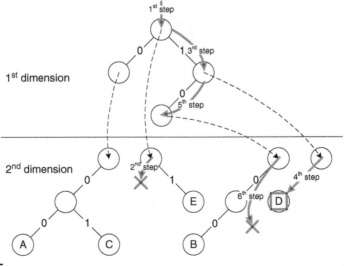

FIGURE 8-5

Lookup process on hierarchical trees data structure.

- Classification complexity: $O(l^d)$ because up to l search steps are necessary in each dimension and each search step triggers a full search in higher dimensions.
- Space requirement: $O(ndl)$ because each rule may require l nodes in each dimension.

Set-pruning trees

Set-pruning trees use the same ideas as hierarchical trees, but improve on the problem of having to traverse back and forth between dimensions. The main idea is that trees in the second dimension should include all rules for shorter prefixes in the first dimension. Using this approach, the lookup becomes simply a longest prefix match in the first dimension followed by a longest prefix match in the second dimension. Searches on shorter prefixes are not necessary since all matching rules for shorter prefixes are included in the trees of longer prefixes.

Figure 8-6 shows the data structure used for set-pruning trees. Note that rule E is replicated in the tree for prefix 0*, 1*, 10*. Rule D is replicated in the tree for prefix 10*. These replications do not change the classification outcome, as they only get added to prefixes that are longer (i.e., more specific) than the original rule.

To perform the classification for fields (1010/0111) with this data structure, a longest prefix lookup is performed in the first dimension. This lookup yields 10* as the longest match. Then, in the second dimension, another longest prefix match is performed. This lookup yields rule D (since the search falls off the tree when attempting to match 01*). Thus, the result is rule D.

The complexity of this matching algorithm and the space requirements of the data structure are:

- Classification complexity: $O(dl)$ because there are d longest prefix matches to be performed and each takes up to l search steps.

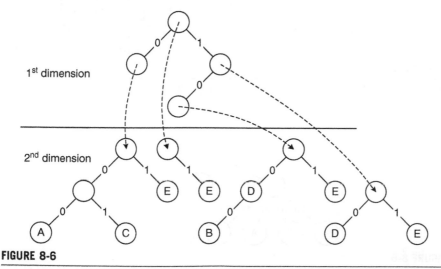

FIGURE 8-6

Set-pruning trees data structure for rule set from Table 8-2.

- Space requirement: $O(n^d dl)$ because each rule may have to be replicated n times in each dimension and each rule may require l nodes in each dimension.

A possible improvement that reduces space requirements is the grid of trees, where pointers are used to connect subtrees in the second dimension. This process avoids the repeated storage of subtrees. However, it only can be used under certain conditions and only for a two-dimensional rule space.

Area-based quadtree

The classification algorithms discussed previously have separated lookup in each dimension into separate steps. A classification algorithm that performs lookups in multiple dimensions at the same time is the area-based quadtree. We explain this algorithm for a two-dimensional space. In practice, it can be extended to more dimensions.

The quadtree divides the two-dimensional space into four areas as shown in Figure 8-7. This cutting is applied recursively to each area until only one rule remains in an area. The resulting quadtree data structure is shown in Figure 8-8. When performing a lookup, the first bit of each dimension is used to traverse the first step of the quadtree. In our example, the 1 from first dimension and the 0 from

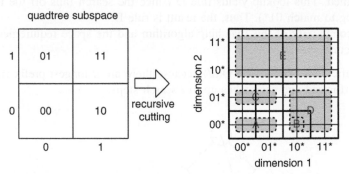

FIGURE 8-7

Division of classification space using area-based quadtrees.

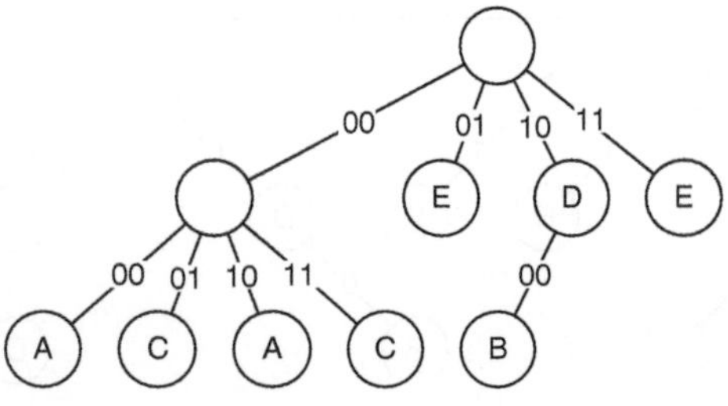

FIGURE 8-8

Area-based quadtree data structure for rule set from Table 8-2.

the second dimension are concatenated and the 10 edge is traversed. Because there are no further children on the node that is reached, the result of the classification process is rule E.

The computation complexity and space requirements for area-based quadtrees are:

- Classification complexity: $O(l)$ because the quad tree has a maximum of l levels.
- Space requirement: $O(nl)$ for two dimensions because n rules need to be stored at possibly multiple levels in the tree.

Hierarchical intelligent cuttings

The HiCuts algorithm uses a heuristic approach to classifying packets. The algorithm exploits the fundamental structure of typical classification rules to develop a data structure that provides fast lookup times in most cases. HiCuts cuts the search space into areas such that there are only a small number of rules remaining in each area. A decision tree is built to traverse the cuttings. The set of remaining rules is then searched using linear search.

A cutting for our example rule set is shown in Figure 8-9. In the first step, the second dimension is cut into four areas. In the second step, the 00* child of the first cut is cut into two areas. These cuttings are represented in the decision tree shown in the same figure. Leaf nodes of the decision tree contain one or more rules that need to be evaluated with linear search.

The key to HiCuts is to determine a suitable cutting heuristic. The goal is to keep the number of cuts low because each cut introduces an additional node in the decision tree. At the same time, the number of rules that need to be searched linearly should also be kept low to avoid expensive linear searches. Because the cutting heuristic depends on the rule set, it is not possible to provide a reasonable bound on processing complexity or space requirements. Poor cuttings can lead to very poor performance. However, good cuttings can provide a good trade-off between cuttings and rules per node.

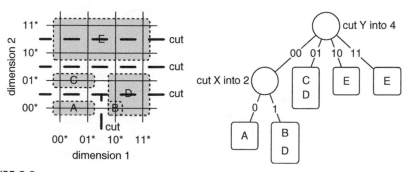

FIGURE 8-9

Hierarchical intelligent cuttings of rule space and results data structure for rule set from Table 8-2.

Hardware-based algorithms

The aforementioned algorithms are designed for software implementations on conventional general-purpose processors. However, there are also specialized hardware solutions to flow classification. These are based on the same type of ternary content-addressable memory discussed for hardware prefix lookups in the network layer. Because the search word does not have to have contiguous blocks of don't care symbols, it is easy to split it into sections that are used by each dimension.

The TCAM configuration for our example rule set is shown in Figure 8-10. Because rules are ordered by priority, they can simply be used in that order in the TCAM. A lookup in the TCAM will return the highest priority rule that matches the values of the packet fields.

A TCAM can achieve classification in a single memory access. However, TCAMs consume much more power than conventional memories and thus can only be used in systems with a sufficient power budget. In addition, there are limits on the size of a TCAM. Recent research has explored a variety of solutions on how to split large classifiers over multiple physical TCAMs.

Other classification algorithms

Packet classification is an important aspect of modern network systems, and there is much ongoing research on how to improve classification algorithms further. The survey by Taylor [177] presents several methods that go beyond the ones discussed here.

Transport layer systems

To further illustrate the role of transport layer systems in the network, we present several example systems used in today's networks.

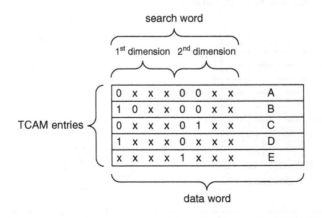

FIGURE 8-10

Packet matching with ternary content-addressable memory for rule set from Table 8-2.

Firewalls

A firewall is a device typically used to protect a local subnetwork from malicious attacks [125]. Security issues are discussed in more detail in Chapter 10. For this discussion, we simply assume that an end system on the subnetwork should only be able to receive traffic that belongs to a (bidirectional) connection that was initiated by that end system. All other traffic should be dropped at the firewall. This process is illustrated in Figure 8-11.

To accomplish this type of traffic filtering, a firewall needs to keep track of the connections that have been initiated by any end system in the subnetwork, classify each packet received, and determine if it may be forwarded or not:

- Connection tracking: To track active connections, the firewall simply identifies all TCP SYN packets that originate from the subnetwork. These SYN packets identify the 5-tuple of traffic directed from the subnetwork to the Internet. Because most connections are bidirectional, traffic that matches the 5-tuple with source and destination fields swapped is permitted to enter the subnetwork.
- Packet classification: Using a simple packet classification process as in this chapter, the firewall attempts to match an incoming packet's (reverse) 5-tuple to an entry in the connection table. If a match is found, then the packet is considered a response to a connection that was initiated from an end system in the subnetwork.

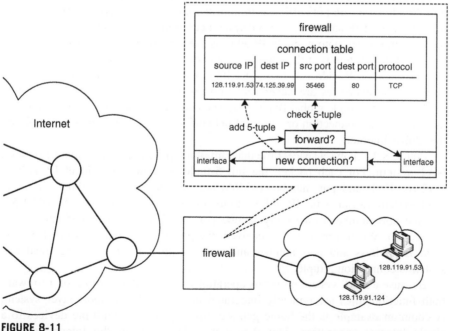

FIGURE 8-11

Firewall operation used to identify packets that belong to connections initiated from within the protected subnetwork.

- Forwarding decision: If a packet is identified as belonging to an active connection, then it is forwarded into the subnetwork. All other traffic is discarded. This packet dropping is typically done "silently," that is, without generating a control message to inform the sender.

Because connections typically only exist for a limited amount of time, entries in the connection table eventually time out and get removed.

Overall, a firewall makes an end system unreachable from the Internet unless a connection is initiated by that end system. However, in some cases an end system should be reachable (e.g., a server). To accommodate such end systems in a subnetwork protected by a firewall, static rules can be added to the connection table. These typically contain wildcards, as the source of the connection request is not known a priori. On some end systems, firewall functionality is also implemented in software in the operating system.

Network address translation

Closely related to firewalls, and often implemented in the same system, are network address translators (NAT). These NAT systems address one of the main problems in today's Internet. The IP address space is limited to 32 bits due to the size of the IP address field in the IP header. With the enormous growth in the number of devices connecting to the Internet (desktop computers, servers, cell phones, game consoles, set-top boxes, sensors, etc.), the roughly four billion available IP addresses are not sufficient to allocate one to each interface. To overcome this shortage of IP addresses, a NAT system can multiplex the traffic of numerous network interfaces onto a single IP address [48]. Similar to firewalls, the typical use of a NAT system is at the edge of a subnetwork as shown in Figure 8-12. Only locally routable IP addresses (e.g., 192.168/16 or 10/8) are used on the local network. These addresses are never sent into the global Internet. On the Internet, the NAT uses a single global IP address. The connection table maintains the information of what connection on the local network matches with what connection on the global Internet.

Figure 8-12 shows a space–time diagram of a typical connection that traverses a NAT system. For each packet, the full 5-tuple is shown. The local IP address (192.168.1.12) and port number (35466) are only used in the subnetwork. The NAT system translates the IP address to its own global IP address (128.119.91.53) and the port number to a locally unique port number (9387) that identifies this connection. When a response is received, the port number is used to look up the local IP address and port number and reverse the translation to the local end system's connection 5-tuple.

Because a NAT system performs operations very similar to those of a firewall, both functionalities are typically integrated into a single transport layer system. A common example is the home gateway used to connect multiple devices to a single Internet connection. This device provides NAT, as the Internet service provider typically only provides a single IP address. It also provides firewall functionality to protect local devices from intrusion attempts.

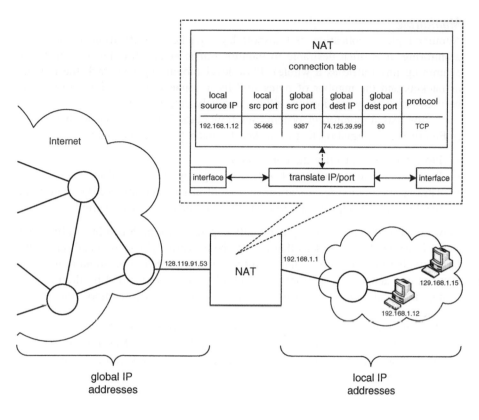

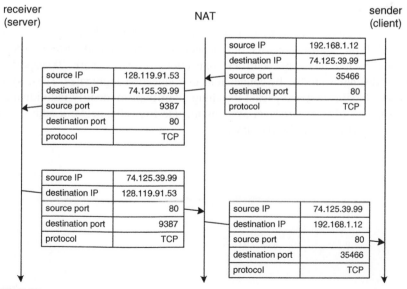

FIGURE 8-12

Network address translation.

Monitoring

Another typical application of transport layer packet classification is for traffic monitoring. It is often desirable to monitor traffic at the flow level (rather than examining link traffic as a whole). Flow level monitoring can track the number of packets and the number of bytes sent by a connection. This information can be used for security monitoring, billing, anomaly detection, etc.

A flow-based monitoring system uses flow classification similar to that shown in Figure 8-2. Information that is tracked for each flow can include:

- Flow 5-tuple to identify the connection.
- Packet and byte count to track network usage by the connection.
- Timing information (e.g., start time, time of last packet observed) to determine bandwidth consumption and to clear flow records that have expired.

Flow classification can be computationally expensive for high-bandwidth links due to the large number of packets that have to be classified per second and due to the large number of active flows that need to be tracked. Therefore, some monitoring systems use sampling where only a subset of packets is recorded by the monitor. Using statistical methods, an estimate of the original traffic composition can be obtained.

A well-known commercial monitoring system is Cisco's Netflow. Netflow reports per-flow information at intervals of 5 min. Typical Netflow information includes flow 5-tuples and packet and byte counts. Netflow can also be used in a mode where sampling is used.

SUMMARY

This chapter discussed the basic functionality of transport layer systems. At the transport layer, traffic consists of connections between end-system processes. The flow 5-tuple uniquely identifies connections in the network. Transport layer systems distinguish traffic by connections or connection aggregates. These systems use flow classification and packet matching algorithms to identify individual packets. Examples of transport layer systems include firewalls, network address translators, and network monitoring devices.

Application layer systems

APPLICATION LAYER

The application layer is responsible for implementing distributed applications and their protocols. This layer implements functionality accessed by end users. When considering distributed applications that use the network for communication, numerous examples come to mind: electronic mail, access to Web documents, interactive audio, streaming video, real-time gaming, etc. Permitting such an incredible diversity of applications at this layer is one of the main successes of layered Internet architecture. With only a small number of protocols at the transport layer and only a single protocol at the network layer, all these applications can be supported. As discussed in the Appendix, the hourglass architecture of Internet protocol stack is at the core of this design.

The application layer can be viewed as consisting of several sublayers: session layer, presentation layer, and application layer. In the OSI layered protocol model, these sublayers are numbered layers 5–7, respectively. However, in Internet architecture, they are combined into a single application layer. The reason that they are not treated independently is that these layers often provide functionality that is tuned to higher layers. For example, mechanisms implemented to maintain sessions in layer 5 are often specific to the application used in layer 7. Therefore, it can be justified that these three layers are treated as a single application layer. Note that in some cases this combined application layer is referred to as layer 7, layer 5, or layers 5–7.

This chapter discusses network system design and implementation issues related to the application layer. In some cases, we discuss specific protocols as examples of the application layer in general. However, there are also general functions (e.g., payload inspection) that are implemented on network systems independently of a specific application layer protocol. The questions we address are:

- Functionality of the application layer: What functions are provided by sublayers of the application layer?
- Payload inspection: How can a network system scan packet payloads efficiently to identify certain content?
- Application layer functions in network systems: What are examples of network systems supporting end-system applications?

Functionality of the application layer

The application layer uses end-to-end communication abstractions provided by the transport layer to implement distributed applications. The application layer can be structured into session, presentation, and application sublayers. However, many applications do not formally distinguish these sublayers. Instead, features from each layer may be implemented as part of the distributed communication of the application.

Session layer

The session layer, which corresponds to OSI layer 5, handles connection aggregates, called sessions. A session represents the information exchange that takes place between end systems in the context of a specific distributed application. A session encompasses possibly multiple (sequential or parallel) transport layer connections. Typical examples of distributed applications with multiple transport layer connections in a session are video conferencing (where multiple parallel transport layer connections transmit voice, video, and control information) and online shopping (where multiple sequential transport layer connections are used to add items to a shopping cart followed by a purchase).

There are several services that the session layer implements that may be used by higher sublayers of the application layer.

- Robust communication: The session layer needs to deal with coordination between multiple parallel transport layer connections and recover from failures in transport layer connections (e.g., disconnection due to mobile user moving from one access point to another and thus changing IP addresses). By providing a robust communication service, higher layers do not need to deal with the mechanics of coordinating individual transport layer connections. The session layer may use checkpointing and recovery mechanisms to achieve robustness.
- Authentication and access control: Verification of which end-system applications may communicate can be implemented at the session layer. The communicating end systems identify themselves to each other and validate access control permissions. More detail on security protocols related to authentication and access control can be found in Chapter 10.

Presentation layer

The presentation layer, which corresponds to OSI layer 6, handles the representation of information used in the communication between end-system applications. Data can be encoded in a number of different ways, and the presentation layer ensures that they are translated appropriately for transmission on the network and to be useful to the end-system application.

Services provided by the presentation layer are:

- Translation: The translation service provided by the presentation layer is important for end systems and end-system applications that use different representations for data. For example, text can be represented by a number of different codes (e.g., ASCII, EBCDIC). If the two sides of a communication use a different encoding, a translation is necessary to avoid corruption of data. Similarly, different hardware architectures use varying representations for numbers (e.g., big-endian, little-endian), and translation is necessary to ensure correct interpretation by the application. Note that translation services can also be implemented for more complex data structures (e.g., strings, XML content).

• Encryption/compression: Encryption/decryption and compression/decompression can be seen as one form of translation. However, these functions do not simply translate from one data format to another, but convert data into an intermediate format (ciphertext or compressed data) for transmission over the network. Note that encryption can also be performed in other layers of the protocol stack (see Chapter 10).

Application layer

The application layer, in this case the sublayer corresponding to OSI layer 7, performs all processing related to communication between distributed end-system applications not handled in any of the other layers. The functionality implemented at this layer is often very specific to a particular distributed application. Thus, no general service is provided by this layer. Instead, application-specific protocols are used. Some examples of such protocols are discussed in the following section.

Application layer protocols

There is a large diversity of application layer protocols, as any application may define its own protocol for distributed communication. We discuss two examples of widely used application layer protocols: Hypertext Transfer Protocol (HTTP), which is used to transmit Web documents, and SIP, which is used to set up multimedia communication. These examples are intended to only provide a small insight in the design and operation of the application layer.

Domain name system

Many application layer protocols require that users identify specific end systems. For example, to access Web documents using HTTP (see later), a user needs to specify the Web server from which a document needs to be retrieved. As discussed in Chapter 7, each network interface contains its own global interface address (unless it is shared using a NAT system). Thus, a user could provide the IP address of the server's network interface. However, memorizing IP addresses is difficult for humans. Instead, "domain names" are used to refer to networks (i.e., sets of IP addresses with matching prefix) and specific interfaces within them. Domain names typically use more intuitive names and thus are easier to remember (e.g., www.google.com or www.umass.edu). The Domain Name System (DNS) is an application layer system that provides mapping between domain names and the associated IP addresses. DNS is described in detail elsewhere [123, 124]. DNS is widely used in the Internet, as practically all Web addresses and email addresses contain domain names.

Domain names are structured hierarchically with each domain name belonging to a top-level domain (e.g., ".edu" for educational institutions or ".de" for Germany). Continuing from the top-level domain, domain names replicate some of the hierarchical structure of IP prefix assignments. Domain names are structured by zones (e.g., "umass.edu" for the University of Massachusetts Amherst). Domain name zones can have subzones that manage part of the name space (e.g., ecs .umass.edu is a subzone of umass.edu). Within each zone or subzone a name server ("authoritative name server") maintains the local mapping between IP addresses and names. The IP address of the name server is known to the next higher zone as well as all hosts within the zone.

To retrieve a DNS mapping for an application on an end system, the end-system DNS resolver (typically part of the operating system) initiates communication with name servers. Because the resolver does not know the address of the name server that maintains the IP addresses for the domain name in question, a step-wise process is necessary. The domain name can be resolved iteratively by parsing the domain name in reverse order and querying the corresponding name server. First, the top-level domain name server needs to be queried. To determine the IP address of the top-level domain name server, one of the root name servers is contacted. The root domain name server provides the IP address of the top-level domain name server, which is contacted next. The top-level domain name server provides the address of the name server of the next level domain. The resolver queries that name server and continues this process until it reaches the authoritative name server that manages the IP address of the domain name in question, where the IP address of the domain name can be retrieved.

To make the query process more efficient and to avoid an overload on name servers high up in the hierarchy, name servers can cache mappings. If a query for a mapping is received that can be answered from information in the cache, the name server responds with this information and no further queries are necessary. To implement this caching process effectively, the resolver typically does not directly contact the top-level domain server, etc., but has its local name server do it. Thus, the local name server can learn the DNS mapping and provide a cached response to repeat queries on the same domain name. (The end-system resolver also maintains a local cache to reduce DNS traffic.) Figure 9-1 illustrates the iterative query process when a domain cannot be resolved locally. It is also possible to use recursive queries, where a queried name server automatically sends more specific queries to other name servers before responding (not shown).

The DNS queries are sent as UDP packets, as a query can typically fit into a single packet. Also, the lossy operation of UDP has limited impact on DNS. If a query or response is lost, retransmission can be triggered by the application (or the resolver). The benefit of UDP is that no transport layer connection needs to be established and thus less delay is incurred. Numerous additions have been implemented for DNS, including security extensions (e.g., DNSSEC) and extensions to support email (e.g., Mail Exchanger record).

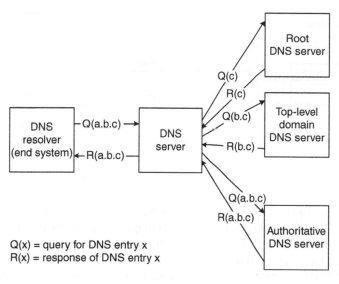

FIGURE 9-1

Iterative DNS queries for domain name a.b.c.

The DNS system plays a critical role in operation of the Internet. Without DNS, many application layer applications fail, as applications and users do not know the IP addresses of the systems they need to communicate with. Therefore, there is much concern about the protection of top-level name servers from denial of service attacks (see Chapter 10). Also, there is ongoing debate on which national or international organization should manage (and thus have control over) this critical component of Internet infrastructure.

Hypertext transfer protocol

One of the most widely used application layer protocols in the Internet is the Hypertext Transfer Protocol. This protocol is used to communicate between clients and servers to exchange World-Wide Web (WWW) documents. The most common use of HTTP is for a client program (e.g., a Web browser) to fetch a document from a server to display its information to a user. The HTTP protocol is defined in RFC 2616 [52]. Protocol headers in HTTP use human-readable ASCII text (rather than a binary representation) and thus can be interpreted more easily than headers used in the transport and network layer. The HTTP protocol follows the client–server design: client applications connect to the server to issue requests for documents (or control information) and the server responds to these client requests. A number of different types of requests can be issued in HTTP, but the basic protocol steps and header formats follow the same principles.

The basic setup for a Web client and server is shown in Figure 9-2, which illustrates how the user agent (e.g., a Web browser) interacts with the server by sending requests for documents. The document that is transmitted in response is then rendered by the

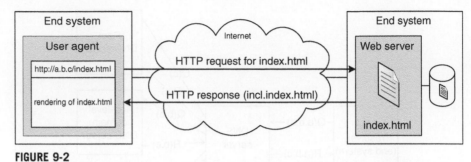

FIGURE 9-2

Exchange of request and response between user agent and Web server.

user agent to display. Documents can be of different formats [e.g., HTML for Web documents (see RFC 1866 [17]) or JPEG encoding for images]. While there is ongoing competition between different browser software (e.g., Mozilla Firefox, Microsoft Internet Explorer) on performance and functionality, all these user agents use the same HTTP request and response mechanism. Their difference lies in how they render the document and what additional functions they implement (e.g., security).

HTTP requests

An HTTP request consists of up to four components.

1. A request line: The request line indicates the type of operation that is to be performed, the document to which the operation refers, and the HTTP protocol version that is being used. Examples of operations are GET (to fetch a document from the server), POST (to submit data, e.g., from a Web form), PUT (to post a document to a server), and HEAD (to retrieve meta-information without a document body).

2. HTTP headers: These headers contain more detailed information about the request (e.g., the type of encoding to be used, preferred languages). There can be multiple headers and each header uses its own line. Examples of HTTP headers used in a request are Accept (indicating the types of encodings that can be used, e.g., Accept: text/plain), Accept-Language (indicating the languages preferred for a document, e.g., Accept-Language: en), and User-Agent (indicating the type of user agent used, e.g., User-Agent: Mozilla/5.0 (Linux; X11)).

3. An empty line (to indicate the end of the request header).

4. An (optional) message body: This message body may contain a document or data for requests that transmit information to the server (e.g., a POST request).

An example of a complete HTTP request is shown in Figure 9-3.

HTTP responses

An HTTP response consists of the following.

1. Status code line: The status code line indicates the type of response the server provides. The line consists of the HTTP version used by the server, the status

```
                         HTTP request
GET /index.html HTTP/1.1
Host: www.umass.edu
User-Agent: Mozilla/5.0 (Linux; X11)
Accept: text/plain
Accept-Language: en
```

FIGURE 9-3

Example HTTP request.

code, and a verbal description of the status code. Examples of status codes (and their verbal description) are 200 ("OK"), 404 ("Not Found"), and 503 ("Service Unavailable").

2. HTTP headers: Similar to HTTP headers in the request, the response also uses them to provide more additional information. Examples are Content-Language (indicating the language of the document in the message body, e.g., Content-Language: en), Content-Length [indicating the size of the document in the message body (in bytes), e.g., Content-Length: 1793], and Last-Modified (indicating the time the document was last modified, which is relevant for caching, e.g., Last-Modified: Sat, 07 Jun 2003 18:43:00 GMT).

3. An empty line (to indicate the end of the response header).

4. An (optional) message body: The message body may contain a document that is sent in response to the request.

An example of a complete HTTP response to the request shown in Figure 9-3 is shown in Figure 9-4.

Persistent HTTP connections

The performance of an application layer protocol can be measured by how efficiently the required communication can be completed. At first glance, the request

```
                         HTTP response
HTTP/1.1 200 OK
Date: Mon, 23 May 2005 22:38:34 GMT
Server: Apache/2.0.41 (Unix)
Last-Modified: Fri, 11 Sep 2009 15:29:33 GMT
Content-Length: 3488
Content-Type: text/html; charset=UTF-8
Content-Language: en
Connection: close

(content of page)
```

FIGURE 9-4

Example HTTP response.

and response process of HTTP seems to leave little room for improvement. However, interactions between the application layer protocol and the lower layers in the protocol stack (the transport layer, in this case) show that there are potential performance bottlenecks.

When issuing an HTTP request for a document, a connection to the server is set up and the request is transmitted. HTTP uses TCP as the transport layer protocol, as reliable data transfer is a paramount requirement. As discussed in Chapter 8, setting up a TCP connection requires an exchange of messages between the sender and the receiver before data can be transmitted. This setup takes roughly one round-trip time between client and server. The actual data transfer (assuming a small document that fits into a TCP segment) also takes one round-trip time. When requesting subsequent documents from the same server, the same delay of two round-trip times is incurred.

Persistent HTTP connections offer an improvement to reducing the delay caused by transport layer connection setup. When HTTP uses a persistent connection, the transport layer connection can be used for multiple requests and responses. Thus, at the end of the initial document request, the TCP connection remains active and subsequent requests are sent over the same connection. Thus, the delay for setting up a transport layer connection is incurred only once (for the first document). All subsequent documents can be retrieved in a single round-trip time. The operation of persistent HTTP connections is illustrated in Figure 9-5.

Persistent connections are optional under HTTP/1.0, where clients and servers can use the "connection: keep-alive" header to indicate that they want to support this feature. In HTTP/1.1, persistent connections are used by default, but can be

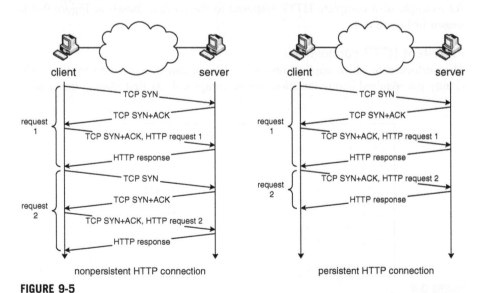

FIGURE 9-5

Comparison of two HTTP requests using nonpersistent and persistent HTTP connections.

overridden by the client or the server. If a "connection: close" header field is sent, then the connection is terminated at the end of the transfer.

Caching in HTTP

The HTTP provides a great example of how devices inside the network (i.e., not on the client or server side) can support application layer functionality. If multiple clients from one subnetwork request the same pages on a server (e.g., multiple users retrieving the same Web document from a news site), then transferring the same document multiple times is redundant. In particular, multiple transfers of the same document over slow network links or over large distances waste network resources. To address this problem, HTTP supports the use of caches (also called caching proxy).

An HTTP cache is a device that can store copies of HTTP documents and respond to requests (similar to a server). By configuring the user agent to use the cache, all requests for Web documents are redirected to the HTTP cache. There, the cache checks its local storage if the document is available. If so, the cache responds to the HTTP request. Operation of the HTTP cache is illustrated in Figure 9-6. If the document is not available, the cache requests it from the server, stores a local copy, and forwards it to the client. Thus, if a document is requested by multiple users that use the same cache, only the first request triggers interaction with the server. The second and all further requests are handled by the cache without communication to the server. As a result, bandwidth is saved and the response to the user agent is provided faster than when communicating with the server directly.

There are several restrictions on the types of documents and circumstances when caching is suitable.

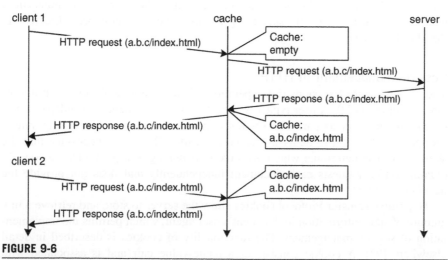

FIGURE 9-6

An HTTP caching example with two clients requesting the same document.

- Document freshness: Many Web documents change over time. Therefore, the cache should only provide copies of documents considered "fresh." Freshness can be specified by the server when transmitting the original copy (i.e., how long the document may be cached before a new copy needs to be retrieved). Also, the cache may actively check the freshness of a document by requesting the HTTP control information (i.e., the HTTP header using the HEAD command). If the checksum or hash value of the original document matches the checksum or hash value provided in response to the HEAD command, then no update is necessary.
- Explicit cache control: End systems involved in an HTTP transfer may explicitly specify the functionality used by any cache that is encountered. A user agent may specify to explicitly fetch the most recent document from the server and bypass the cache. The server may specify that a response may not be cached. The latter case may occur specifically in the context of dynamic Web content. Some Web documents are created dynamically in response to specific user requests (e.g., results from a database query, a personalized shopping portal, or a Web-based email system). Because these documents are specific to one user (or one instant in time), there is no value in caching them. Also, some documents may contain information that the user may not want to have cached (e.g., personal email).

The operation of HTTP caching is "transparent" to the end systems. A transparent operation means that client and server applications do not need to be aware of caching operations and do not see any difference in the requests and responses that they send and receive. (Note that the only necessary change is to configure the user agent to make transport layer connections to the caching proxy device rather than the server. However, this change does not affect the operation of application layer protocols.) HTTP also allows end systems to explicitly override the transparent behavior of caches (e.g., by specifying a "no-cache" or "no-store" directive in the HTTP header).

Session management in HTTP

The management of sessions (i.e., operation of the session sublayer) is an important aspect of HTTP. A user typically accesses Web documents not independently of one another, but as part of a session (e.g., reading of multiple emails, online shopping with multiple items in the virtual cart). Thus, it is necessary that the Web server can determine which Web requests belong to a particular session. By default, HTTP requests each document independently and does not provide the necessary context.

Hypertext Transfer Protocol cookies allow the server to store and retrieve a tiny amount of state information in the client's user agent, which permits the implementation of session management. The functionality of cookies is described in detail elsewhere [93]. A cookie consists of a name-value pair and is associated with the domain name of the Web server. The server can transmit the cookie in the

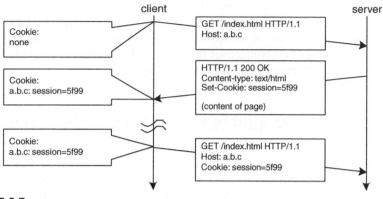

FIGURE 9-7

An HTTP exchange with cookies to maintain session information.

HTTP header of a response. The client stores the cookie and transmits it to the server along with every subsequent request to the site. The process is illustrated in Figure 9-7, where the client stores a cookie and sends it with later requests. The server needs to maintain the session state (e.g., shopping basket) associated with the identifier (not shown in Figure 9-7).

The server can use this mechanism to store a session identifier with the client's user agent when the first Web document is requested. All subsequent requests carry the session identifier value and thus can be associated with the session by the server. Clearly, the server needs to maintain the bulk of the session information (e.g., the content of the shopping cart) since the cookie only stores an identifier and no further content.

Cookies are optional and neither servers nor clients are required to support them. In many cases, users may chose to disable or restrict the access to cookies to avoid leaking information that could be used to track their Web activities.

Session initiation protocol

The Session Initiation Protocol (SIP) is an application layer control protocol that coordinates multimedia communication sessions. The SIP implements the signaling necessary to initiate communication between two or more parties, but it does not implement the actual protocols for sending data. This design allows SIP to be a general control protocol that can be adapted to different communication scenarios. Details of SIP are presented elsewhere [149].

The SIP uses uniform resource identifiers (i.e., the type of string used to identify Web documents in the Internet) to identify user agents, which are implemented on end systems. SIP user agents can act both as clients to send requests and as servers to respond to requests. User agents interact with proxy servers, registrars, and redirect servers to reach other user agents. The SIP operates with several different transport layer protocols, including UDP, TCP, and Stream Control Transmission

Protocol. Signaling implemented by SIP is a superset of that used in the public switched telephone network, and thus SIP can interact with telephony networks.

The SIP is an example of an application layer protocol that interacts with a diverse set of applications (voice over IP clients, video conferencing, etc.), as well as with several other protocols at the transport layer.

NETWORK SYSTEM SUPPORT FOR APPLICATION LAYER

The application layer protocols discussed in the previous section have very limited interactions with devices inside the network. Most application layer protocols simply use TCP (or UDP) sockets to create a point-to-point connection to the other end system. In such a scenario, network devices along the path of the communication simply forward packets at the network layer. In some cases, application layer proxies (e.g., HTTP, SIP) interact with some specific network traffic that is directed to them. However, there are few application layer network devices that work broadly on all network traffic. The reason for this situation is that very few functions can be applied to any application layer traffic independently of what protocol is used.

This section discusses a few examples of general application layer functions that are implemented on network devices. These examples are payload inspection, which scans packet payload to find specific patterns, and load balancing, which can redirect traffic based on application layer information.

Payload inspection

One function that can be applied to network traffic from any application is payload inspection. Payload inspection parses the payloads of packets (i.e., application layer headers and data) to classify traffic. We discuss the uses of payload inspection in the context of several scenarios. Because payload inspection requires access to the entire packet (application layer headers and data), it is a function that is very expensive to implement. Not only does it require considerable processing power to perform all the necessary computations at line speed, but it also puts considerable demands on the memory subsystem. Therefore, efficient scanning algorithms have been developed to minimize the resource demand of payload inspection. We discuss a variety of algorithms and their implementation here.

Payload inspection scenarios

Payload inspection is a very general term for accessing the payload of a packet. It is also referred to as deep packet inspection. Example scenarios where packet payloads are inspected on a network device are as follows.

- Monitoring: Traffic monitoring is used to understand properties of the traffic aggregate (e.g., distribution of application layer protocol use in aggregate) or to track individual sources or connections (e.g., lawful interception of individual's digital communication). In the case of monitoring of aggregates, payload inspection may be used to determine what application layer protocol is used in a particular connection. In this case, the payload is scanned for particular strings that identify specific application layer protocols. In the case of lawful intercept, packet payloads are recorded and reassembled for forensic purposes.

- Security: To protect end systems from malicious network traffic (e.g., hacking attacks, worms, viruses), network security devices inspect the payload of packets to identify suspicious patterns. These patterns can consist of specific strings (e.g., worm signature) or more general patterns (e.g., sequence of strings over multiple packets indicating a hacking attack).
- Content blocking: Content blocking may be used by network providers to limit the exchange of data that infringes copyright, violates local laws, or is considered obscene. Similar to payload scanning for security-related patterns, packet payloads are inspected to determine if the packet content matches criteria of the search.
- Quality of service: Certain types of network traffic may consume large amounts of networking resources (e.g., peer-to-peer file sharing). Therefore, network service providers may attempt to identify traffic from these sources and throttle their bandwidth consumption in the network. Payload inspection can be used to determine if packets belong to such traffic types.

Applications related to security and quality of service are discussed more in Chapter 10. We now discuss how specific strings and patterns can be found in packet payloads.

Search patterns

Different types of patterns can be considered for payload inspection. Patterns are expressed with a notation that allows an unambiguous statement of what bit sequences match. In principle, individual bits in the payload could be specified. However, in practice, pattern matches are aligned with 8-bit bytes. Because many protocols use regular text coding for protocol headers, patterns are typically expressed with conventional characters (noncharacter bit sequences are expressed in hexadecimal using an escape character). For the discussion of patterns in this section, we assume a simple alphabet with only four characters: {a,c,k,t}.

In principle, two types of patterns need to be distinguished.

- Strings: Strings are a sequence of characters that need to be matched exactly. For example, to match the string attack, the exact same sequence of characters (i.e., a, t, t, a, c, k) needs to be encountered.
- Regular expressions: Regular expressions consist of a combination of strings, alternatives, character sets, wildcards, and character repetitions. Alternatives allow a choice of matching one subexpression or another [e.g., (ac|ct)]. Character sets allow the choice of one character out of a set (e.g., [a,c,t]) matches if any character out of the set (i.e., a, c, t) is encountered. Wildcards represented as a period (.) match any character out of the alphabet (which is equivalent to a character set with all possible characters). Character repetition matches if the repeated

character is observed zero or more times (expressed by *, e.g., a*) or one or more times (expressed by $^+$, e.g., a$^+$). An example of a regular expression is a[c,t]a$^+$[k,c], for which acaaak and atac match, but attac does not.

Note that more complex patterns are possible (e.g., those expressed by context-free or context-sensitive grammars). An example of a pattern generated by context-free grammar is mathematical expressions where the number of opening parentheses is balanced with an equal number of closing parentheses. Expressions with such a balancing constraint cannot be generated by regular expressions. To match expressions that are generated by grammars, it is necessary to use a parser (and even then, not all possible types of expressions can be matched). In the networking domain, such complexity is typically limited to end-system applications and is not implemented in network devices. Therefore, we limit our discussion to strings and regular expressions.

There are different techniques to match packet payloads with search patterns. The main distinction is between what kind of matching is necessary (i.e., exact match of string or general matching of regular expression) and what type of hardware is used for the match. We describe the most common matching algorithms next. Payload inspection is an active area of research and new algorithms continue to be developed.

Exact string matching algorithms

String (and regular expression) matches can be translated elegantly into finite state automata (i.e., "state machines"). A finite state automaton consists of a set of states (typically illustrated by circles) and a set of possible transition edges between states (illustrated as arrows between states). As the automaton processes the input that is provided to it, it transitions between states along the edges. Annotations on transition edges show on what input a transition can be taken. Some states are annotated as "accepting states" (illustrated by double circles), which are reached when the automaton has detected a pattern successfully. Differences between various types of finite state automata are discussed. Performance trade-offs consider the size of the automaton and how complex the state transition computations are.

In a practical scenario, the payload of packets is inspected for multiple patterns in parallel (e.g., to find one or more possible signatures indicating a hacking attack). In the examples discussed here, we aim to match one of the following four strings: attack, act, aka, cat.

Nondeterministic finite automaton

The simplest translation between the set of strings that need to be matched and finite state automaton can be accomplished using a nondeterministic finite automaton (NFA). Each character in the string corresponds to a state. State transitions are set up to "chain" the characters to create the strings. The final character of each string is an accepting state to indicate a match. An NFA for the four strings used in our example is shown in Figure 9-8.

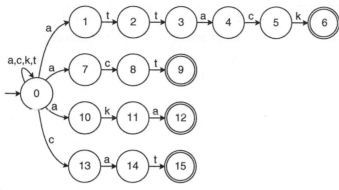

FIGURE 9-8

Example of nondeterministic finite automaton for string matching.

The left most state in Figure 9-8, labeled as state 0, is the starting state of the NFA. When one of the string patterns is input into the NFA, the state transitions traverse the states that match up each character of the string. At the end of the string, an accepting state is reached and the string match is reported. The main problem with an NFA is that the automaton does not know a priori when an input leads to a string match. For example, when observing an a on the input, the automaton cannot know if this is the first character of attack (which would lead to a match) or akkk (which would not lead to a match). Knowing this information would defeat the purpose of the string matching automaton. However, because the NFA is nondeterministic, it simply performs the correct transition.

To implement such nondeterministic behavior in practice, the automaton must pursue all possible state transitions. Once it becomes clear which transition was the correct choice, the other possibilities are discarded. For example, when an a is observed in state 0, the automaton transitions into the set of states {0,1,7,10}. If the next input is a c, then there are no valid transitions for states 1 and 10 and these options are discarded. Based on states 0 and 7, all possible valid transitions are considered and the new set of states is {0,8,13}. This process is repeated until an accepting state is in the set of valid states, at which point a match is reported. Note that it is not possible that the set of valid states becomes empty (i.e., the automaton becomes "stuck"), as state 0 transitions to itself for any of the four possible input characters. To illustrate the operation of the NFA for a complete example, Table 9-1 shows the progression of the set of states for the input acaattack.

While it is easy to construct an NFA given the set of string patterns that need to be matched, the computation to determine the set of active states is quite complex. When processing an input character, each active state needs to be checked for possible transitions. Even for the simple example shown earlier, there can be a very large number of active states at any given time. On conventional processors, this processing can require considerable amounts of time. Thus, a nondeterministic

Table 9-1 State Transition Table for NFA in Figure 9-8

Input	Set of states	Match?
–	{0}	No
a	{0,1,7,10}	No
c	{0,8,13}	No
a	{0,1,7,10,14}	No
a	{0,1,7,10}	No
t	{0,2}	No
t	{0,3}	No
a	{0,1,4,7,10}	No
c	{0,5,8,13}	No
k	{0,6}	Yes ("attack")

finite automaton for string matching at high performance (as it is necessary for payload scanning) is typically not the best choice.

Deterministic finite automaton

For payload scanning in network systems, where fast and deterministic performance is important, string matching is typically performed by a deterministic finite automaton (DFA). In a DFA, there is only one active state at any given time and there is only one possible transition for each input character. While the pattern matching steps for a DFA are straightforward, the construction of a DFA that matches multiple strings is slightly more complex.

A DFA can be constructed from an NFA through a general process called "subset construction." In this process, all sets of states generated by an NFA for any input are considered as states for the DFA. Subset construction is a process for converting any NFA into a DFA and thus is applicable to string matching. There is also a (possibly simpler) process for constructing a string matching DFA from scratch, which is described here.

Because a DFA can only use a single state for representing parts of strings that have already been matched by the automaton, it is necessary that strings sharing common prefixes also share states that represent a match of these prefixes. In our example, attack, act, and aka share a as a common prefix. Thus, there is a single state that represents the match of an a at the input. With shared prefixes, we obtain the (still incomplete) DFA shown in Figure 9-9.

The deterministic behavior of a DFA no longer allows "guessing" of the NFA when any particular pattern starts. Thus, any input character sequence that matches the prefix of a string needs to be treated as a potential match. When a partial match fails because an incorrect character is observed, then the failed sequence may already be a match for another string. For example, if attac is followed by an a (and thus fails the matching of attack), the last two characters, ca, may already

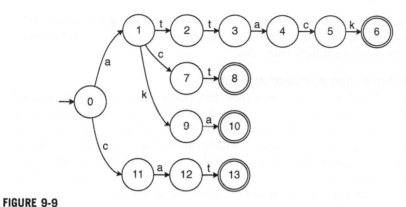

FIGURE 9-9

Example of deterministic finite automaton for string matching (without failure transitions).

be the first two characters of cat. These failure transitions require careful consideration in construction of the DFA. (To determine systematically where to transition to on each character that is not a match, the longest postfix of the failed pattern that matches any prefix of a string needs to be found. In the example, attaca (which is the longest postfix) is not matched with any prefix, ttaca (the next longest postfix) is not matched with any prefix either, etc., until ca is matched with the prefix for cat.) The complete DFA for our examples with all resulting transitions for failure scenarios is shown in Figure 9-10.

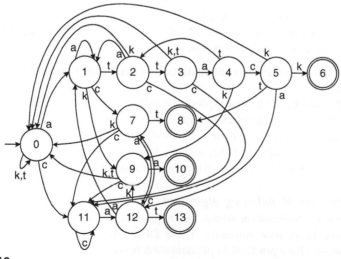

FIGURE 9-10

Example of complete deterministic finite automaton for string matching.

In this deterministic finite automaton, there is only a single transition valid for any given input in any given state. Thus, the processing complexity is low enough to perform matching at high data rates.

Regular expression matching algorithms

As discussed earlier, regular expression matches include alternatives, character sets, wildcards, and character repetitions. By extending the NFA technique discussed for strings, these features can be implemented. Note that some of these transformations require ε-transitions, which can be taken without consuming a character on the input. Once the construction is completed, these ε-transitions can be removed by determining the closure of any state (which is the set of states that can be reached by traversing zero or more ε-transitions).

- Alternative: An alternative allows the choice of matching one out of two (or more) subexpressions. To implement alternatives, both subexpressions are constructed and ε-transitions are added such that either subexpression can be traversed.
- Character set and wildcard: A character set simply provides between which characters trigger a transition. Instead of listing identical transition for all the character in the set, the character set simply allows an annotation of the transition that includes all characters in the set. We have used such notation already (e.g., in the DFA shown in Figure 9-8, where any character from set [k,t] transitions from state 0 to state 0). To implement a character set, the state transition is simply repeated for all characters in the set. A wildcard is a character set that consists of the entire alphabet. Thus, on any input character, the transition takes place.
- Character repetitions: A character repetition permits the same character (or subexpression) to occur an arbitrary number of times. To represent zero or more repetitions (i.e., a "star"), a "loop" transition back to the same state can be used. To enforce one or more repetitions (i.e., a "plus"), a state is added to "count" the first instance of the character. That state is followed by a state where a loop for zero or more repetitions is placed.

The construction process for alternatives and character repetitions is shown in Figure 9-11.

Once the NFA for the regular expression has been constructed, it can be transformed into a DFA by determining the closure of all states and by performing subset construction to identify all possible sets of states used in the NFA. An example of a regular expression in our example alphabet is $([a,t](ck|t)t^+|c(ak)*c)$. The corresponding DFA is shown in Figure 9-12. To simplify the figure, failure states are not shown.

Implementation of matching algorithms

The matching algorithms for strings and regular expressions can be expressed with deterministic finite state automata. These DFA were illustrated in previous sections. However, for a practical implementation on network systems, these automata need to be implemented on a real computer system. Different techniques are used for DFA processing on different platforms.

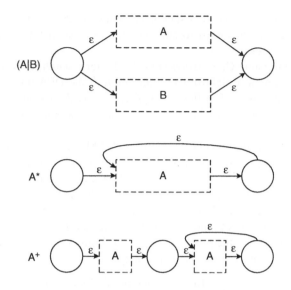

FIGURE 9-11

Construction process for alternatives and character repetitions in regular expressions.

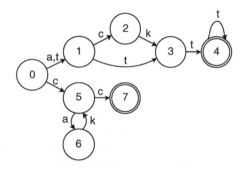

FIGURE 9-12

Example deterministic finite automaton for regular expression matching (without failure transitions).

- General-purpose processor: The DFA can be implemented by creating a data structure that maintains state transitions in table format. All states are represented by a row in the table, and all possible inputs are represented by a column. The entry in the table indicates the next state that the DFA transitions to for a given character input (column) and state (row). The table also maintains an indicator if a particular state is an accepting state. To perform the matching, the processor maintains a variable with the current state. When a character is processed, the table entry at the row of the current state and the column of the character is indexed. The processor updates the current state and repeats the process until an accepting state is encountered. A number of software tools ("scanner generators") exist to automate the process of table construction and parsing input files.

- Field-Programmable Gate Arrays (FPGA): Pattern matching with FPGA can be accomplished by a straightforward translation of the DFA into sequential logic. On-chip storage (e.g., flip-flops or register) is used to store the current state. Combinational logic is used to implement state transition computation for given input characters.
- Ternary Content-Addressable Memories (TCAM): TCAM are particularly useful for matching strings (with wildcards). Assuming that the TCAM width is sufficiently large, each string can be stored in one TCAM entry (with wildcards and unused characters encoded with don't care bits). To match strings, as many characters as the TCAM is wide are input to the TCAM. If a TCAM entry exists, then a match is found. If no match is found, the input window is shifted by one character and the process is repeated. Longer patterns can be implemented by performing multiple TCAM lookups.

The techniques just described for string and regular expression matching have been refined in a number of ways (lower storage requirements for state information, faster matching speed, etc.). For an overview of some of these techniques, see Becchi and Crowley [14].

Load balancing

Another example of application layer support in network systems appears in the context of load balancing for an application-layer end system. A load balancer aims to distribute workloads among multiple systems to avoid overloading a single system and to make use of replicated resources. One example of load balancing is used on large Web server systems. Many of the large Web sites in the Internet cannot be handled by a single Web server. Instead, Web content is split and replicated among a large number of Web servers, which are typically housed in large data centers. Each Web server has its own network interface with a distinct IP address. Users who access the Web site do not (and should not have to) know about these IP addresses. To allow users to access the Web site through a single, well-known IP address and to permit distribution of work among multiple Web servers, a load balancer can be used as the front end of a Web site. Figure 9-13 shows a simple configuration, where the load balancer distributes Web traffic between several Web servers.

For large Web sites, it is not possible that a single server hosts all content. Thus, the Web content is often split between different servers. Figure 9-13 shows subdirectories covered by a particular server. In this setup, the load balancer needs to direct traffic for a particular subset of Web content to one server and that of another subset to another server. Also, within servers that handle the same subset, load balancing can be used to ensure that users get the best performance. Thus, the main challenge is to make sure that each Web request received at the front end is directed to the right server.

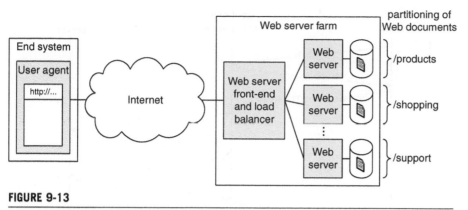

FIGURE 9-13

System configuration of Web front-end and load balancer.

The problem in such a system is that HTTP requests are sent via TCP connections. These TCP connections are initiated through a three-way handshake, where a connection's sequence numbers are chosen by the end systems. This setup takes place before any HTTP information is sent and thus the load balancer does not know to which server to direct the TCP traffic. To solve this problem, Apostolopoulos and colleagues [5] have proposed an elegant solution that involves the following steps.

1. The load balancer receives the TCP handshake and responds to it without forwarding it to any server. The load balancer chooses a sequence number for the TCP connection.
2. After establishing the TCP connection with the load balancer, the end system sends the HTTP request, which contains the information on which content is requested. The load balancer identifies the Web server(s) that can handle the request and chooses one of them. Using a new TCP connection, the load balancer sets up a connection between itself and that Web server. During the setup, the Web server chooses a sequence number for the TCP connection.
3. The load balancer forwards the Web request from the end system on the connection to the Web server.
4. For all further communication, the load balancer acts as a "middleman" and forwards all data between the two connections that have been set up. To improve the performance of this process, the load balancer "slices" the two TCP connections by simply adjusting the sequence numbers (and the TCP checksum). The adjustment of the sequence number is simply addition or subtraction (depending on the direction) of the difference between the sequence number chosen by the load balancer and the sequence number chosen by the Web server ($s_l - s_w$).

A space–time diagram of an example exchange is shown in Figure 9-14. This type of interaction shows how a network system uses application layer information (i.e., HTTP request) to handle packet forwarding.

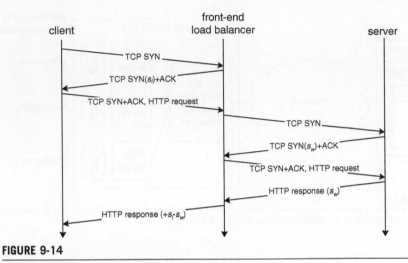

FIGURE 9-14

Space–time diagram of a load balancer operation.

SUMMARY

This chapter discussed the functionality and structure of the application layer. The application layer is highly diverse and a multitude of protocols exist. Many protocols use some of the functions of the session and presentation sublayer. We discussed the Domain Name System, the Hypertext Transfer Protocol, and the Session Initial Protocol as examples of application layer protocols. Network systems play a limited role in implementation of the application layer, but some functions related to payload inspection are used. We discussed pattern matching algorithms to identify particular payload content and load balancing to redirect traffic at the application layer.

Quality of service and security

CROSS-LAYER ISSUES

Previous chapters explored design issues that were tied to one particular layer in the protocol stack. This chapter addresses issues that cross layer boundaries and appear in several or all layers of the protocol stack.

- Performance: To achieve high-throughput performance in a network system, it is important to avoid performance bottlenecks that limit the achievable data rate. Therefore, all aspects of input/output, storage, and processing in all layers of the protocol stack need to be designed for efficient operation.
- Performance guarantees: The goal of performance (noted in the previous bullet) aims at achieving high throughput in a best-effort sense. Performance guarantees provide quantifiable guarantees or bounds on certain metrics (e.g., minimum bandwidth, maximum delay). To provide such guarantees, all layers in the protocol stack need to support this functionality.
- Security: Security aims at ensuring certain properties (e.g., privacy) on packet payloads and certain header fields. Depending on security requirements and attack scenarios, security protocols can be employed at different (and even multiple) layers in the protocol stack.

Chapter 3 discussed general performance requirements for network systems. This chapter focuses on the other two issues: performance guarantees (i.e., quality of service) and security.

QUALITY OF SERVICE

The layered architecture of the protocol stack is designed to hide the complexities of one layer from others. As a result, the network is agnostic to the specifics of any application using the network. From the perspective of transport and network layers, applications set up connections or send packets and there is no difference between different types of applications. In practice, however, there are applications that have specific requirements on the performance of the network. To accommodate such applications, the network can be extended to provide "quality of service" (QoS). That is, the network handles traffic in such a way that certain performance guarantees can be provided. These guarantees can be hard guarantees or of a probabilistic nature.

Note that standard Internet architecture does not inherently provide QoS mechanisms. Several network architecture designs have been developed to support QoS, but their deployment in the current Internet is limited. There are, however, some simple mechanisms (e.g., link scheduling) that can be used to improve the current network's ability to support applications with QoS requirements.

Quality of service concepts

Quality of service is necessary to implement a number of applications. We discuss examples of such applications here and explore their performance requirements. Because the network inherently uses shared resources, it is often necessary to explicitly set up connections that require QoS. In the context of reservations of limited resources, the question of fairness arises. Fair allocation of resources is a central issue for link scheduling algorithms discussed here.

Application requiring QoS

Quality of services is typically only required by applications that have some sort of real-time constraint. If time is not an issue, reliable data transfer is the only remaining concern. The Transmission Control Protocol provides such reliability (see Appendix A) and no further QoS functionality is necessary. However, if time is an issue, then an interesting problem needs to be solved: depending on the state of the network, reliable data transfer (which involves retransmissions of packets that have been lost or corrupted) may not be feasible within the timing constraints of the application. Thus, the network may need to provide additional QoS support to accommodate such an application.

To illustrate what types of performance requirements can be found in different applications, several examples are discussed.

- Internet telephony: Interactive voice communication in the Internet—also referred to as Voice over IP—has very strict requirements on end-to-end packet delay and loss rate. End-user perception of call quality degrades significantly with end-to-end delays of more than 150 ms or packet loss. Packet losses can be hidden through the use of transport layer protocols that provide reliable data transfer. However, notifying the sender of a packet loss and waiting for the retransmission incurs so much additional delay that the delay bound cannot be met in many cases. Therefore, many voice communication applications use unreliable data transfers and tolerate packet losses. To support Internet telephony, the network needs to transmit packets with as little delay as possible.
- Video conferencing: Video conferencing is similar to Internet telephony, but consists of two data streams: one for audio and one for video. The delay and loss requirements for the audio stream are similar to that of Internet telephony. The delay requirements for the video stream are similar, as audio and video need to be displayed in sync. Because video quality is perceived as less

important than audio quality, more loss can be tolerated for that stream. Network support for this application involves low delay. Because video requires considerably more data than audio, it is also necessary that the network supports a higher data rate for the connection.

- Video streaming: Video streaming is used for noninteractive video distribution (e.g., video on demand). The real-time constraints are less demanding than in video conferencing, as a user is likely willing to wait a few seconds for a video stream to buffer before playback starts. In such a scenario, video quality is more important. Thus, reliable data transfer protocols may be employed. To ensure continuous playback, the network needs to provide sufficient bandwidth (and limited packet loss).
- Cyber-physical control: Numerous physical systems are controlled remotely through a network. Examples include factory control, remote-controlled unmanned aerial vehicles, and, in the near future, telemedicine. Such control requires low delay and very low (or no) packet losses. Some applications in this domain involve high-quality video, which requires high bandwidth.
- Online gaming: Interactive games that involve multiple players require low delay between the interacting parties to provide for a realistic gaming experience. Networks need to support low delay communication with low packet loss.

From these applications, we can see which quality of service metrics need to be considered in a network.

Quality of service metrics

The following metrics are typically considered in the context of quality of service. As discussed earlier, an application may not have requirements for all metrics, but a specific subset.

- Bandwidth: The bandwidth metric captures the bandwidth required by an application. This metric assumes that data are transmitted continuously (rather than sending data in a best-effort fashion over an arbitrary interval of time). To accommodate bandwidth requirements, all links along the path of a connection need to have that much bandwidth available. (Note that "available bandwidth" refers to the data rate that can actually be used for transmission rather than the data rate of the physical (unloaded) link. With more traffic being transmitted across a link, its available bandwidth decreases.)
- Delay: The delay metric specifies how long it can take for packets to reach their destination. The metric is typically expressed as a bound that should not be exceeded (because packets that arrive faster can be delayed artificially at the receiver). In most cases, the delay is specified as the one-way delay (rather than the round-trip delay).
- Jitter: The jitter metric measures the variation in delay that different packets of the same connection experience. This metric can be expressed as a distribution or by minimum and maximum bounds.

- Loss: This metric expresses the fraction of packets that may be lost during transmission (due to queue overflow under congestion, bit errors, etc.). Typically, packet loss is expressed as a percentage. The metric is computer at the level of packets (and is therefore independent of packet size).

Other metrics that may be relevant to applications are out-of-order packet delivery, end-to-end network reliability, etc.

Each QoS metric can be defined strictly or probabilistically. For example, an application may have a strict requirement for packet delay (e.g., all packets must arrive within a certain delay limit (or are considered lost at that point)). Another application may require that a certain percentage of packets arrive within a delay limit.

Quality of service techniques

Within a network, there are certain limits on what level of QoS can be achieved for a connection. For example, the propagation delay of electromagnetic signals within a network cable or fiber provides a lower bound for the end-to-end delay of communication. No matter how the network handles traffic, it is not possible to achieve a lower end-to-end delay. Similarly, the available end-to-end bandwidth is limited by the data rate of the link layer at the bottleneck link. Within these constraints, a number of techniques can be employed to achieve the quality of service that is required by a particular connection.

- Routing: QoS routing is an extension to conventional shortest-path routing where QoS metrics are considered. For example, available bandwidth information can be used to identify links that can meet the requirements of a connection. To find a path that provides the minimum bandwidth requirements, all links with lower available bandwidth can be ignored when solving shortest-path routing.
- Queuing: QoS queuing (or QoS scheduling) is the process of determining packet order on the outgoing link of a router. When multiple packets compete for access to the outgoing link, the order of transmission has a direct impact on the delay that is experienced by different connections. This delay directly impacts the end-to-end delay experienced by a packet and thus may need to be kept at a minimum.

Thus, QoS routing ensures that traffic traverses links in the network that can provide the necessary QoS guarantees, and QoS queuing ensures that traffic is handled appropriately on the links that have been chosen.

Reservations and connection setup

For a network to provide quality of service, it is necessary that connections specify what their requirements are. Without knowledge of the existence of a connection and its requirements, it is difficult, if not impossible, to provide the necessary quality of service. Communicating the requirements of a connection (as well as announcing its presence) can be done at time of connection setup. During the connection setup, the end system can specify its requirements, the network can determine if and what QoS guarantees it can provide, and hardware resources can be reserved to ensure availability once packets are transmitted.

A protocol widely used for this reservation and connection setup process is the Resource Reservation Protocol (RSVP). Details of this protocol are described in RFC 2205 [22]. RSVP reserves resources for a flow along a path. The sender initiates a reservation request and propagates it through the network along a path. The reservation request contains information on the requirements of the flow (flow specification), as well as how to identify packets belonging to that flow (filter specification). When the request reaches the receiving end system, a confirmation is returned to the sender along the reverse path stating the reserved resources. Using such a reservation mechanism, the sender can inform the network about its requirements, the network can allocate the required resources, and the path of the reservation can be established.

Network support for QoS

The support for quality of service in the network is based on the techniques discussed earlier. The network needs to support QoS at the level of network architectures as well as the level of network systems.

Quality of service in network architecture

One of the key issues related to quality of service is that support for QoS needs to be built into all components of the network. If there is single hop in the network that causes long packet delays or limits the available bandwidth for a particular connection, then QoS requirements may not be achievable—even though all other hops support QoS. Thus, it is essential that QoS be considered at the level of the overall network architecture, as well as at the system level.

At the network level, there are several options of how to realize quality of service.

- Overprovisioning: This "technique" does not change the network behavior to explicitly support QoS, but relies on statistical properties. By implementing a network that has significantly more available bandwidth than is necessary to carry all traffic, delays on routers due to queuing rarely occur. Therefore, all traffic appears to be forwarded without delay—similar to how it would be forwarded in a network with explicit QoS support. The main benefit is that no modifications to routers, end systems, or the protocols used are necessary. Overprovisioning is by far the most widely used approach to providing quality of service for Internet telephony, streaming video, gaming, and so on in today's Internet.
- Integrated Services (IntServ): In integrated service architecture, all routers (and end systems) support quality of service. Routers implement three fundamental components for QoS: admission control (i.e., explicit setup of connections) using RSVP, packet classification to identify to which flow packets belong, and packet scheduling to determine the order of packets on the outgoing link. Because all systems along any path implement this functionality, quality of service metrics can be assured. More details on IntServ are described in RFC

1633 [21]. The main drawback of this architecture is that it demands that all systems support IntServ. Because most of today's routers do not support quality of service, most of the currently deployed network infrastructure would need to be replaced.

- Differentiated Services (DiffServ): In differentiated service architecture, quality of service is not provided at the fine-grained level of flows as in IntServ, but at a coarse-grained level of classes. When entering a DiffServ domain, traffic is classified and marked as belonging to a particular class of traffic. Routers inside the DiffServ domain provide quality of service forwarding based on this marking. The main advantage of such an approach is that it simplifies the implementation of forwarding on routers inside the DiffServ domain. Classification and admission control only needs to be performed at the edge of the domain. The DiffServ architecture is described in more detail in RFC 2475 [20].

There are also more advanced network architectures that use different paths for connections with different QoS requirements (i.e., QoS routing) or send traffic along multiple paths to achieve higher reliability.

Quality of service in network systems

Both integrated services and differentiated services require some fundamental QoS functionality in their router systems. Typical functions for the control plane and data plane of these systems are:

- Control plane: At the control plane, QoS requires admission control in the broadest sense. If the network is unaware of what traffic to expect, it is difficult to provide quality of service. Thus, connection setup (in IntServ) or admission control and traffic conditioning at the network edge (for DiffServ) are necessary.
- Data plane: In the forwarding path of a router, two main functions are related to QoS. Packet classification is used to determine how to handle a particular packet, and link scheduling is used to determine when a particular packet is transmitted. Traffic classification can be based on techniques discussed in Chapter 8 or simpler approaches as discussed later. The problem of packet scheduling is at the core of quality of service implementations as it ensures that QoS requirements are met.

The main focus of the remaining discussion on quality of services focuses on different link scheduling algorithms that can be used to implement quality of service.

Link scheduling algorithms

Link scheduling algorithms, also simply called scheduling algorithms or queuing algorithms, determine the order of packets on the outgoing link. Because packet-switched networks typically use statistical multiplexing, it is not uncommon that packets that arrive (nearly) simultaneously on different input ports of a router need to be transmitted on the same output port of that router. Scheduling algorithms determine how this competition for the output link is resolved.

The most basic link scheduling algorithm uses a single packet buffer. While this approach is simple to implement, it fails to provide any level of quality of service. Therefore, more complex link scheduling algorithms are necessary that separate traffic into different queues and provide priority of fair scheduling among them.

First-in-first-out queuing

The most basic link scheduling algorithm uses a single queue to store all packets. Packets are entered into and retrieved from the queue in first-in-first-out (FIFO) order. Thus, the only relevant metric to determine transmission order is the timestamp at which a packet was received on the router. The process for FIFO queuing is illustrated in Figure 10-1.

To illustrate timing in operation of a FIFO queue, we show its operation in Figure 10-2. Three input links are present, and the arrival times of packets from each link are illustrated along three synchronized timelines. (It is assumed that all packets are forwarded to the same outgoing link.) The order of outgoing packets is shown on a fourth timeline, which represents the outgoing link after scheduling. For simplicity, it is assumed that transmission of a packet of size B requires B time units. The size of each packet is noted within each packet (and the illustrated size of each packet is proportional to its size). Note that a packet cannot be transmitted before it has arrived in its entirety. An arrival event is shown as an arrow pointing into the queue and a departure event is shown as an arrow leaving the queue. If the queue is empty, a packet does not get delayed (i.e., there is an arrival and departure event at the same time).

Clearly, it is not possible to provide quality of service guarantees to traffic that traverses a link with such a scheduler. Depending on the level of competing traffic, a packet may be queued for a long time if it arrives shortly after a burst of packets

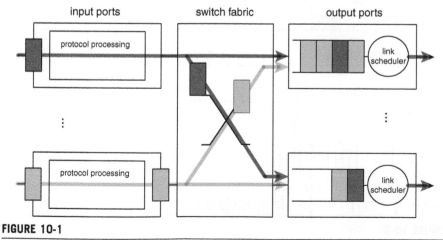

FIGURE 10-1

Link scheduling with single FIFO queue.

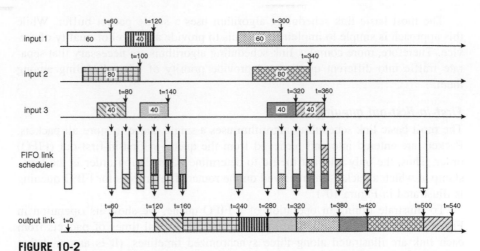

FIGURE 10-2

Scheduling example for FIFO queuing.

arrives from other links. With more inputs that compete for the outgoing link or longer packet bursts, this delay can be increased considerably.

It is also possible that packets get dropped due to lack of buffer space. This scenario is illustrated in Figure 10-3. The second packet from input 3 is dropped because the queue is already full. (For simplicity, we assume that a queue has a fixed number of slots independent of the size of the buffered packets.) When using a single queue, traffic from one input can "crowd out" other packets and cause packet drops for inputs that send at much lower rates.

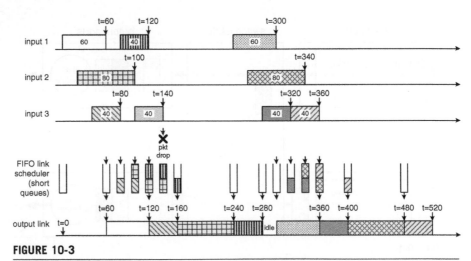

FIGURE 10-3

Scheduling example for FIFO queuing with short queues.

Thus, the main shortcoming of FIFO queuing is that there is no distinction of packets from different connections. It is not possible to accommodate different QoS requirements without separating packets by their requirements.

Traffic classification for QoS scheduling

The premise for any link scheduling algorithm (other than simple FIFO queuing) is that the scheduler can distinguish between different types of traffic. Ways in which traffic can be classified include the following.

- Quality of service bits in IP header: The Internet Protocol has 3 bits in its header that can be used to identify quality of service requirements by a packet. There is no commonly accepted standard for how to use these bits, and thus they are not used commonly in link scheduling.
- Transport and/or application layer protocol. The transport layer protocol (and application layer protocol if it can be identified) can provide some information on the quality of service requirements of traffic. For example, Internet telephony traffic using a UDP packet in the transport layer may require low packet delay.
- Source address: The network layer source address of a packet can be used to identify the end system (and thus the customer) that sent the packet. Based on the service level agreement between the customer and the network provider, packets can be treated differently. For example, traffic of customers with a more expensive data plan may receive higher bandwidth.
- Destination address: Similar to the source address, the destination address identifies a customer. An online business may pay a premium to ensure that traffic destined to its servers receives better performance, for example, experiences a lower loss probability.
- End-to-end connection: Using 5-tuple classification, individual end-to-end connections can be identified. This information can be used to provide more or less network resources to any particular connection. For example, a secure tunnel between corporate campuses (using virtual private networking as discussed later) could be given a certain minimum bandwidth.
- Aggregates: Any traffic classification based on addresses can be aggregated beyond individual sources and destinations. Instead, entire subnetworks can be identified and their traffic scheduled according to requirements.

The basis for distinguishing traffic is that the router system can perform some level of flow classification (ranging from very simple classification to generic 5-tuple matching as discussed in Chapter 8).

Priority queuing

Based on the classification of traffic, packets can be categorized to receive different levels of quality of service. One simple distinction is to separate packets into different levels of priorities. For example, a router may support two different categories of packets: those sent by paying customers (and thus should have higher priority in accessing network resources) and those sent by nonpaying customers (and thus should only access network resources not needed by traffic in the other category). Using the classification discussed earlier, packets are separated into different queues. When the link is available for transmission, the link scheduler decides from which queue the next packet is chosen. Within each queue, the order of packets is FIFO. Within each priority level, several queues can be maintained to distinguish between different traffic (e.g., different connections, different customers) with the same level of priority.

Priority queuing provides preferential link access to traffic that belongs to higher priority classes. The scheduler determines which packet gets transmitted by checking the queue of the highest priority class, then the next higher priority, and so on. (Note that the relationship between priority and class number (e.g., "class 1") is ambiguous. In some systems, lower numbers indicate higher priorities; in some systems, higher numbers indicate higher priorities.) As long as packets are ready for transmission in a higher priority class, any lower class may be "starved" (i.e., does not get to transmit any packets).

An example of the operation of a priority link scheduler is shown in Figure 10-4. Packets from input 3 are placed into the high-priority queue; packets from inputs 1 and 2 are placed into the low-priority queue. Whenever the link is empty, packets are first drawn from the high-priority queue. Only if there are no high-priority packets, then a low-priority packet is sent.

The same example of operation, but using short queues, is shown in Figure 10-5. As expected, the packet drop happens for a low-priority packet as the low-priority queue is more likely to fill up and trigger a packet loss.

Priority systems can operate in either a preemptive or a nonpreemptive way. If preemption is used, transmission of a lower priority packet is terminated when a

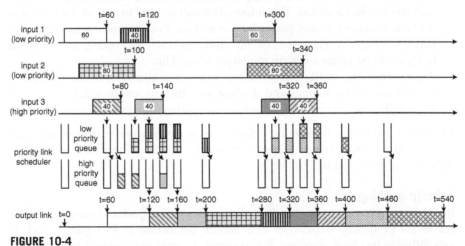

FIGURE 10-4

Priority link scheduler operation.

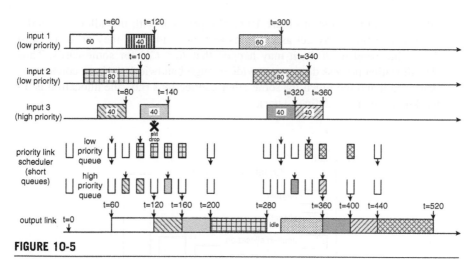

FIGURE 10-5

Priority link scheduler operation with short queues.

higher priority packet arrives. This kind of preemption is rarely used in networks as the work committed to partially transmitting the lower-priority packet cannot be recovered after the preemption (unlike preemptive processing where partial computations can be stored and continued at a later point). Instead, most link schedulers operate in a nonpreemptive fashion.

Fair queuing principles

In contrast to providing strict priorities, a scheduler may want to provide fair sharing between different queues. Before discussing several fair queuing link scheduling algorithms, we define "fair sharing" formally to augment our intuitive understanding of what fairness implies.

Max–min fairness

A formal definition of fairness helps us in determining how access to a shared resource can be divided among several parties. This definition can also be used to verify that link scheduling algorithms indeed achieve fairness.

To simplify the discussion of fairness, we look at the scenario where multiple connections need to be accommodated on a bottleneck link at the same time. Assume n connections requests an amount of bandwidth $R_1, \ldots, R_n$. The bottleneck link capacity C is the maximum bandwidth that can be allocated in total. The question is what a fair allocation of bandwidth $A_1, \ldots, A_n$ is for each connection. (We assume $\Sigma_{i=1\ldots n} R_i > C$, otherwise all requests can be accommodated: $A_i = R_i$.)

There are several intuitive ways to allocate bandwidth to connection requests that do *not* lead to a desirable outcome. Examples include the following.

- Equal share for all requests: One simple way to partition available bandwidth is to allocate an equal amount to all requests (i.e., $A_i = C/n$). Equal share allocation is illustrated in Figure 10-6. The problem with this allocation is that some connections may get assigned more bandwidth than they need. Because C/n is independent of R_i, it may happen that $R_i < C/n$ for some cases. Thus, this allocation process does not provide enough bandwidth to those connections that need it and too much for some other connections (i.e., the allocation is not work-conserving as defined later).

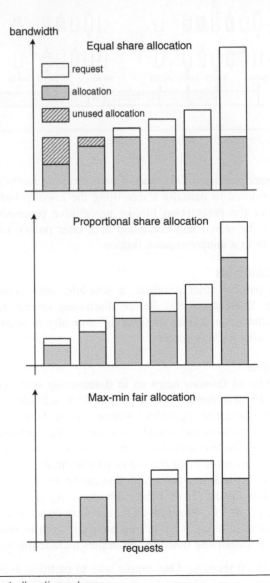

FIGURE 10-6

Example of different allocation schemes.

- Proportional share for all requests: Another simple way to partition available bandwidth—while considering requests R_i—is to allocate an amount proportional to the request, i.e., $A_i = R_i/(\Sigma_{j\,=\,1\ldots n}R_j)$. Proportional share allocation is also illustrated in Figure 10-6. Because the sum of all requests exceeds the capacity, the allocation does not allocate more than requested and thus solves the problem of equal share allocation. However, this allocation process raises the problem that the entity making the request can influence the amount that is allocated to it by increasing its request R_i. Thus, if one tries to game the system, one could always request as large amount as possible ($R_i \to \infty$), knowing that this will increase the allocation that is received. Of course, once this strategy is understood by all requesting parties, all requests will increase and allocation approaches that of equal share.

Because both of these simple allocation strategies have shortcomings, we need to identify a different definition of fairness. One such definition used broadly in the networking domain is max–min fairness. An allocation of rates is max–min fair if an increase of any allocation must be at the cost of a decrease of some already smaller allocation (all within allocations that do not exceed C). This definition describes properties of a max–min fair allocation, but does not provide a constructive process for obtaining it.

To construct a max–min fair allocation, the following iterative process can be used. For simplicity, we assume that requests are sorted by increasing size ($R_1 \le R_2 \le \ldots \le R_n$). The allocation process iteratively allocates A_i, $i = 1..n$, starting with the smallest request. Let C_i be the amount of unallocated available bandwidth in step i (i.e., $C_i = C - \Sigma_{j\,=\,1\ldots i}A_j$). Then, the max–min fair allocation is $A_i = \min(R_i, C_i/(n - i + 1)$. Thus, the max–min fair allocation assigns the requested amount of bandwidth to small requests and shares the remaining bandwidth equally among large requests.

An example of a max–min fair allocation is also shown in Figure 10-6. Note that small requests receive exactly the requested amount. Larger requests share the remaining bandwidth equally. These large requests receive more than the equal share among all requests (C/n). Thus, the max–min fair allocation redistributed the bandwidth that was not used by the smaller requests (and thus maintains the work-conserving property).

Another important aspect of the allocation process is the use of weights. In practice, scenarios exist where some categories of traffic should receive larger shares of link bandwidth than others (e.g., paying customers vs nonpaying customers). This bias toward more or less access to resources can be represented by weight w_i that is assigned to each category of traffic (i.e., to each request R_i). A larger weight w_i implies a larger allocation of link bandwidth.

Work-conserving property

One key property of (fair queuing and other) link schedulers is that they are work conserving. This means that if any packets are queued for transmission, then the scheduler will assign one to the transmitted. In particular, the outgoing link is never idle as long as packets are queued for transmission. This property ensures that the scheduler does not let an opportunity pass to transmit a packet. (In contrast, time-division multiplexing (TDM) schedulers that assigned fixed slots to each type of traffic are not work conserving, as they keep the outgoing link idle if no packet is available for a particular type of traffic—even if other types of traffic have packets queued.)

Fair queuing link schedulers

The scheduling algorithms discussed in this section aim at fair sharing of the transmission link between several queues of equal priority. To simplify the discussion, we assume that all queues are "back-logged," that is, always have packets available for transmission. The example setup and the scheduling sequence for all fair queuing link schedulers are shown in Figure 10-7. The packet sizes are noted in the queues, and the transmission rate is assumed to be one bit per time unit.

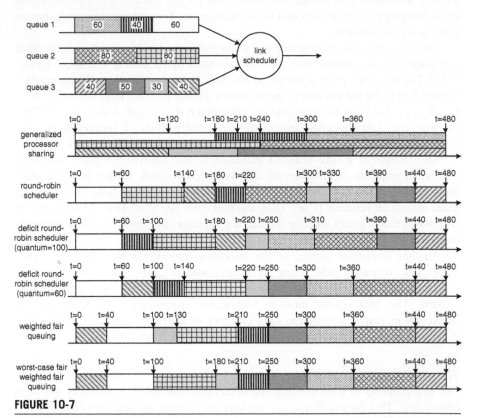

FIGURE 10-7

Fair queuing link scheduler examples.

Generalized processor sharing

Generalized processor sharing (GPS) represents ideal sharing on a link assuming a fluid model. In a fluid model of the link, all packets that compete for the link are transmitted at the same time, each at a rate that is the fair share fraction for that packet. Clearly, such a transmission process cannot be implemented on a realistic network. However, GPS provides a basis to compare how well realistic algorithms achieve the idealized scheduling by GPS. The GPS scheduling of the example scenario is shown in Figure 10-7.

Round-robin scheduler

Following the idea of GPS, where all packets are transmitted in parallel, one can attempt to make the fluid transmission discrete to allow its implementation on a realistic system. To accomplish sharing among different packets, each packet gets access to the link in turns (i.e., round-robin).

The key question is at what level of granularity scheduling should happen. In computer systems, the smallest amount of information is a single bit. While it is conceivable to implement bit-wise round-robin scheduling, it is impractical for a network system. In networks, packets are the smallest entity of transmissions. If a packet needs to be broken into smaller fragments, the control information (i.e., packet header) needs to be replicated and attached to each fragment. For bit-wise round-robin, this approach would not be feasible. Therefore, it is more suitable to perform round-robin scheduling at the level of packets. Operation of a packet-wise round-robin scheduler is shown in Figure 10-7.

To accommodate weights in a round-robin scheduler, a queue with weight w_i should receive, on average, $w_i/(\Sigma_{1..n}w_j)$ of the turns. Depending on the value of weights w_i, it may not be possible to achieve an exact value of $w_i/(\Sigma_{j\,=\,1..n}w_j)$ over any reasonable window of time. In such cases, the fraction of rounds assigned to any queue may need to be approximated.

The main drawback of packet-wise operation of the link scheduler is that it may introduce considerable unfairness. Because packet size can vary significantly between connections, the amount of allocated bandwidth between connections may differ considerably. A connection that attempted to gain the most bandwidth would send packets with the largest possible packet size. With each round of the scheduler, this connection would be able to send more data (or at least equal amounts of data) than other connections.

Deficit round-robin scheduling

The shortcoming of systematic unfairness due to large packets in round-robin scheduling is addressed in deficit round-robin scheduling. This scheduling algorithm was first described in Shreedhar and Varghese [166]. The main idea is to track the amount of bandwidth consumed by each queue. The waiting time enforced between the transmissions of packets increases with larger packets.

In deficit round-robin (DRR) scheduling, a "deficit counter" is associated with each queue. This counter tracks the credit that each queue has with the link scheduler. Credit is accumulated when a packet is delayed in the queue, and credit is used when a packet is transmitted. The round-robin operation is as follows: Every time the scheduler visits a queue, the deficit counter for this queue is increased by a fixed amount (i.e., "quantum size"). Then, the queue can use the credit to transmit packets. A packet can be transmitted if the accumulated credit is equal to or larger than the packet size. Once the packet is transmitted, the credit of the queue is reduced by the size of the packet. While the remaining credit is sufficient to send the next packet in the queue, the process continues. (Note that the credit is incremented by the quantum size only once per round, but multiple packet transmissions may be performed.) The process of DRR scheduling is shown in Figure 10-7. There are two scheduling examples using quantum sizes of 100 and 60.

The quantum size determines how fine-grained the scheduler operates. Larger quantum sizes increase the (temporary) unfairness between connections. Smaller quantum sizes provide better fairness, but also increase the computational requirements for the link scheduler as more rounds need to be computed before a packet can be transmitted. Also, note that inactive queues (i.e., those without packets) cannot accumulate credit. When using weights, the amount of credit allocated to each queue can simply be scaled by the queue's weight. Larger weights lead to larger amounts of credit, which allow more use of the link.

Weighted fair queuing

While DRR achieves fairness and overcomes the problems of packet-wise round-robin, it is still only an approximation to GPS at the granularity of the quantum size. A link scheduling algorithm that tries emulating GPS more closely is weighted fair queuing (WFQ). WFQ is described in detail elsewhere [171].

In weighted fair queuing, the link scheduler emulates bit-wise round-robin to determine when each packet would have completed its transmission. Using the finish times of all packets, the WFQ scheduler determines the order in which packets get transmitted on the outgoing link. Note that this process is equivalent to using DRR with a quantum size of 1. The problem with emulating a round-robin process with this fine level of granularity is that it is very expensive to compute. For a transmission of a packet with B bits, B rounds of computation are necessary. This processing overhead cannot be sustained for high link speeds.

For an explicit computation of the finish times of packets, the fluid model of GPS can be used. For the ith packet of a traffic class, the start time of transmission, S_i, in GPS is either the finish time of the previous packet, F_{i-1}, or the arrival time of the current packet, t_i. Thus, $S_i = \max(F_{i-1}, t_i)$. The transmission time of a packet of size B requires B rounds with each round requiring as many bit times as there are competing queues, n. Thus, the transmission time, T_i, is $T_i = B \times n$. The finish time is the sum of the start time and the transmission time: $F_i = S_i + T_i$. Using this finish time, the order of packet transmissions can be determined.

The result of the WFQ link scheduler for our example is shown in Figure 10-7.

Worst-case fair weighted fair queuing

One of the problems of WFQ is that of "run-ahead." Queues with many short packets get many transmission opportunities before queues with longer packets get to transmit. In our example in Figure 10-7, Queue 3 transmits its second packet before Queue 2 transmits its first packet. In Bennett and Zhang [16], the authors illustrate with an extensive example this potential unfairness of WFQ. To solve this problem, a modification to WFQ can be made to ensure fairness in the worst case as described [16].

Worst-case fair weighted fair queuing (which is typically abbreviated incorrectly as WF^2Q) does not allow transmission of a packet before the time when GPS would have started its transmission. The resulting schedule for our example is shown in Figure 10-7. Note that the second packet of Queue 3 is delayed until after $t = 120$, which is the packet's start time in GPS.

Quality of service summary

Quality of service is necessary for applications with various requirements for timing, bandwidth, and reliability. To provide a quality of service path for these applications, a network needs to support quality of service in its architecture and on its network systems. Network systems need to perform some type of packet classification to distinguish packets with different QoS requirements. The link scheduling algorithm determines in which order packets are sent from different queues. Through link scheduling, transmission priorities or fair sharing can be achieved.

SECURITY

Security is an important topic for the design for network architecture and systems due to its considerable impact on many of the usage scenarios for which networks were designed. Many data transfers for military, commercial, and even for personal communication require the network to provide basic security features. We discuss what security properties are necessary and how they can be provided. We also present typical network protocols used to provide security in different layers of the protocol stack.

Security concepts

Security is a very broad term and can mean a variety of things in different context. In computer networks (and information systems in general), there are four key aspects to data security:

- Confidentiality prevents the disclosure of information to unauthorized users. One way of achieving confidentiality is to encrypt information in such a way that only authorized users can successfully decrypt and access it.

- Authenticity ensures that the source of information is genuine. One way to achieve authenticity is for the source to encrypt information in a way that it can only be done by that source. All others can decrypt the information and verify its source in the process.
- Integrity is a property that ensures that information is not modified by unauthorized users. One way to achieve integrity is to compute a digest (i.e., compute the results of a hash function over the information) that is then encrypted by the source (as done for authenticity). The integrity property includes nonrepudiation, which means that a source cannot deny having generated a particular piece of information.
- Availability ensures that access to information (and the network in general) is possible for authorized users. Unlike the other three properties, availability cannot be solved through cryptographic operations. Instead, the system has to be designed with the ability to distinguish accesses by authorized users from others and deflect malicious traffic.

Before discussing how different layers in the network provide different types of security, we briefly discuss the types of cryptographic functions used in this domain.

Cryptography overview

Cryptography is a field of mathematics and computer science that provides the theoretical foundations for hiding information. Cryptographic algorithms ("ciphers") are used to implement confidentiality, authenticity, and integrity. In the context of confidentiality, cryptography provides the mechanism for translating information from its "cleartext" representation into "ciphertext" (and back). This encoding and decoding process typically uses a "secret key" that ensures that the ciphertext can only be decoded by users who have access to that secret key. Two examples of broadly used cryptographic algorithms are discussed briefly.

One important aspect of cryptography is that most practically used ciphers only provide limited secrecy. Given sufficient computational resources and time, these ciphers can be broken by an adversary through cryptanalysis. While cryptographers aim to make the analysis of their ciphers as difficult and expensive as possible, the progress in computing technology over the last decades has reached the point where algorithms that were extremely costly to break 20 years ago can now be broken with moderate effort. In response, new algorithms have been developed and deployed. Additionally, larger secret keys are used for encryption to make the analysis of an encrypted message more difficult. Thus, there is a trade-off between the cost of encryption (larger keys require more computational effort) and the level of secrecy that can be achieved.

One exception to this trade-off is encryption with "one-time pads," which can provide perfect secrecy. A one-time pad consists of a truly random sequence of bits that is used for encryption and decryption (e.g., simply XORing each information bit with a unique bit of the pad). The size of the pad needs to be at least as large as the amount of data transmitted, and the pad needs to be available to both parties a priori. These constraints make it cumbersome and costly to use such an encryption process in practice and thus one-time pads are not used in networking.

Symmetric key cryptography

Symmetric ciphers use the same secret key for the encryption and decryption of information. Parties that want to use such a cipher need to agree on the same secret key before using the cipher. For example, the secret can be shared by the parties when they meet in person, or the key can be exchanged using a different security protocol (e.g., using a trusted third party).

A very simple example of symmetric key cryptography is shown in Figure 10-8. The sender shown on the left uses the encryption algorithm to convert the cleartext information into ciphertext (shaded). The encrypted information is sent across the network. On the receiver side on the right, the decryption algorithm uses the same secret key to decrypt the ciphertext back into plaintext. This illustration does not show practical considerations for secure network protocols (e.g., packets need a cleartext IP header to be handled by the network).

A very important aspect of this (and any other) encryption and decryption process is that the algorithm used for the process is not secret—only the keys are secret. In fact, most practically used symmetric key algorithms are standardized and well documented. Thus, anyone can program the same encryption and decryption algorithm. This approach to limiting secrecy to key material only is an important principle of security engineering. Kerckhoffs' principle summarizes this idea by stating that a cryptosystem should be secure even if everything about the system, with exception of the secret key, is publicly known. In contrast, developing an encryption/decryption process that relies on secrecy for the algorithm has several disadvantages. First, if any information about the algorithm is leaked, all instances of the system become vulnerable. Second, the lack of public scrutiny of the algorithm in the design phase makes it more likely that there are fundamental flaws in the system not detected by the designers.

Two symmetric key encryption algorithms are widely used in networks. These are:

- Data Encryption Standard (DES): The DES encryption algorithm is a "block cipher" that encrypts information in blocks of 64 bits (8 bytes). Using a 56-bit key, DES encrypts each block in 16 identical rounds. Each round operates

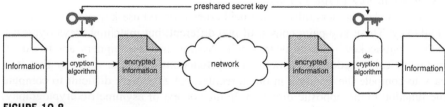

FIGURE 10-8

Symmetric key cryptography in network setting.

on alternating 32-bit halves of the block and uses different 48-bit subkeys derived from the original key. The main operation in each round is the substitution of input bits through 8 S-boxes, which perform a nonlinear transformation based on a lookup table. The final step of each round is a permutation of the outputs of the S-boxes. The design of DES allows the same sequence of operations to be used for encryption and decryption. The only difference is that the sequence of subkeys needs to be reversed. DES was published as a U.S. federal standard in 1977. Triple DES, an improvement to DES, was published in 1999. Triple DES uses three encryption steps with different keys to improve the better security. More details on the functionality of these algorithms can be found elsewhere [130].

- Advanced Encryption Standard (AES): The AES encryption algorithm is also a block cipher with 128-bit blocks. The block is arranged in a 4×4 grid of bytes. There are three variants with key sizes of 128, 192, and 256 bits. Larger key sizes increase the security of the algorithm but require more processing: 128-bit keys use 10 rounds, 192-bit keys use 12 rounds, and 256-bit keys use 14 rounds. In each round, each byte is substituted with another based on a lookup table. Then, the columns of the 4×4 grid are shifted cyclically. Next, each column is multiplied with a fixed polynomial. Finally, each byte is combined with the key used in that round. AES was published as a U.S. federal standard in 2001. The algorithm was chosen among numerous competitors through an extensive selection process. One of the concerns when selecting the algorithm was to ensure that it can be implemented efficiently in software and in hardware. The latter allows for high-throughput encryption in systems that need to support high data rates (e.g., network devices). The details of AES are described elsewhere [131].

Symmetric key encryption algorithms are widely used to encrypt data traffic in networks. However, their main limitation lies in the need for a preshared key. In a large-scale network it is impractical to assume that all pairs of end systems have a secret key setup. Therefore, it is necessary to have an additional system for the exchange of keys that can be used by symmetric key algorithms. Asymmetric key cryptography can provide such a key exchange mechanism (as well as other security functions).

Asymmetric key cryptography

Asymmetric key ciphers (also called public-key ciphers) use key pairs instead of a single key. These key pairs consist of two different, but matching, keys (typically called "public key" and "private key"). Asymmetric key ciphers are based on mathematical "trapdoor" functions. These functions have the property that it is easy to compute the function in one direction, but extremely difficult to compute the function in the opposite direction. In the context of asymmetric cryptography, the trapdoor function allows for computationally easy encryption from cleartext to ciphertext with one of the keys. The interesting point is that even if that key is known, it is computationally difficult to extract the cleartext from the ciphertext. When using sufficiently large keys, a brute force attempt to crack the computationally difficult reverse direction would take a conventional computer longer than the existence of the universe. However, if the matching key is used, a computationally easy decryption is possible. This asymmetry of requiring one of the keys for encryption and the other for decryption leads to a number of interesting uses of such ciphers. The mathematical foundations of asymmetric cryptography are described elsewhere [42]. This work led to the widely used RSA cryptosystem, named after the inventors Rivest, Shamir, and Adelman. The importance of this cryptographic technique was recognized when the inventors received the prestigious Turing Award in 2002.

There are numerous ways in which encryption and decryption using public or private key on parts or all of the information can be applied. Some commonly used examples are described here (in all cases, it is assumed that the public key is publicly known and the private is only known to its owner).

- Confidentiality: To encrypt information such that only the receiver can decrypt it, the public key of the receiver is used for the encryption process. This public key is publicly known and thus is easily accessible to the sender. Due to the asymmetry of the cryptographic system, only the receiver can decrypt the message with its private key. Note that this process does not authenticate the message or ensure its integrity.
- Digital signature: A digital signature attempts to emulate the characteristics of a signature on a physical document. A signature achieves authentication and integrity/nonrepudiation. Authentication could be achieved by having the source sign the information with its private key—everyone could use the matching public key to verify that only the source could have performed the encryption. However, this process does not protect the information from being truncated (i.e., integrity). To achieve all properties of a signature, the information is condensed by a hash function attached to the original information. This hash is encrypted using the source's private key. To verify the correctness of the signature, the hash is recomputed and compared to the decrypted version attached to the document. This process of using asymmetric cryptography to implement digital signatures is illustrated in Figure 10-9. Note that this process does not ensure confidentiality (but could be combined with confidentiality as described earlier).

Asymmetric key encryption can also be used to establish keys for symmetric key encryption. While asymmetric key encryption provides the ability to achieve confidentiality, it does so at a very high computational cost. For most practical data transfers it is more efficient to use asymmetric key encryption to verify the identity of the communication partner (using digital signatures) and then establish a temporary symmetric session key (that can be transmitted securely using confidentiality in asymmetric cryptosystems). Once the session key is set up, symmetric key algorithms are used for high-throughput secure transmission.

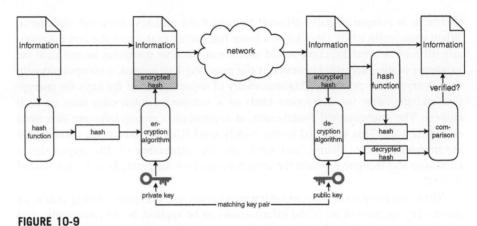

FIGURE 10-9

Asymmetric key cryptography used for digital signature.

Security in network protocols

Network protocols can implement security features at different levels of the protocol stack. Depending on the layer, there are differences in the security guarantees provided and the way keys are established. However, all layers use symmetric key cryptography to ensure confidentiality in the data transfer. Figure 10-10 shows the format of packets using security protocols at different layers in the protocol stack. Shaded regions indicate encrypted fields.

Link layer security

At the link layer, security is used mainly in wireless networks. Due to the broadcast nature of wireless transmissions, it is much simpler for an eavesdropper to access transmissions than in a wired infrastructure. Thus, the use of encryption to achieve confidentiality is much more important.

There are several standards for encryption in wireless Ethernet. Examples are Wired Equivalent Privacy (WEP) and Wi-Fi Protected Access (WPA and WPA2).

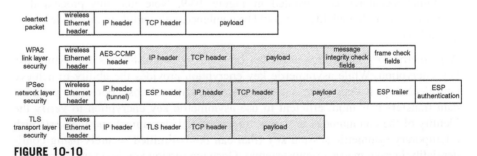

FIGURE 10-10

Comparison of security protocols at different layers.

The structure of encrypted frames is shown in Figure 10-10. The AES-CCMP header contains information about the frame's packet number and the key used for encryption. The IP header, TCP header, and payload are encrypted (e.g., using AES). There are also fields that contain values for integrity checks. Because the packet is encrypted at the IP layer and up, an eavesdropper cannot determine between which hosts it is sent. The only information available in cleartext is which wireless hosts are involved in the transmission. In cases where the wireless link connects to an access point, this information is sufficient to determine the host that originates the TCP/IP connection (since most end systems do not act as routers).

One major shortcoming of link layer security is that the packet headers and payload are only protected on links that use security. Even if multiple consecutive links use such security protocols, the packet still gets converted into cleartext on every node.

Network layer security

Network layer security is used to provide secure tunnels between subnetworks. The general outline of a Virtual Private Network (VPN) that connects two networks through a secure tunnel is shown in Figure 10-11. All traffic between networks 1 and 2 is protected through network layer encryption. It is also possible to connect a single end system to a subnetwork through a VPN (as is commonly done by business travelers who need to connect to their corporate networks).

Network layer security is achieved through the IPSec protocol. Figure 10-10 shows the header fields used for data transfers in IPSec. The packet headers include a new IP header that is used by the tunnel. The IP source and destination addresses correspond to the external interfaces of the VPN gateways that are the end points of the tunnel. The ESP header contains information about the key material used for encryption and the sequence number of the packet. The trailer contains padding (to ensure alignment to a multiple of the block size of the cipher) and a next protocol field to ensure correct handling of the embedded packet. There is also an authentication trailer that verifies the source of the tunneled packet.

In IPSec, the encapsulated packet remains encrypted along the path between the tunnel end points. Within networks connected by the tunnel, the packet is sent in cleartext.

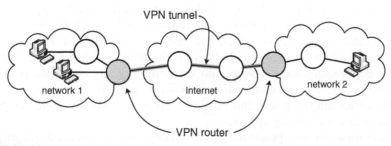

FIGURE 10-11

Virtual Private Network providing network layer security between subnetworks.

Transport layer security

Transport layer security provides security between two end systems using the Transport Layer Security (TLS) protocol. As shown in Figure 10-10, a TLS header with information about the encrypted content is inserted between IP and TCP. The TCP header and payload are encrypted by TLS.

Because encryption is performed in the protocol on one end system and decryption in the protocol of the other end system, the packet payload remains encrypted along the entire path. However, the IP header is transmitted in cleartext and thus it is possible for an eavesdropper to determine the source and destination of the connection.

Public key infrastructure

In the discussion of security protocols in different layers of the network, it is assumed that suitable keys are established between the entities that perform encryption and decryption. Shared secret keys are typically used for link layer security, where the user needs to provide the secret key to use a wireless link. While this approach is feasible for wireless links due to proximity between the communicating entities, it is not feasible for network-scale communication.

To allow for secure communication between parties that have no prior shared secret, the Public Key Infrastructure can be used. This system can be used to verify the identity of entities by establishing a "chain of trust" to a trusted third party. To use asymmetric key cryptography successfully to establish session keys, it is important to have access to the correct public key of the entity at the other end of a connection. In particular, it should not be possible for an attacker to pose as the other entity and intercept communication (i.e., "man-in-the-middle attack"). Therefore, it is important to correctly associate a public key with an identity. This association can be achieved through the use of unforgeable public key certificates.

A public key certificate contains information on the identity of an entity and its public key. The certificate is signed digitally by a certification authority (CA). This authority certifies that the binding between identity and public key is correct. If the communicating parties trust the certification authority, then they can trust that the identities of the other party are correct (assuming the digital signature in the certificate can be verified correctly). To make this approach scalable to a large number of identities, it is possible that the issuing of certificates can be delegated by the certification authority. To verify a certificate issued by a sub-CA, the identity and public key of that sub-CA are verified by a certificate from the original CA. Once this certificate has been validated, the sub-CA's certificate for the entity can be verified. Thus, a chain of certificates can be established. An illustration of this process is shown in Figure 10-12.

The only requirement for successful verification of any certificate is that the public key of the top level certification authority is known to the receiving end system. To avoid tampering with this public key, it is typically distributed as part of the end system's operating system.

Using these security protocols, confidentiality, authenticity, and integrity can be achieved. However, to provide the fourth aspect of security, availability, a different approach is necessary.

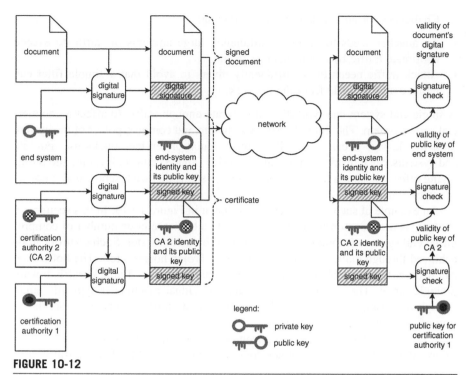

FIGURE 10-12

Certification authority providing authenticity for public keys.

Denial-of-service attacks

Distributed applications are designed to use software components running on different computers connected through the network. If access to some of the end systems used by a distributed application is not possible, the application may fail. Thus, the availability of networking resources (and thus access to end systems) is an important aspect of security. Denial-of-service (DoS) attacks aim at making certain resources unavailable to legitimate users.

Denial-of-service attack scenarios

Denial of service is typically achieved by overwhelming a system with apparently legitimate traffic. For example, to make a Web server unavailable, an attacker would send large numbers of connection requests to that Web server. The server, which cannot distinguish between requests from attack traffic and those from legitimate traffic, attempts to serve as many requests as possible. The larger the proportion of attack requests to legitimate requests, the smaller the probability that a legitimate request can be served. Similarly, attacks can aim at making other end-system services unavailable or at using up buffer space on routers to trigger packet drops.

Challenges for an attacker are the following:

- An attacker needs to generate sufficiently large amounts of traffic to exceed legitimate traffic by a considerable factor.
- Attack traffic needs to be sufficiently divers to avoid that a simple filter can remove attack traffic from the network.

A single end system can typically not generate enough traffic to affect a commercial server system. The limited access bandwidth and compute power of the system limit the damage it can cause. Thus, most denial-of-service attacks use multiple end systems. Such distributed denial-of-service (DDoS) attacks leverage the multiplying effect of using a large number of end systems that each send small amounts of attack traffic.

An example of such a DDoS attack is shown in Figure 10-13. In this scenario, a "botnet" is used to coordinate attack traffic. In a botnet, a large number of compromised end systems ("zombies") are controlled by a bot master. Such control can be achieved through malicious software (viruses, Trojan horses, etc.). The bot master can instruct these zombie machines to send small amounts of attack traffic toward a single target. The attack traffic by each individual machine is typically small enough to remain undistinguishable from legitimate traffic. Thus, a simple detection of such attacks is not possible.

It is also possible to use a few machines to send large amounts of attack traffic. To avoid identification of the attack sources, the header fields of attack traffic may

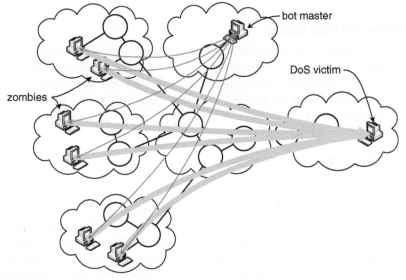

FIGURE 10-13

DDoS attack through a botnet.

contain incorrect values (e.g., spoofed IP source address). This technique of address spoofing is widely used to hide the source of malicious traffic.

Mitigation techniques

There are a large number of techniques to identify and block malicious traffic in the network. We discuss just a few of these approaches that illustrate possible solutions.

- Overprovisioning: A straightforward way of reducing the impact of a denial-of-service attack is to make enough resources available such that the attack does not have any practical impact. Such overprovisioning is typically expensive and may trigger an arms race where attackers try to use more sources to increase traffic, etc.

- Packet marking to identify true source: If the true source of attack traffic can be identified, it becomes easier to block its traffic (e.g., in the access network). However, IP source address spoofing makes it easy for an attacker to disguise the origin of traffic. To limit the effectiveness of address spoofing, it has been proposed to augment the functionality of routers to add information about the path of traffic in the network. For example, if every router was to add its identity to the packet, the complete path of the packet could be reconstructed and the source could be identified. Recording the entire path in every packet incurs a significant overhead. It has been observed that this overhead can be amortized over several packets that belong to the same connection. If the route of a connection through the network is stable, then all its packets traverse the same routers. Thus, the path can be recorded progressively over numerous packets. Packet marking techniques use just a few bits in the IP packet header (e.g., ToS bits that are typically not used) to store a very small amount of information about the packet's path. Marking techniques often operate probabilistically, where a router uses the few available bits only with a small probability to avoid overwriting the information that has been provided by another router earlier in the path. While many of these techniques have been studied, they have not been widely deployed in the Internet.

- Checkpoints throughout network: A very different approach to separating attack traffic from legitimate traffic is to place explicit checkpoints into the network. At these checkpoints, cryptographic techniques can be used to verify the identity of the communicating end system (or user). Only if the identify can be verified positively and the access control policies confirm that access to network resources is permitted, the traffic is forwarded. To avoid that such verification has to be performed on every packet of a connection, a token can be provided to the source of the connection. This token is included in every packet and the checkpoint is configured to let packets with valid tokens pass. This technique is referred to as "network capabilities." The main challenges of this approach are the need for verifiable identities and the complexities associated with obtaining and enforcing capabilities.

- Anomaly detection: This technique uses data from traffic monitors to detect unusual patterns. Typically the anomaly detection algorithm characterizes baseline traffic (i.e., legitimate traffic) in order to be able to detect deviations that indicate anomalies. If an anomaly is detected, an operator is notified to intervene manually.

While there are a range of approaches to deal with denial of service attacks, there is no single system that solves this problem satisfactorily. Therefore, there is much current interest in developing new approaches to address this challenge.

SUMMARY

Security is an important aspect of any information system. In networks, security protocols are used to ensure confidentiality, authenticity, and integrity of data transfers. Most protocols use block-based ciphers with symmetric session keys. These session keys are established through cryptographic techniques based on asymmetric keys that do not require preshared keys. Additionally, availability of access to network resources is an important consideration that cannot be addressed by cryptographic protocols. To mitigate the impact of denial-of-service attacks, additional functionality in network systems is necessary.

Specialized hardware components

HARDWARE SUPPORT FOR PACKET FORWARDING

Correct functionality of network systems is critical for correct operation of the Internet. In addition to correct functionality, it is nearly equally important that network systems perform their operations efficiently. Optimization goals for network systems include high throughput performance, low power consumption, and low implementation cost. While software implementations of router functions on general-purpose workstation processors can provide the necessary functionality, these systems often lack in performance, power efficiency, and cost. Instead, specialized components have been developed to improve the operation of network systems.

This chapter explores these specialized hardware components. Specifically, we address the following topics:

- General-purpose hardware: multicore embedded network processor systems for high-performance packet processing.
- Special-purpose hardware: hardware accelerators for specific functional tasks (e.g., lookups, cryptographic operations).

These issues tie in closely with power issues discussed in Chapter 12 and run-time support systems discussed in Chapter 14.

GENERAL-PURPOSE PACKET PROCESSORS

The functionality of a network is determined by the protocols implemented on the end systems connected to the network and on the nodes inside the network. In the case of the Internet, the Internet Protocol (IP) is one protocol that is common among entities. Every Internet router implements the packet processing steps necessary for IP, as discussed in Chapter 7. Figure 11-1 shows that the packet processing system is typically located on a router's input port. Traffic on the output port side typically also traverses the packet processing system for link scheduling.

Because the speed at which packet processing occurs determines to some extent how fast the network can operate, it is important to develop network systems that

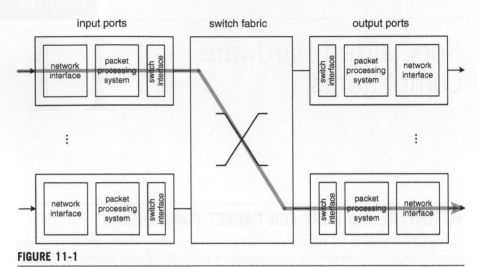

input ports   switch fabric   output ports

FIGURE 11-1

Packet processing system within router system.

can achieve high packet processing throughput. More recently, it has also become critical to be able to expand the functionality of routers after they are deployed (e.g., introducing new features in the packet forwarding process). This need for performance and flexibility exhibits an inherent tension with respect to the design of the packet processing system.

Performance vs flexibility

In general, there is a trade-off between high performance and flexibility. If the functionality of a system does not change over time (leading to low flexibility), then its implementation can be optimized for this scenario (leading to high performance). If the functionality changes during the lifetime of the system (i.e., high flexibility), the optimization process should not be too specific, as future changes need to be accommodated (leading to low performance).

In network systems, this trade-off can be observed when considering implementation of the packet processing steps in the data path of routers. The highest performance implementations of IP forwarding are based on custom logic designs. These implementations use an application-specific integrated circuit (ASIC) that can perform packet forwarding functions at high data rates by employing specialized logic functions and finely tuned optimizations. However, this circuit cannot do any other processing. In particular, its functionality cannot be changed once it has been manufactured. Thus, any changes to the packet processing functionality of the router (to add new features, e.g., traffic management or security) would require the design and manufacturing of an entirely new ASIC. This approach to deploying new functions can only be used rarely, as typical ASIC development requires a large design team, takes well over a year, and incurs considerable cost.

In contrast, designs for a packet forwarding system that focus on flexibility rather than performance are typically based on a general-purpose processor. This processor can be programmed to perform packet forwarding functionality using software. An example of such a system is the packet forwarding functionality implemented in a general-purpose operating system. When new functions need to be introduced into the system, the software can simply be modified. This approach clearly provides flexibility. However, its drawback lies in the relatively lower performance compared to an ASIC implementation. General-purpose processors do not achieve processing rates as high as custom ASICs, as a processor is optimized for the general case rather than specific networking functions.

From the perspective of a commercial router vendor, the use of ASIC-based router systems provides a competitive advantage in terms of providing high throughput performance (and low power consumption). However, the use of ASICs limits the flexibility to customize the functionality of systems for specific customers, adapt to new protocol standards, and support emerging packet processing functions. Use of a general-purpose processor can provide this flexibility, but has limitations in forwarding performance. To meet a balance of both requirements, a programmable system with high throughput performance is necessary. Network processors, which are based on system-on-a-chip design, are an example of such a system. Figure 11-2 illustrates how network processors relate to ASICs and workstation processors in terms of performance and flexibility.

Systems-on-a-chip

There is continued progress in integrating more and more logic functions onto a single chip. Moore's law [127], which has predicted and quantified this trend, continues to apply, despite several fundamental and technological hurdles. As a result, it is possible to implement processing systems that contain all the important functions of computation, memory, and input/output on a single chip. These

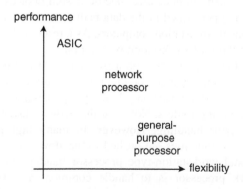

FIGURE 11-2

Relationship of ASICs, workstation processors, and network processors in terms of performance and flexibility to adapt to new functionality.

"systems-on-a-chip" (SoC) can implement processing at higher speeds and/or lower power consumption than multichip solutions, as the processor components are integrated on a single chip. Interfaces can be clocked at higher data rates because components are more closely colocated.

Since the first broad use of SoC in the late 1990s, the complexity and the level of integration of SoC devices have continued to increase. A key trend for SoC designs has been the integration of multiple processor cores on a single die. These multiprocessor systems-on-a-chip (MPSoC) can contain processor configurations ranging from two to four high-end processor cores to dozens of lower end cores.

This move toward parallel processing has significantly increased the overall processing power that can be achieved by a single chip system. On single-core systems, performance gains are typically tied closely to the increase in system clock rate and the exploit of potential instruction-level parallelism. The limits of this growth in performance lie in the super-linear increase in system cost when increasing the processor clock rate. In addition, there are limits to the amount of instruction-level parallelism that can be exploited in typical processing workloads. When using multiple parallel processors, each processor core can be clocked at a relatively lower rate (which allows for a simpler, more space-efficient implementation on the chip). By using a larger number of these simpler processors, the total processing power of the MPSoC can exceed that of a single-core chip.

Network processors

One type of multiprocessor system-on-a-chip, which is specialized for packet processing tasks, is the network processor. Network processors are MPSoC devices optimized for the workloads encountered in the networking environment.

Processing workload

The characteristics of the workload that need to be processed by a system determine greatly the overall system architecture, specific design choices, and optimizations. The type of processing performed in the data path of a router is very different from the workload on typical workstation computers. As a result, network processor architectures differ from those of workstation processors.

The processing that is performed on a router port to handle a packet is determined by the protocols implemented on that router. In practically all cases, a router implements at least IP and the necessary link layer processing to receive and transmit packets to neighboring routers. Note that the network layer also involves routing protocols and error handling. However, in many high-performance router implementations, these functions are pushed to the slow path or the control plane, where a conventional workstation-type processor handles these tasks. Thus, the focus of a network processor is to handle common-case data path functions. (As shown later, some network processor designs use a control processor on-chip for slow path and control processing.) In addition, network processors may implement additional packet processing functions (e.g., firewall or intrusion detection functions as discussed in Chapters 8 and 9 or next-generation network protocols as discussed in Chapter 15).

The handling of each packet on the network processor can be seen as a separate processing step. When considering the workload generated from processing a single packet, the following observations can be made.

- Processing of a single packet requires a small amount of processing: Network protocols are designed to require only small amounts of processing on routers. For example, to implement fully compliant IP forwarding, only a few hundred instructions are necessary (depending on the processor instruction set architecture). Because this code has very few—if any—loops, it can be executed in a few hundred cycles. Protocols that require the processing of packet payloads (e.g., TCP checksum computation, IPSec payload encryption) lead to processing requirements in the tens of thousands of cycles.
- Processing of packets is very regular and repetitive: Practically all packets that traverse a router require very similar processing. There may be some differences in systems where different flows receive different processing (e.g., forwarding and decryption for flows where VPN is terminated and plain forwarding for other flows). However, all packets require basic link and network layer processing. In most protocols, there are very few processing alternatives (other than error handling, which is offloaded to the control processor). Thus, the processing steps executed by the packet processing platform are nearly identical for most packets. This regularity and repetitiveness help in optimizing network processor systems for efficient processing.
- Processing of packets is performed with very simple computations: The types of computations used for protocol processing are typically based on very simple comparisons, arithmetic, and logic operations. Practically no network protocol requires floating-point operations or other complex computation or data manipulation functions. Thus, processor cores used for network processor systems are typically based on very simple reduced instruction set computer (RISC) architectures.

For a more comprehensive evaluation of processing characteristics of network processing workloads, see Ramaswamy and colleagues [146].

The simplicity of packet processing has immediate implications for the input/output system of the network processors. Because each packet spends very little time on the processor, the relative amount of input/output bandwidth is much higher than in workstation processors, where processing tasks have higher computational demands. This increase in data input/output over computation also impacts the demand on the memory system, which needs to handle read and write accesses when data are accessed. The designs of network processor MPSoCs are based on these workload characteristics.

System architecture

The overall architecture of a generic network processor is shown in Figure 11-3, which shows the main internal components of the network processors and the external memory and input/output interfaces to which it connects. The specific

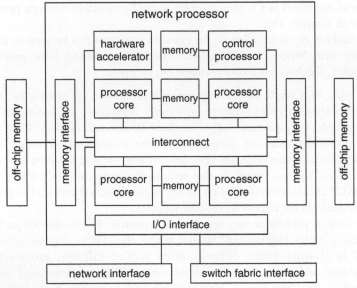

FIGURE 11-3

System architecture of network processor.

architecture of network processors differs among models, but their main components typically include the following.

- Multiple processor cores for data path processing. These processors are used for the processing of network traffic and are typically simple RISC cores. The number of cores can range from tens to several hundred. Processor cores are typically very simple and not capable of running their own operating system. Each processor core may have hardware support for multiple processing threads.
- Single processor core for control operations. This processor is used for control operations and slow-path handling of packets. It is often based on an embedded RISC system that is capable enough to run a full-blown embedded operating system.
- On-chip memory. On-chip memory consists of instruction and data memory for data path processors and control processors. Often, some portions of the memory are shared among all processors and others are dedicated to individual processors. More recently, some of these memories are built as caches similar to those found on conventional workstation processors. In most cases, on-chip memory uses SRAM technology, as a combination of DRAM and processing logic within a single MPSoC is more difficult to manufacture.
- Several interfaces for off-chip memories. The amount of on-chip memory that can reasonably be included on network processors usually does not provide enough storage for packets that need to be buffered or for programs and

program state. To expand the available memory space, off-chip memories are used. Interfaces to access these memories are included in the network processor chip. Typically, there are multiple interfaces to heterogeneous types of memory (e.g., SRAM and SDRAM) to exploit the benefits of different memory technologies (e.g., access speed vs memory density).

- High-bandwidth interface for network interface(s). The router ports on which network processors are located typically interface with one or more physical links on one side and the router switching fabric on the other side. Because network links use a wide variety of physical layer protocols (e.g., copper wiring, optical fiber), network processors do not connect directly to the physical medium, but send network traffic to separate physical interface components. The same interface is also used to interface with the switching fabric of the router.
- High-bandwidth interconnect between internal components. The various components inside the network processor (data path processor cores, control processor core, memory interfaces, input/output interface) need to be connected to allow for movement of data through the system. The bandwidth of this interconnect needs to be sufficiently high to pass network traffic through at full bandwidth as well as to accommodate memory accesses and other processing-related communication. There are various approaches on how to design such an interconnect. In the simplest case, a bus can be used to fully connect all components. While this approach is straightforward and allows any component to communicate with any other, it may present a performance bottleneck. Other approaches include arrangement of data path processors in a physical pipeline with local interconnects or other hybrid topologies. The choice of interconnect has a considerable impact on programming and run-time management of network processors, as it may constrain which components can communicate with each other.
- Specialized hardware accelerators. Optional but very commonly used components of network processors are hardware accelerators. These blocks implement networking-specific processing tasks in custom logic and achieve much higher performance than typical software implementations. Examples of common hardware accelerators are lookup engines (using specialized logic and/or TCAM), cryptographic coprocessors, content inspection engines, etc. Hardware accelerators are typically shared among all data path processor cores and thus need to be accessed via the on-chip interconnect.

These system components on a network processor interact closely with each other. These interactions are illustrated here by considering the path of a packet through the network processor. We also discuss the trade-offs that need to be considered when designing a network processor.

Operation of network processor

The process of forwarding a packet through a network processor is shown in Figure 11-4. Packets that are received on the network interface are stored in memory and control information is sent to one of the data path processors. The processor

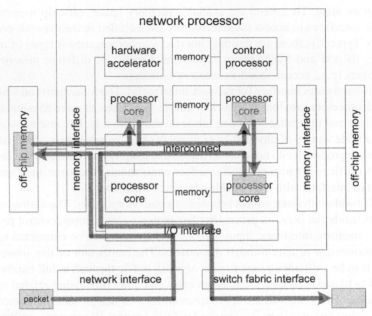

FIGURE 11-4

Flow of network traffic through a network processor.

fetches some part of the packet (e.g., protocol header) and performs the processing operations required by the protocols that are implemented on the router system. During processing, the packet may be passed to another data path processor. If the packet needs to be passed to the control plane or the slow path, the control processor is notified (not shown in Figure 11-4). At the end of these processing steps, the packet is queued and scheduled for transmission (e.g., into switch fabric or on output interface). This scheduling process is typically also done in software.

The interconnect that provides communication between data path processors determines the physical topology of the network processor. The software used on the network processor determines the logical topology of the network processor. Physical topologies with fewer constraints allow a broader range of logical topologies and thus are more flexible. Examples of physical and logical topologies of network processors are shown in Figure 11-5.

The simplest topology to use is a full interconnect (e.g., using a bus as shown in Figure 11-5). Any processor core can communicate with any other core. This topology does not scale well to large numbers of processor cores because it is a single centralized component that needs to handle all communication. A pipeline is the opposite of a full interconnect. In the pipeline, each processor is only connected to its neighbors. Each interconnect needs to handle at most the full data rate of the system. The drawback of a pipeline is that the slowest element determines the maximum performance of the system. In cases where processing bottlenecks occur

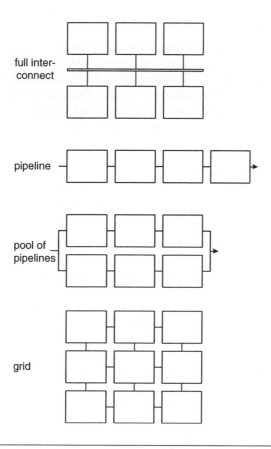

FIGURE 11-5

Topologies for data path processors in network processors.

(or where the workload is not split evenly among processors), the pipeline topology performs poorly. The other two topologies, pool of pipelines and grid, present a combination of the full interconnect and the pipeline topology. They are based on local interconnects to ensure scalability, but provide multiple paths to avoid bottlenecks. The pool of pipelines uses multiple pipelines in parallel and thus can continue to operate efficiently even if there is a bottleneck in one pipeline. The grid topology uses local interconnects to neighboring processors and provides numerous paths in the 2-D processor space.

The software used on a particular network processor needs to be adapted to the underlying hardware topology. In particular, the processing workload needs to be partitioned among processor cores to allow effective operation of the network processor. As long as the underlying hardware topology is less restrictive than the software, an implementation is possible (e.g., software pipelining on top of a full interconnect). More details on software for network processors can be found in Chapter 14.

Design choices

The cost of design and manufacturing of a chip is roughly dependent on its physical size. Larger chips contain more logic gates, which increases the design cost. Larger chips are also more costly to produce, as fewer fit on a waver (and are more likely to contain faults, which reduce the yield). Thus, there is a practical limit on how large the physical implementation of a network processor can be. This limit requires designers to make choices on how to use the silicon real estate available to them.

System design parameters

As shown in Figure 11-3, a number of components are necessary for operation of the network processor. Numerous parameters can be tuned in the design of a network processor. The key parameters are:

- Number of data path processors: A larger number of data path processors can perform more processing tasks to handle packets.
- Clock rate of data path processors: A higher clock rate implies that more processing can be performed by data path processors.
- Amount of on-chip data and instruction memory: A larger number of instruction memory means that more complex packet processing applications (or more of them) can be used by the system. A larger amount of data memory can store more program state and packet data on-chip and reduces accesses to off-chip memory. If data path processors use caches, then the access to instruction and data memories becomes more efficient.
- Bandwidth and topology of internal interconnect: A higher bandwidth of the interconnect can improve the amount of internal communication that can be performed (e.g., to move packets between processors). In some cases, a higher bandwidth can also reduce the delay for communication.
- Number and type of memory interfaces: More and faster memory interfaces allow for faster access to off-chip memory and a higher amount of data transfer into and out of memory.
- Number and type of hardware accelerators: More types of hardware accelerators imply that more processing steps can be performed by high-performing specialized logic. A larger number of hardware accelerators reduce the contention for this shared resource.

These design parameters need to be considered in context of each other to ensure a balanced design that leads to an efficient operation of the network processor.

System design trade-offs

When choosing design parameters, a large numbers of devices, higher clock rates, more memory, and bandwidth are desirable to achieve higher performance. However, it is also intuitively clear that such performance increases come at a cost. Higher-performing versions of components typically require more chip area than their lower-performing counterparts. For example, to increase the clock rate of a processor, the number of pipeline stages needs to be increased. This increase in processor complexity leads to a more complex logic design, which requires more area on the chip.

Because the maximum chip area is limited by the cost of the system, increasing the chip area for one component implies that other components need to fit into a smaller area. This tension between integrating a higher-performance version of a component and saving the chip area for other components on the network processor leads to a number of important design trade-offs. While optimization of the afore-mentioned parameters of a network processor system design is complex and involves many details, several key design choices need to be considered by a designer.

- More processors vs faster processors: Given a limited amount of chip real estate, a designer can choose to implement a larger number of slower (and thus smaller) processor cores or a smaller number of faster processors. While faster processors are able to process a single task more quickly, they typically do not achieve the aggregate performance of a larger number of slower processors. Thus, this design trade-off is equivalent to optimizing a processor system for throughput vs delay. High throughput can be achieved with a large number of slow processors, but the delay of any particular task is high. In workstation systems, processors are typically optimized for fast processing of a single (or few) task(s). This design optimization meets the needs of an impatient user waiting for their application to execute. In network processing, where the system throughput is the main optimization goal, the design choice typically falls toward more, but slower, processors to achieve higher aggregate processing power.

- Higher processing power vs more memory: Another important trade-off relating to the processing performance of a network processor is the choice between dedi-cating chip area to processors and using the area for memories instead. All proces-sing requires access to memory (for both instruction and data accesses). If the memory system cannot supply data to processors fast enough to sustain effective processing, then the memory becomes a performance bottleneck. To avoid memory bottlenecks, a designer can increase the size of on-chip memories (cache or regular) or add more memory interfaces to reduce contention for off-chip memory accesses. The right balance between processing and memory is highly dependent on the type and complexity of the processing application. In network-processing scenarios, the amount of on-chip memory is typically small (in the order of tens to hundreds of kilobytes), as network processing applications are usually simple and do not require much instruction store or complex data structures.

- General-purpose processors vs hardware accelerators: General-purpose proces-sors can perform any packet processing function, but their processing speed is slower than a hardware accelerator with the same functionality. However, a hardware accelerator is limited to one (or a few) specific function and cannot be used for anything else. Thus, an important design decision is to determine how many hardware accelerators of what type should be used. These accelera-tors can increase system performance, but also take away space that could be used for general-purpose processors. In many network processors, the number of accelerators is limited to very few that implement functions that are commonly used on all packets (e.g., IP lookup).

• Higher interconnect bandwidth vs software complexity: The interconnect determines what types of software and hardware pipelining can be implemented on a network processor. The most general type of interconnect is a full connection between all system components (e.g., bus). However, implementing a high-performance interconnect that connects a large number of system components requires a large amount of chip area. Using a larger number of high-performance, point-to-point connections requires less chip area, but imposes constraints on which components can communicate with each other. With a constrained interconnect, the development of software becomes more challenging and run-time management of system resources becomes more difficult. This issue is discussed further in Chapter 14. Many network processors use a full interconnect or implement a simple pipeline architecture.

With all the aforementioned system components and their related design trade-offs, an important question is how well each can be utilized during operation of the network processor. A large number of data path processors is only useful if the remaining system components can transfer enough data from the interfaces to the processors and program and instruction data to and from memory. Similarly, accelerators are only useful if the processing workload can utilize them.

Power constraints

In addition to performance considerations that aim at high throughput of the network processor, the power consumption of the router system needs to be considered. As discussed in Chapter 12, lowering power consumption through system design and implementation techniques is important.

In the context of the system design trade-offs discussed earlier, the focus on throughput in network processor systems helps with the goal of lowering power consumption. When using many processors clocked at a lower rate, less power is dissipated than when using a few processors that run at a much higher clock rate. Similarly, the use of on-chip memories and local interconnects can help reduce system power consumption.

In addition to the goal of lowering power for economic and environmental reasons, there is also a hard limit on the power consumption that is technically feasible for a router (and thus for the system components inside the router). Many routers are located within data centers that house racks and racks of equipment. These systems require cooling through air conditioning to ensure that they remain within an operating temperature where no damage occurs from overheating. Based on the availability of air conditioning, there is a limit on how much heat can be dissipated by any given device. This heat is directly correlated to the power consumed by the device. Thus, peak power consumption needs to be limited accordingly. In a typical data center, the available power is 5 kW per rack, which is about 120 W per rack unit.

Due to this power limit for router system, the design constraint for network processors has mostly focused on limiting the total power consumption while achieving the necessary throughput rate. As energy efficiency becomes more important, this design goal is expected to change toward minimizing power consumption (possibly at the cost of reducing the overall system throughput).

Example systems

With a basic understanding of the design trade-offs in network processors, we briefly review three specific systems that have been implemented and deployed. These network processors differ in their system configuration, their interconnect topology, and the software support that is available. Table 11-1 provides a comparison of the system characteristics of three network processors. The systems compared are as follows.

Table 11-1 Comparison of Network Processor Configurations

	Intel IXP2855	Cisco QuantumFlow	Cavium CN5860
Maximum throughput	10 Gbps	20 Gbps	20 Gbps
Data path processors	16 32-bit RISC processors, eight threads per processor, up to 1.5 GHz	40 32-bit RISC processors, four threads per processor, up to 1.2 GHz	16 64-bit RISC processors, up to 800 MHz
On-chip memory	32-kB instruction and 32 kB data memory per processor	16-kB cache per processor, 256-kB shared cache	32-kB instruction cache and 8-kB data cache per processor, 2 MB shared cache
Control processor	32-bit XScale RISC core, 32-kB instruction cache, 32-kB data cache, up to 750 MHz	Off-chip	Off-chip
External memory interfaces	Three DRAM interfaces, four SRAM interfaces	DRAM, SRAM, and TCAM interfaces	DRAM and TCAM interfaces
Hardware accelerators	Cryptographic coprocessor	Classification, traffic policing, etc.	Cryptographic coprocessor, TCP acceleration, regular expression matching, etc.
Maximum power dissipation	32 W	80 W	40 W

- Intel IXP2855 [76]: The Intel IXP2855 network processor uses 16 processor cores, called microengines, for data path operations. Each microengine supports eight hardware threads and has its own local instruction and data memories. The on-chip control processor can run an embedded operating system. Off-chip memory interfaces provide access to different memory types. Hardware acceleration is provided for cryptographic operations. The peak throughput of this network processor system is 10 Gbps.
- Cisco QuantumFlow [32]: The Cisco QuantumFlow network processor uses 40 processor cores with four hardware threads each. Compared to the Intel IXP2855, this is a larger number of processor cores, but a smaller number of hardware threads per core. Each processor has its own local cache memory, but also access to a larger, shared cache. There is no control processor on-chip. Memory interfaces for DRAM and SRAM as well as TCAM are provided. Hardware acceleration functions include packet classification and traffic policing. This network processor is used in routers with a peak throughput of 20 Gbps.
- Cavium OCTEON Plus CN5860 [24]: The Cavium CN5860 multicore processor uses 16 RISC processors. The clock rate of the processors is considerably lower than for the Intel and Cisco products, but the data path is 64 bits wide instead of 32 bits. Each processor has 32 kB of instruction cache and 8 kB of data cache in addition to a 2 MB shared cache. There is no on-chip control processor. Memory interfaces for DRAM and TCAM are available. Hardware acceleration support includes cryptographic functions, TCP processing, and regular expression matching.

While significant differences exist in the specific implementation details of these systems, it can also be seen that there are many similarities. All systems support tens of processor cores (with the number of hardware threads reaching into the low hundreds). On-chip memory is in the order of tens of kilobytes per processor core. There are also similarities in the memory interface and hardware acceleration configuration.

As technology progresses, the specific configuration details will change. However, the overall system architecture of network processors, which is based on a large number of simple, parallel processor cores, is expected to remain the same.

SPECIAL-PURPOSE HARDWARE ACCELERATORS

In contrast to general-purpose network processors, which can be programmed to perform any packet processing function, special-purpose accelerators can only perform one or a few different functions.

Trade-offs in use of accelerators

The main benefit of using special-purpose hardware is that these accelerators can perform certain functions faster than possible with conventional processors. In general, reasons for using specialized accelerators or coprocessors include the following.

- Processing performance: As the name indicates, accelerators are designed to do certain computations faster than general-purpose processors. Speedup can be achieved through the use of custom logic functions that can implement the desired functionality without having to follow the standardized instruction set of a conventional processor. In addition, custom logic can utilize high levels of parallel processing on workloads with inherent parallelism. Custom logic circuits often can be clocked faster or accomplish more work per clock and thus achieve a higher processing performance.
- Energy consumption: The amount of energy consumed to perform a particular task may be lower in a specialized hardware implementation compared to a software implementation on a general-purpose processor. General-purpose processors have some inherent overhead due to their generality.
- Special functionality: Some coprocessors can provide functions that simply cannot be implemented on a general-purpose processor. For example, a true random number generator requires information from a physical process (e.g., decay of nuclear material). This process can be built into a coprocessor, but cannot be emulated on a general-purpose processor. Another example is a trusted platform module, where cryptographic keys are stored and cryptographic operations are performed. The secure storage of cryptographic keys cannot be provided by a general-purpose processor, but requires dedicated logic.

A key concern when deciding on the use of accelerators in a router design is what level of utilization can be achieved during operation. The cost of integrating an accelerator into a router design needs to be offset by leveraging the aforementioned benefits and processing as much traffic as possible on the accelerator component. Fortunately, the highly repetitive nature of packet processing makes it easier to achieve high utilization on these accelerators than is possible with general-purpose workloads.

Example accelerators

Examples of hardware accelerators used in the networking domain include the following.

- Cyclic redundancy checks (CRC)/checksum computation: Link layer protocols such as Ethernet and AAL5 use CRC to detect bit errors that may have occurred during transmission of a frame. CRC computation requires computation of polynomials and can be slow when implemented on a conventional processor. However, the streaming nature of CRCs lends itself to an efficient implementation in hardware. Typical CRC accelerators can operate at line speed and are widely used to implement link layer processing.
- Prefix lookup: As discussed in Chapter 7, IP prefix lookup is one of the computationally demanding functions in IP forwarding. Special lookup engines can be used to accelerate the forwarding process. These accelerators can be based on specialized data structures or TCAM implementations.

- Pattern/regular expression matching: As discussed in Chapter 9, regular expression matching is used to inspect packet payloads. The process of scanning data streams and matching a set of regular expressions can be accelerated with accelerators that implement specialized matching algorithms.
- Cryptographic functions: Cryptographic computations are computationally complex. Network systems that provide SSL termination or VPN termination (see Chapter 10) need to provide this functionality at high data rates. Modern cryptographic algorithms (e.g., AES) are optimized for fast operation in custom logic implementations. Cryptographic coprocessors provide this basic encryption and decryption functionality, as well asymmetric cryptographic operations, and key generation and management.
- Instruction set extensions: A special case of hardware acceleration is the extension of instruction sets for network processing operations. Some network processors (e.g., Intel IXP family) are equipped with special instructions that are particularly useful for network protocol processing (e.g., bit selection and modification operations). This type of specialization is becoming less common, as the complexity of software development for custom instruction sets may outweigh the performance gains.

As network processors move toward higher levels of integration, the size (and implementation cost) of accelerators continues to decrease. This trend lowers utilization threshold where the use of an accelerator breaks even with the cost of integrating it into the system. Therefore, it can be expected that an increasing number of accelerators for more specialized functions will be developed.

Accelerator implementations

Hardware accelerators can be integrated into the packet processing system in different ways. If the accelerator is packaged as a separate chip, then it can be integrated with other packet processing components on the router line card. If the accelerator is a logic block, then it can be integrated within a network processor design. The latter approach leads to higher system integration and thus better performance, but may not be feasible in practice due to restrictions on intellectual property. It also limits the flexibility of the system since the logic block gets locked into the system at design time.

Coprocessors and hardware accelerators can be implemented in a number of different ways.

- Custom logic: Hardware accelerators can be based on a custom logic design that implements the accelerator's functionality. This custom logic block can be used as a stand-alone chip or as an intellectual property core integrated in another chip design. This approach has the benefit of imposing no constraints on implementation of the accelerated functionality. In addition, custom logic can be optimized to meet performance targets.
- Programmable logic: Hardware accelerators can also be based on programmable logic, e.g., field-programmable gate array (FPGA). The benefit of using

programmable logic rather than a custom design is that FPGAs are broadly available and do not require fabrication of a custom chip. Also, an FPGA integrated into a network system design could be used for different accelerators and thus allows a level of customization not possible with custom logic accelerators.

Many existing network processing systems use custom logic for their accelerators since they provide better performance than FPGA-based implementations. The need for flexibility may change this balance toward more programmable logic implementations in future networks (see Chapter 15).

SUMMARY

This chapter explored some of the specialized hardware components used for packet processing in router systems. Network processors use multiple parallel processor cores to implement packet forwarding and more advanced functions. These network processors provide a general-purpose platform, where the router operation can be changed by updating software. In contrast, hardware accelerators provide a fixed set of functions specialized for the networking domain. Hardware accelerators typically use custom logic implementations that achieve higher performance than software, but cannot be reprogrammed. Both general-purpose network processors and special purpose hardware accelerators are used in modern router designs.

Power issues in network systems

12

INTRODUCTION

Power consumption constitutes a significant issue in the emerging green computing environment. The effort for power optimization addresses computing systems at all fronts, but is significantly more important for embedded systems. Power optimization of embedded systems, especially handheld, battery-operated systems, is a requirement that leads to practical and successful systems. Failure to reduce power consumption below a threshold leads to systems that are costly, with short market life, and practically difficult or impossible to use. The recent focus of the research community on power optimization for embedded systems has led to a large number of techniques and parameters that designers need to consider for power-efficient embedded system designs [153].

The adoption of embedded systems in a range of heterogeneous applications has led to several specialized methodologies for reducing power in common, widespread application environments. For example, the effectiveness and usefulness of wireless sensor networks have led to the development of network systems with specialized processors, addressing the requirements of wireless sensor networks. A designer focusing on this specific application area can take advantage of the event-driven nature of many sensor network workloads and reduce power requirements of the employed processors equipping them with event-based, fine-grained low power mechanisms [63].

Network systems are special-purpose embedded computing systems. The power consumption of most network systems is constrained by their deployment environments. Many network systems are installed in densely utilized equipment racks. Limits on cooling of this equipment put a bound on how much energy can be consumed (and dissipated as heat). Some network systems are used in handheld, battery-operated systems or in application areas that require battery-operated, and thus power limited, systems. The current state of the art of low power embedded system design does not enable the development of systematic approaches for power efficient systems overall; importantly, several results have been developed for embedded subsystems, such as processors and sensors. For network systems, the major effort to date has been on the most power-consuming system components.

This chapter surveys the main results for low power network systems development in the context of two specific system components: lookup engines and network processors.

LOOKUP ENGINES

One of the important operations in network systems is determining how to handle incoming packets. Routers need to determine how to forward a packet based on the destination address (see Chapter 7). Similar operations are performed by transport layer systems for packet classification (see Chapter 8). These types of lookups are performed on every packet and thus are an important aspect of data plane processing in network systems.

As discussed in Chapter 7, lookup operations in Internet Protocol implementation are based on Longest Prefix Match. This IP lookup is an important and interesting problem because it needs to be performed with increasingly faster links and with an increasing number of address prefixes. Requirements for more efficient lookups in larger configurations have led to several approaches in the design of lookup data structures in order to reduce the average number of memory accesses required for longest prefix matching [29, 133, 169, 173]. The complexity of data structures, as well as the necessity for several memory accesses per search operation, has led to the development of several specialized memory architectures and the adoption of several memory technologies for efficient IP lookup, such as Content Addressable Memory (CAM), reduced-latency DRAMs, etc. In all cases, the proposed solution constitutes a trade-off among lookup delay, update speed, and memory size. Importantly, because memory is a power-hungry component, special attention has been paid to decrease the power consumption of table lookups. The remainder of this section surveys techniques for power-efficient IP table lookups. Considering the main approaches for IP lookup subsystem designs discussed in Chapter 7, we classify the architectures into two categories: (i) Ternary CAM (TCAM) based and (ii) SRAM based.

Ternary CAM-based IP lookup

Exploitation of parallelism is the typical technique adopted when performance improvement is required. In the case of routing, as with IP table lookup, a straightforward employment of parallelism is to search all table routes simultaneously. Content Addressable Memories are memories that enable such parallel search: the target destination address is entered as input and the matching entries are extracted. Considering the specific requirements of longest prefix matching, however, one needs to extend the typical CAM operation to enable the use of *wildcard* or *don't care* bits. Ternary CAMs constitute a technology that enables the use of don't care bits. (TCAMs include one don't care bit for every tag bit; when the don't care bit is set, the tag bit matches any value.) Figure 12-1 presents the logical view of a classical TCAM, assuming, for simplicity, that prefixes have a maximum length

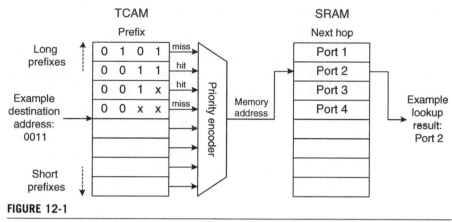

FIGURE 12-1

Ternary CAM organization and operation.

of 4. Each entry includes a matching pattern for a route, where "x" indicates a don't care bit. As Figure 12-1 shows, an incoming packet with destination address 0011 arrives at the TCAM. The TCAM compares the destination address of the incoming packet against all the prefixes in parallel. Two matches occur and the priority encoder selects the first matching entry—the longest prefix match. If the routing table is loaded sorted, the longest prefix match appears at the highest hit in the TCAM (lower memory address).

Ternary CAMs were introduced as an important technology for IP-lookup operations [114], but they were immediately identified as an expensive, power-hungry solution that provided significantly smaller density than conventional SRAM. Furthermore, prefixes stored in TCAMs need to be sorted in order to enable identification of the longest prefix matching easily. Sorting is also a time- and power-consuming process. Since their introduction, several research efforts have focused to solve the high power consumption problem of TCAMs. Their approaches can be classified as optimizations at two levels: (i) algorithmic–architectural and (ii) circuit. We describe briefly several of the promising contributions in this direction.

One of the algorithmic optimizations is addressing the sorting and updating problems of the routing table, which is stored in the TCAM. TCAMs automatically report the topmost (lowest address) matching. Thus, the longest prefix matching is guaranteed to be the TCAM response only if it appears first; thus, prefixes need to be sorted so that longer prefixes appear before the shorter ones. This leads to significant complexity and results in significant power consumption in the case of a table update. One proposal to avoid sorting the table is to introduce priorities in the table entries (the TCAM addresses) and use additional specialized hardware to select the correct matching entry (with the highest priority) in case of multiple matches [90]. This solution is effective in terms of avoiding sorting of prefixes, but it reduces performance because it adds latency to the time-critical lookup operations. Alternatively, one can avoid sorting using a technique that keeps empty spaces in the TCAM so that some of the table updates can be implemented fast, with $O(1)$ complexity, without the requirement for sorting [162]. A third solution reduces the number of sorting operations by relaxing the requirement to sort the complete set of prefixes in TCAM. Actually, one can observe that longest prefix matching is possible even when sorting has not been performed completely on the whole set but only partially on overlapping prefixes. For example, two prefixes overlap if one is a subset of the other; for example, 01* overlaps with 0101*, but not with 001*. This observation enables designers to reduce memory-swapping operations during the insertion/deletion of new routes [162]. Apparently, these approaches are useful to all operations that require some type of sorting, sequencing, and classifying. The last method, for example, has been shown to apply to TCAM-based packet classifiers as well.

An alternative approach to reducing power consumption is that of compacting prefix tables through removal of redundancy. An interesting technique that uses a combination of pruning and logic minimization algorithms achieves reduction of power consumption by 30–40%, depending on the performance of the logic minimization algorithm [102]. However, the method places significant overhead on the table-updating process, making it unsuitable for environments with frequent routing updates. Alternatively, others attack the problem by compacting the TCAM active area [147]. Ravikumar and colleagues [147] combine several techniques, such as prefix aggregation and expansion and a new paging scheme, to limit the number of TCAM entries searched during an IP-lookup operation. More specifically, they propose a two-level memory architecture, with the first level composed of SRAM memory and the second level composed of TCAM memory. The use of SRAM at the first level is based on the observation that the high order bits of the prefixes (8 in the case of this specific technique), called page bits, do not contain wildcard bits in the typical case; thus, an 8-bit-wide SRAM memory can be used for lookup at the first level. The technique accommodates the case when page bits contain wildcards as well, using a controlled prefix expansion technique. Use of the SRAM at the first level reduces the number of the required TCAM bits, which are included in the second level. If the used prefix bits for the first level are 8, the TCAM memory array is 24 bits wide for the IP protocol, achieving significant reduction in power consumption.

An additional approach to power reduction is the use of parallel routing tables, that is, parallel TCAM chips, where only one TCAM chip is selected for searching at every time instant. In such an approach, one can power only the chip (part of the table) that is being searched, reducing power consumption. Analogously, if all partitions are used in parallel, power consumption increases, but so does performance due to the parallel searches that increase throughput. Several algorithms are used for the partitioning of prefix tables [136, 196]. In an effort to develop techniques that target to implement searching only where necessary, an alternative technique targets to avoid searching for nonmatching packets by using a multilevel Bloom filter to eliminate a fraction of the nonmatching packets before passing them to the TCAM-based classifier [28].

Ternary CAM manufacturers have been addressing the issue of power consumption as well. One of their major directions is the inclusion of mechanisms that enable system designers to use only portions of a TCAM chip at a time for searching. In this fashion, each TCAM chip does not consume power fully, only the portions that are enabled at every time instant. Such TCAMs are called blocked TCAMs. Considering the structure and functional characteristics of blocked TCAMs, it is important to develop algorithms that map prefix table portions to the blocks of the TCAMs in order to achieve efficient operation for the lookup operations overall. Several such methods are feasible. For example, a bit selection algorithm (for selecting route prefixes) is combined with a hashing function to direct (and limit) the lookup process to a portion of the TCAM, reducing power consumption [195]. Alternatively, a trie-based algorithm uses an index TCAM, a smaller TCAM, to select one or more of the TCAM blocks for the searching operation [195]. Such efforts achieve significant power savings. Furthermore, a designer can combine these techniques with the page-based scheme described earlier [147] in order to achieve even further power savings [105].

In a different approach, one can try to reduce the number of TCAM entries, reducing power consumption due to smaller memory size. Prefix inclusion coding (PIC) [137] is a promising solution in this direction. PIC encodes address filters in codewords of small size and replaces the conventional address lookup with codeword lookup, which is equivalent to longest prefix matching operation. PIC is effective by using appropriate coding of the filters and leads to 70% to over 90% smaller memory sizes and thus to significant improvement in power consumption [137].

At the circuit level, there are two main optimizations. The first one targets the design of a TCAM in such a way so that when a prefix mismatches, searching does not proceed to any additional bits of the word with the mismatched prefix [126]. The developed VLSI design of the TCAM adds a new signal to every TCAM line. During a search operation, bits are compared from higher order to lower; when a mismatch occurs, this new signal stops the searching (comparison) of the remaining TCAM bits of the same TCAM line, thus reducing power consumption significantly.

The second circuit level optimization targets the storage of don't care bits. In a typical TCAM design, the requirement to store three values (0, 1, and don't care) at every memory location leads to the use of 2 RAM bits per single TCAM ternary value; that is, each single TCAM digit uses 2 RAM bits to store. Thus, if a TCAM has a width of w digits, each TCAM entry uses $2w$ RAM bits. The optimization, named Prefix TCAM (PCAM), introduces a different encoding scheme for storing prefixes in the memory array that is very suitable for TCAM implementations [2] and that reduces the $2w$ required RAM bits to $(w + 1)$ bits. The scheme takes advantage of the fact that all the masked bits in a prefix are adjacent and located at the low order bits of the route bits; for example, 1100110010* is a valid 10-bit IP prefix shown in binary with the 22 lower bits masked, whereas 11x01* ("x" denotes a don't care bit) is not a valid prefix because it has a masked bit surrounded by valid bits. Specifically, the scheme replaces low-order don't care bits with an equal number of 0 bits headed by a bit with value "1", which functions

TCAM array

Prefix (8 bits) ⟶

1	1	1	1	0	0	0	0
1	1	1	1	0	0	0	x
1	1	1	1	0	0	x	x
1	1	1	1	0	x	x	x
1	1	1	1	x	x	x	x
1	1	1	x	x	x	x	x
1	1	x	x	x	x	x	x
1	x	x	x	x	x	x	x

Prefix TCAM array

⟵ PCAM entry (8+1 bits) ⟶

1	1	1	1	0	0	0	0	1
1	1	1	1	0	0	0	1	0
1	1	1	1	0	0	1	0	0
1	1	1	1	0	1	0	0	0
1	1	1	1	1	0	0	0	0
1	1	1	1	0	0	0	0	0
1	1	1	0	0	0	0	0	0
1	1	0	0	0	0	0	0	0

FIGURE 12-2

Prefix TCAM for 8-bit routes.

as a preamble. Figure 12-2 shows an example of PCAM, assuming a prefix length of 8 bits. The encoding of each 8-digit TCAM entry leads to a 9-bit entry with the rightmost "1" indicating the beginning of don't care digits. The reduction of the $2w$ RAM bits to $(w + 1)$ leads to significant reductions in memory usage and thus to power consumption. For $w = 32$, that means a 48.4% reduction in memory usage [2]. Based on this observation, the inventors of the scheme offer a new VLSI implementation dedicated for TCAMs in which the extra mask bits were removed, reducing the number of transistors by 22% relative to a conventional TCAM.

SRAM-based IP lookup

The high power consumption of TCAM-based lookup subsystems has led to the development of SRAM-based lookup solutions, which are characterized by lower circuit complexity. As discussed in Chapter 7, special efforts have been made to develop appropriate systems for efficient lookups when using SRAM memories due to the specifics of the longest prefix matching algorithm. Several efforts have been made to develop and implement ASIC designs that support trie-based, software level IP-lookup algorithms [29, 133, 169, 173]. However, these solutions do not provide the flexibility required by conventional IP-lookup search engines; for example, they have no or limited capability for updating the prefix table entries and, in general, require a significant number (typically more than 4) of dependent (serialized) memory accesses, stressing conventional memory architectures to the limit in their effort to meet conventional link speed requirements.

Caching has been exploited for the reduction of memory operations and thus reduction of power consumption due to searches in smaller sets. In these configurations, prefixes are stored in main system memory, usually using a trie-based data structure, and a cache stores the portion of the most common prefixes. The use of associative caching has been explored in this environment, proving to be a useful technique that takes advantage of locality characteristics in IP traffic and reaching miss rates less than 10% in configurations [33]. However, the update process is complex in these environments due to requirements of the longest prefix matching algorithm mentioned earlier. Importantly, the effectiveness of caching in such environments improves significantly when the cache stores IP prefixes rather than IP addresses [138]. The resulting caches, called supernode caches, reduce the number of main memory accesses, leading to a fast IP lookup. In the environment introduced for supernode caches, original results report avoidance of up to 72% memory accesses using a 128-KB supernode cache, an achievement of less than 4% miss ratio for the supernode cache, and a 77% energy reduction relative to a TCAM of the same size [138].

Another category of solutions consists of SRAM-based lookups that use set-associative memory structures to store prefix tables. The main difference between this category and the previous one is that a cache holds a small part of the data set, but the SRAM memory holds the entire prefix table. That is, the SRAM is the main storage for the prefix table and not just a cache for it. A representative approach in this category is IPStash [87, 88]. IPStash is a hash-based scheme that uses SRAM hash tables to store prefixes. Unlike trees, hash tables are flat data structures that have the desirable property of key length-independent latencies (i.e., $O(1)$ lookup complexity) and are easy to implement in hardware. Importantly, IPStash scales well as table sizes increase and also overcomes many problems faced by TCAM designs, such as the complexity to manage the prefix table (sorting and partitioning), the high power consumption, the low density/bit, and the high cost. In general, hashing schemes have two main drawbacks. First, hashing leads to collisions and thus requires conflict resolution techniques that may lead to unpredictable lookup performance. Second, IP prefixes include don't care bits, and these bits may be used as hashing bits. In this case, one would need to expand all affected IP prefixes to eliminate the don't care bits or would simply give up hash functions that depend on any of these bits. IPStash achieves good space utilization and fewer expansions by classifying prefixes according to their lengths (e.g., ≤ 16, $17 - 21$, ≥ 21) and using different hash indices for the prefixes of each class to a single multihash table. As a result, wildcard bits are excluded from hashing, while good hashing results are achieved. IPStash claims to be twice as fast as top-of-the-line TCAMs while offering up to 64% power savings (for the same throughput) over the best commercial TCAM of the same technology [87, 88]. Finally, an advanced hashing scheme, combined with extra hardware for parallel hash table lookup, can lead to improved performance [41].

NETWORK PROCESSORS

Network processors are another component of network systems, where techniques for low power consumption have been explored and applied. The motivation for this effort is due to the fact that network processors constitute highly parallel and specialized hardware components composed of functional blocks that may be active in parallel. As discussed in Chapter 11, network processors typically contain several packet processors, caches, memory interfaces, specialized hardware units, and I/O components on a single die. These components address different functional requirements of network systems and can be active in parallel, leading to high performance and high power consumption. Trends toward increasing chip functionality and increasing link bandwidth make power consumption of network processors a challenging issue.

Addressing the issue of low power network processors, methods have been developed for design space exploration of typical network processor parameters, including configuration of the processing elements and the memory subsystem [54]. Interestingly, this research work includes an analytical power model suitable for CMP network processors, which leads to proof that the greedy power consumer is the system clock during stall cycles, that is, while a packet processor waits for memory accesses to be served. To address this problem, a scheme has been developed to reduce the dynamic power consumption of components not in use [107, 108]. This method exploits the fact that in low traffic load, most processing elements in network processors are almost idle, although consuming dynamic power. The scheme monitors the average number of idle threads during a time window and calculates the number of processing elements necessary to process the incoming traffic load. The remaining number of processing elements is gated off the clock network and thus neither performance is sacrificed nor is dynamic power consumed by idle processing elements. This method achieves significant power consumption reduction (up to 30%) with little impact to the resulting throughput.

Memory references in network processors present high divergence in terms of their locality characteristics. Based on this observation, a methodology to classify the memory references of a packet stream has been developed [119]. Based on results of the classification, data with high temporal locality are directed to a data path with caches and branch prediction hardware, where high locality is exploited; in contrast, data with low locality are directed to dedicated hardware engines. In this fashion, the memory subsystem achieves higher utilization, improving system power consumption, bus utilization, and performance overall.

Methods for reducing power consumption in highly parallel network processors do not focus only on systems with identical processing elements, but on systems with heterogeneous processing elements as well. Such systems use multiple arrays of processing elements with different processing cores in the different arrays, with significant differences in terms of performance and power consumption. Packet scheduling techniques can lead to significant power savings [109].

In addition to approaches that are specific to network systems, general techniques for power reduction are being investigated. At the circuit level, voltage reduction in cache memories, as well as adjustments of clock frequency, provides significant power benefits without significant effect on system reliability [112]. At the architectural and compiler level, optimizations in the resolution of the register allocation problem for both interthread and intrathread register allocations lead to simultaneous performance improvement, as well as power savings [198].

SUMMARY

Network systems are special-purpose embedded computing systems with low power requirements. This chapter surveyed the main techniques that have been developed to date for use in low power network systems. Considering the direction of research and development in the field, we presented the main techniques for low power lookup engines and low power network processors. In the case of lookup engines, we focused on IP lookup systems, examining all proposed memory architectures, including tri-state CAMs and SRAM-based designs.

Networks on chips

13

INTRODUCTION

Significant advances in very large-scale integration (VLSI) circuit technologies have enabled the implementation of complete computing systems on a single chip. Such a complete computing system is called system-on-chip (SoC), as discussed briefly in Chapter 11. A typical SoC, as shown in Figure 13-1, is composed of several subsystems, including a processing element, memory, interconnection, special-purpose subsystems, and so on, although special-purpose SoCs may exist for specialized applications. SoCs are used in products with space and power limitations such as portable devices, in systems with increased security requirements, and as parts of larger systems.

Many SoCs have more than one processing element, effectively being multiprocessor SoCs (MPSoCs). These multiple processing elements can either be homogeneous, with identical processing elements, or be heterogeneous, with differing processing elements, depending on the need of the application. Typically, MPSoCs employ homogeneous processing elements when more processing power is needed (e.g., in a network processor), while heterogeneity is employed when special-purpose computing operations are necessary (e.g., in a mobile phone). Independently of the processing elements, though, the interconnection subsystem of the system-on-chip must provide sufficient bandwidth to all connected subsystems. Due to the large number and diverse functionality of components that need to be connected within an SoC, this interconnect needs to take advantage of state-of-the-art implementation technology to meet functional and performance requirements. The important performance characteristics of an SoC interconnection subsystem are its bandwidth, latency, power consumption, and area, analogous to those of switches described in Chapter 3.

The SoC interconnect can be viewed as a generic interconnection network that connects all system components within a single chip, hence the term Network-on-Chip (NoC) [135]. This on-chip network can adopt architectural models, designs, and techniques from parallel computer networks and local area networks (LAN), as well as wide-area networks (WAN). However, the small scale of SoCs differentiates a network-on-chip from these networks and presents new technical challenges that need to be addressed. These challenges are mainly in three directions: (i) network architectures and topologies, (ii) routing schemes, and (iii) physical characteristics of the

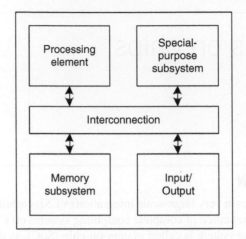

FIGURE 13-1

Generic structure of a system-on-chip.

chips and how the technology and circuit design affects network-on-chip design. This chapter presents these challenges and identifies promising solutions. We also present a framework for analysis of NoC architectures that enables the analysis of architectures by capturing characteristics of the underlying implementation technology.

NETWORK-ON-CHIP ARCHITECTURES

Multiprocessor interconnection networks constitute attractive candidates for network-on-chip designs because of their characteristics in terms of performance and reliability. Multiprocessor interconnections are typically considered as a class of networks with tightly coupled end systems that are colocated, with short latency, high bandwidth, and extremely low bit error rates. These characteristics are different from those of long-distance wide-area networks that emphasize providing high bandwidth rather than low latency and that exhibit higher bit error rates. In addition, NoCs place constraints on power and area beyond the constraints and requirements of multiprocessor interconnections.

Multiprocessor interconnection networks are typically classified into two categories: point-to-point and switch-based networks [44]. Figure 13-2 shows examples of both categories of networks. In point-to-point networks, processing elements are connected directly to each other. In switch-based networks, processing elements are connected to switches that are organized in some topology. Thus, in switch-based networks, processing elements communicate with each other over a connection that includes one or more switches. In point-to-point networks, processing elements communicate with each other either directly (if they are connected directly) or through a path that includes one or more processing

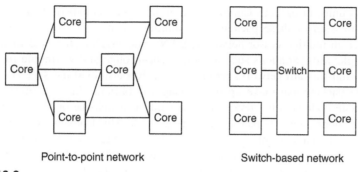

Point-to-point network   Switch-based network

FIGURE 13-2

Point-to-point and switch-based networks.

elements. In either case, each processing node requires an input/output (I/O) component that enables communication with the connected processing element or the connected switch.

Networks are characterized by a range of structural parameters, such as node degree (the number of links per node), diameter (the maximum length of the shortest length paths interconnecting any pair of nodes), etc. Each parameter influences one or more of the physical parameters of the NoC circuit, that is, bandwidth, delay, power, and area. Network topologies can be used for either point-to-point or switched-based networks. A wide range of literature explores the implementation of various networks as NoC, such as mesh and torus networks [36], octagon [84], and fat-tree [58]. Mesh, torus, and octagon networks are examples of point-to-point networks, and the fat-tree network is an example of a switch-based network because it is composed of switches as internal nodes that connect processing elements at the leaves [58].

Despite the similarities of multiprocessor networks and NoC, there are also important differences due to implementation technology characteristics. These differences relate to wiring and buffering, which affect performance characteristics such as bandwidth, delay, and power consumption. In typical multiprocessor networks with chip-to-chip and board-to-board connectivity, the width of the data path has always been limited to a small number of wires, while the density of wires in NoC is in the order of hundreds [194], thus increasing bandwidth significantly. In multiprocessor networks and LAN and WAN networks, low wire density leads to an extensive use of buffers, where data are stored temporarily in case of contention or congestion. In NoC, extensive use of buffers is prohibitive because buffers introduce latency and on-chip memory is costly in terms of power and silicon area.

NETWORK-ON-CHIP ROUTING SCHEMES

The topology of communication networks, including NoCs, is associated with one or more routing algorithms. The choice of routing algorithm, in turn, influences the network design. Most NoC interconnects are based on transmissions of fixed-size basic data units, or packets. Communication of larger amounts of data may require the transmission of these packets. The routing schemes of NoCs are similar to those used in multiprocessor networks, LANs, and WANs: store-and-forward and cut-through, with variations such as virtual cut-through and wormhole routing.

Store-and-forward networks require that each transmitted message (i.e., all the fixed-size packets that make up the message) is buffered in its entirety at every intermediate node (routing processing element or switch) before being forwarded to the next node along the path toward the receiver. This leads to NoC designs that require significant amounts of buffering per node and leads to long end-to-end latency for data transmission. The large amount of buffering leads to high cost in power consumption and circuit area. All these overheads of store-and-forward networks make them inappropriate for NoC implementations.

Virtual cut-through provides an improved alternative to store-and-forward networking because virtual cut-through does not store a message fully at intermediate nodes in the path; in this scheme, a packet is forwarded to the next node along the route as soon as possible, without any requirement to receive any additional packets of the same message. However, when the next node is blocked, for example, due to transmission of another message, the current message needs to be stored at the node in full (the packet and subsequent ones need to be received and stored completely). Thus, virtual cut-through still requires sufficient storage per node, but achieves significantly improved latency. Wormhole routing [44], a virtual cut-through-based scheme, is the best candidate for NoC implementation. In wormhole routing networks, packets of messages are routed as soon as possible (as in the cut-through case) and when the next node is blocked, the whole message is stopped and stored at the nodes where the packets have arrived at that time, waiting for the route to become available. The achieved low latency, in conjunction with the achieved low storage requirements per node, makes the scheme very attractive for NoC; an example is implementation in the SPIN network [4].

An important parameter of data transmission that relates to the routing scheme is the length of the transmitted packets. The importance of the parameter is not only due to performance but to power consumption as well. Power consumption is influenced by three factors: (i) the number of packets in the network, (ii) the energy consumption per packet per hop, and (iii) the number of hops per packet. Clearly, the length of packets influences each of these factors differently [194]. Longer packets lead to fewer packets in the network, while increasing power consumption per transmission. Furthermore, longer packets lead to higher contention, reserving network resources for longer periods, causing other packets to be rerouted through longer paths, etc.

TECHNOLOGY AND CIRCUIT DESIGN

The physical characteristics of the technology and design methods used for NoCs influence several of their parameters, such as bandwidth, delay, and power consumption. Clearly, the topology of an NoC influences its performance and power consumption significantly because of physical system characteristics, as well as architectural and traffic issues. Circuit characteristics play a more significant role in NoC than in networks interconnecting chips, boards, or racks. Therefore, we provide here delay models for two popular NoC interconnects: bus and crossbar switch. These models enable NoC designers to evaluate their decisions before creating detailed NoC designs. These models take into account physical characteristics, such as interconnect and device capacitance, and are parameterized by N, the number of components connected to the NoC. The presented analysis originates from Serpanos and Wolf [160] and assumes that each analyzed NoC supports the attachment of N modules, each capable of I/O operations. That is, the number of inputs (n_i) to the interconnect is the same as the number of outputs (n_o) and $n_i = n_o = N$.

Bus delay model

We consider a typical synchronous bus, composed of control, address, and data lines, delivering data in clock cycles of length T_B. Furthermore, we assume that the bus has N attached devices and that the layout of the bus has equal spacing among subsequent device interconnections; the spacing is normalized to 1, leading to bus length $L_b = N$. The control of the bus is determined by a bus arbiter.

Figure 13-3 shows the circuit model for the bus. The model considers a long bus with short attachment-to-bus connections, rather than a short bus with long attachment-to-bus connections, because of the typical practice in NoC system design. Multiple long attachment-to-bus connections would lead to an area-inefficient design; the depicted tri-state I/O buffers would be replaced with multiplexers/ demultiplexers.

Considering that (i) the main bus wires have length L_b, (ii) each input has its own tri-state buffer/driver (B_1) and a sequence of cascaded buffers to drive the long bus wire (B_2), (iii) each output has its own input tri-state buffer (B_3) with

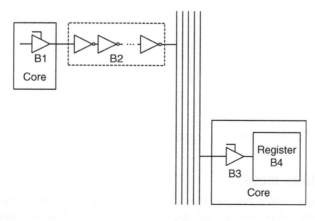

FIGURE 13-3

Bus model.

capacitive load C_L, and (iv) each output drives a register (B$_4$) that stores the incoming data, the total bus delay is the sum of three components:

$$\delta_b = \delta_{in} + \delta_w + \delta_{out},$$

where δ_{in} is the delay to drive buffer B$_1$ and the cascaded buffers B$_2$, δ_w is the latency on the bus wire, and δ_{out} is the delay of B$_3$ driving register B$_4$.

Considering that the sequence of buffers B$_1$, B$_2$, and B$_3$ needs to be sized so that the buffers constitute a cascade driving a load of N buffers B$_3$, that is, $N \cdot C_L$, and disregarding the delay of the long wire, the delay $(\delta_{in} + \delta_{out}) - \delta_{B4}$, where δ_{B4} is the delay of the last buffer B$_4$, is computed using the formula for exponentially tapered buffers [187]:

$$(\delta_{in} + \delta_{out}) - \delta_{B4} = k\left(N\frac{C_L}{C_g}\right)^{1/N} t_{min}$$

In this equation, k is the number of stages in the cascaded buffers and t_{min} is the delay to drive a minimum size load with capacitance C_g, that is, C_g and t_{min} are constants that depend on the technology.

The wire delay δ_w is a function of the length L_b ($L_b = N$) and is calculated as the Elmore delay:

$$\delta_w = \frac{1}{2}RCN(N - 1)$$

Finally, delay δ_{B4} is calculated using a simple τ model by the load capacitance and the delay of buffer B4:

$$\delta_{B4} = 0.69(R_n + R_l)C_L$$

where R_n is the effective transistor resistance for the used technology and R_l is the resistance of the gate connected directly to buffer B$_4$. Disregarding delay δ_{B4}, for simplicity, the aforementioned equation gives a total bus delay as

$$\delta_b = (\delta_{in} + \delta_{out}) - \delta_{B4}$$

$$= k\left(N\frac{C_L}{C_g}\right)^{1/k} t_{min} + \frac{1}{2}RCN(N - 1)$$

$$= k_1 C_L^{1/k} N^{1/k} + k_2 N + k_3 N^2$$

Thus, delay δ_b, that is, the bus cycle T_B, is $O(N^2)$, where N is the number of interconnected systems.

Crossbar delay model

For the crossbar switch, we consider an $N \times N$ switch that enables any-to-any connectivity. Each connection through the switch is composed of data lines only, and the switch is assumed synchronous, with a clock cycle T_s. The selection of the transfers to be performed during a cycle is made by a scheduler. Importantly, data transmission is unidirectional in switches, differentiating these designs from the bus design significantly; unidirectional transmission enables us to insert buffers (repeaters) in the connections and thus obtain improved transmission times. Figure 13-4 shows the two most common crossbar models, the inverter-based model and the multiplexer-based one.

In the case of the inverter-based switch, we note that a transmitting system is attached to the switch with a buffer (B_1) that drives N tri-state buffers B_3 and each tri-state buffer B_3 drives a register B_4 (similarly to the bus), which latches transmitted data at the receiver. Transmission between B_1 and B_3 is performed through a line with cascaded buffers, which is modeled as an RC transmission line with inserted buffers; the collection of repeaters is mentioned in Figure 13-4 as one single buffer, denoted B_2.

The transmission delay (δ_c) through the crossbar is

$$\delta_c = \delta_{ic} + \delta_x + \delta_{oc}$$

where δ_{ic} is the crossbar input delay, δ_x is the transmission delay through the internal crossbar, and δ_{oc} is the output delay through buffer B_3 and to latch B_4. We disregard the delay of latch B_4, as in the case of the bus, and consider that the length of crossbar wires is N in both axes, x and y, and that connections through the crossbar are unidirectional. Then we can calculate the total delay as the delay of the longest path, which has a length equal to $2N$, passing through $2N - 1$ crosspoints, as the maximum length per axis is N, using Bakoglu's formula [12]:

$$\delta_c = 2.5 \sqrt{R_0 C_0 R_{int} C_{int}} = 2.5 \sqrt{N} \sqrt{R_0 C_0 R_{int} C_L}$$

Thus, the delay of the buffer-based switch is $O(N^{1/2})$, resulting in a switch cycle $T_S = O(N^{1/2})$.

In the case of a multiplexer-based switch, a transmitting system is connected to the switch with a buffer (B_1) that drives a 1-to-N demultiplexer, which, in turn, is connected to N N-to-1 multiplexers; the 1-to-N demultiplexers and the N-to-1 multiplexers are shown in Figure 13-4, implemented as trees of 1-to-2 demultiplexers and 2-to-1 multiplexers, respectively. At each output there exists a buffer B_3 that drives a register B_4, which latches the transmitted data at the receiver.

Considering that the crossbar's vertical control lines have length that grows as a function of $N\log N$ [46] and the sequence of (de)multiplexers, which is $2\log N$ in a path through the switch, the transmission delay (δ_c) through the crossbar is the sum:

$$\delta_c = \delta_{ic} + \delta_x + \delta_{oc}$$

where δ_{ic} is the crossbar input delay, δ_x is the transmission delay through the internal crossbar (RC line with inserted buffers B_2), and δ_{oc} is the output delay through buffer B_3 and to latch B_4.

Based on the equation for δ_{B4} in the bus delay model, we can calculate delays δ_{ic} as

$$\delta_{ic} = 0.69(R_n + R_L)C_L$$

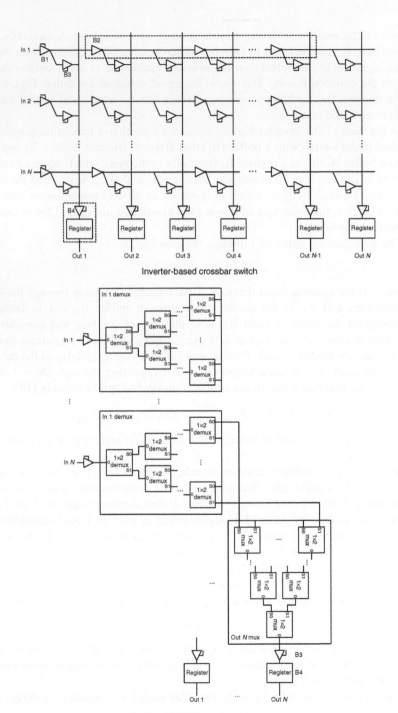

Inverter-based crossbar switch

Multiplexer-based crossbar switch

FIGURE 13-4

Inverter-based and multiplexer-based crossbar switch.

while $\delta_{oc} = \delta_{out}$, as in the case of the bus.

Considering that the capacitance seen from the input of a transmission gate is calculated as [11]:

$$C_{tg} = C_L + \left(\frac{C_{ox}}{2} + \frac{C_{ox}}{2}\right),$$

where the delay through the multiplexers is the sum of the transmission gate and inverter latencies:

$$\delta_c = 0.7(C_L + C_{ox}) + 0.69(R_n + R_L)C_L$$

δ_x is calculated as a delay through a demultiplexer tree and a multiplexer tree:

$$\delta_x = \delta_{mux} \log N + \delta_{mux} \log(N - 1)$$

Considering that delays of input and output buffers are negligible compared to (de-) multiplexer delays, the total crossbar delay is

$$\delta_c \approx \delta_x = 2\delta_{mux} \log(N - 1)$$

Thus, the delay through a multiplexer-based crossbar switch is a logarithmic function of its size, leading to a crossbar cycle $T_S = O(\log N)$.

The analysis can be applied not only to busses and crossbars, which represent the two ends of the interconnection spectrum in terms of connectivity, but also to other significant classes of interconnections, such as multistage networks (e.g., shuffle/exchange, Omega, butterfly), which constitute a significant class of interconnects suitable for NoCs. Such analysis is presented elsewhere [160] and is important not only because it takes account of the physical characteristics of the used technology, but also because it provides improved intuition in new implementations. For example, the presented analysis of bus and crossbar implementations in NoCs indicates that parallelism in data transfers is effective not only because of the high performance of the multiple parallel transfers, but also because it achieves higher clock rates that benefit interconnected subsystems as well since they can exploit the faster clock.

Power issues

Power consumption is important in systems-on-chip and networks-on-chip because SoCs and NoCs are widely used in portable embedded systems, which are battery operated, and in larger systems, which have packaging and cooling limitations [81]. Various analyses have shown that almost half of the energy consumed in a VLSI chip is spent on its wiring system [100], which may include long, high-capacity wires traversing the chip. As the degree of integration increases, more components are integrated on a chip and more wires are necessary to interconnect them. Thus, more power is consumed on on-chip interconnections.

Efforts to design low-power on-chip communication and related interconnects have led to several techniques. Several designs reduce the voltage swing as a method to reduce power consumption. This technique, although successful in terms of transmission power, trades reliability for power, as it decreases a circuit's noise immunity and makes on-chip communication channels less reliable and lossier. Considering that unreliable communication leads to data retransmissions that may eventually require more power than the power saved, designers have come up with a technique that trades transmission speed for power rather than reliability [188]. In this case, the system uses a feedback scheme where voltage swing and operating frequency are determined online (in real time) by monitoring the error rate of transmitted data and the resulting data retransmissions. As the retransmission rate decreases at a given operating frequency, the voltage swing decreases as well. In contrast, an increment in voltage swing occurs when the retransmission rate increases.

An alternative innovative technology that leads to lower power consumption and improved performance in NoC design is that of silicon photonics. Silicon photonics is the application of photonic systems with silicon as the optical medium. Conventional efforts suggest that integration of an optical network can be a viable solution that increases bandwidth, reduces latency, and reduces power consumption of the on-chip network [161].

SUMMARY

Networks-on-chip constitute an emerging technology for systems-on-chip, which can benefit significantly from the techniques of network systems architecture, more specifically from switching architectures. Architectural and circuit design methods are critical in the design and evaluation of NoC architectures, considering the strong dependency of NoCs on implementation technology and the requirements of NoC architectures for high performance in addition to low power consumption. This chapter presented the main technological challenges of NoC architectures and a circuit analysis of NoC architectures using VLSI models, taking into account the interaction of network structure and implementation technology.

Run-time support systems

14

SOFTWARE SUPPORT FOR NETWORK SYSTEMS

Previous chapters explored the hardware design issues of network system components. These components require supporting software to operate correctly and efficiently. Important software components for network systems typically include the following.

- Software development environment: The software components used in a network system need to be developed by a programmer. The software development environment used for the creation of such software is an important component of network systems. The availability of useful programming abstractions, libraries, and so on determines how easily, quickly, and correctly this software can be developed, which in turn may have considerable implications on the acceptance of a system for deployment in the Internet. There are numerous alternatives for software development, but we do not discuss them in detail, as the concepts of creating *static* software are covered sufficiently in software development literature. Instead, we focus on *dynamic* software management, which is essential for, and specific to, the networking domain.
- Software for control plane management: The control plane handles system resource management, route computations, error handling, etc. This software component needs to handle the control of data plane processing operation. We discuss the general operating system issues related to this software component.
- Software for data plane processing: The software used in the data plane handles the processing of network traffic. In this domain, software is somewhat less complex (due to the relative simplicity of packet processing tasks compared to the complexity of control plane software), but highly performance oriented. The management of data plane processing resources is essential to achieve high system throughput. We discuss the run-time management issues that arise in this domain.

Thus, the main focus of this chapter is software used during the run time of the system (i.e., not during offline operations, such as software development for new data plane processing steps).

Network dynamics

As discussed in Chapter 7, the operations that a router needs to perform to forward packets are well defined in RFCs. These standard operations have not changed since they were defined. Therefore, it would seem that functions performed by the software on a router are fixed and do not change over time. However, in practice there are several additional software components in router systems (beyond the standard packet forwarding) that require additional functionality that does indeed change. Examples of changes to software or software components in network systems are as follows.

- Changes to routing algorithms: Routing algorithms are still an active area of research and development. It is challenging to achieve stability in complex routing algorithms (e.g., path-vector algorithms, such as BGP). There is also a need to improve the speed of rerouting in case of link failures. Thus, it can be expected that software that implements routing algorithms may need to be updated as improved versions become available.
- Changes to forwarding implementation: While the functional requirements of packet forwarding in the Internet are fixed, there are no requirements on how these operations are implemented. As more management functions are necessary to maintain operational efficiency (e.g., access control, billing, heavy-hitter flow identification, intrusion detection), the implementation of packet forwarding on a specific network system needs to be updated. These updates may also improve the implementation of route lookup algorithms or flow classification algorithms (as discussed in Chapters 7 and 8).
- Security updates: When using intrusion detection systems (see Chapter 10), the implementation of detecting malicious packets may change when detection rules are updated in response to new attacks.

In addition to these changes, it is also important to note that the diversity of protocols and communication paradigms in next-generation networks will lead to more diverse processing requirements. As discussed in Chapter 15, programmability in the data plane is an essential aspect of next-generation networks. This programmability implies that new software functions need to be accommodated in the network dynamically.

These dynamics require that software changes over time. Therefore, it is necessary to consider how such software can be managed in network systems at run time.

Run-time components

Network systems need to manage software and resources at run time both in the control plane and in the data plane. In a typical router system, each plane uses its own processing resources: The control plane uses a control processor that is similar to a workstation processor and typically runs an embedded or real-time operating system. The data plane uses embedded multicore network processors or other specialized hardware to implement packet processing functions (see Chapter 11). The related software components are shown in Figure 14-1.

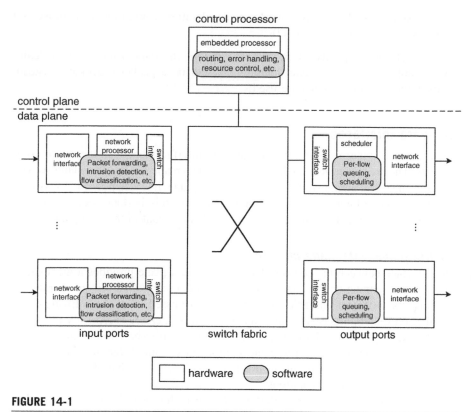

control processor

embedded processor

routing, error handling, resource control, etc.

control plane

data plane

network interface

network processor

Packet forwarding, intrusion detection, flow classification, etc.

switch interface

scheduler

switch interface

Per-flow queuing, scheduling

network interface

network interface

network processor

Packet forwarding, intrusion detection, flow classification, etc.

switch interface

switch interface

Per-flow queuing, scheduling

network interface

input ports

switch fabric

output ports

hardware   software

FIGURE 14-1

Processing resources and software components in control and data plane.

The type of run-time system or operating system needed for each component depends on the complexity of the resource management tasks (e.g., types of resources, complexity of dynamics). In the control plane, the following system components need to be managed:

- Processing resources (typically single-core control processor) for several control or error handling applications.
- System memory for program state, routing tables, monitoring information, etc.

Because control plane processors are typically capable of running a full embedded operating system, the resource management is straightforward to implement.

The system components that need to be managed in the data plane include the following:

- Processing resources (typically multicore packet processing engines) for multiple packet streams requiring possibly different processing applications.
- System memory for packets, program state, forwarding tables, etc.

- Access to shared resources (hardware accelerators at high level, memory and input/output (I/O) at low level).

Because of the simplicity of processors used in the data plane, it is typically not possible to run a complete operating system on a packet processor. Instead, lightweight run-time systems are used.

Software interfaces

Software on a router system uses well-defined interfaces between the major components. The main interfaces are between the control plane and the data plane, as well as between system administrators and the control plane. It is also possible for system administrators to interface with the data plane, but this is done less commonly. Instead, the control plane is used as an intermediary to control the data plane.

Control plane–data plane interface

The interface between the control plane and the data plane provides a mechanism for software running on the control processor to interact with software running on the network processor on each router port. As discussed later, the software functionality on router ports is very limited and thus this interface is typically relatively simple. Attempts to standardize this interface to enable the combination of data plane components with control plane components from different vendors have not been particularly successful. In practice, this interface is based on proprietary specifications and implementations.

Typical interactions for the interfaces between the control plane and the data plane include the following.

- Updates of forwarding tables: The control plane needs to update the forwarding tables used on each router port when routing changes occur. The interface between the control plane and the data plane allows for updates to be sent from the control processor to the network processors that perform packet forwarding.
- Collection of traffic statistics: The data plane may collect information on traffic statistics (e.g., network usage statistics, NetFlow data). This interface can be used to transport this information from the router ports to the control processors where it can be aggregated and processed further.
- Installation of new data plane functionality: The control plane typically can control the processing that takes place in data plane processors. While it does not perform low-level resource management (which is done by the run-time system in the data plane), the control plane can install (and uninstall) processing tasks available in the data plane and thus change the overall functionality of the router.

There are numerous other possible interactions across this interface where the control processor needs to send or receive control and data to or from the data plane (e.g., connection setup, updates to packet processing functions).

System administrator–control plane interface

The interface exposed by the network system to the system administrator provides a way for the system to be configured and to be set up initially. Typical interactions across this interface include:

- Configuration of system (e.g., interface IP addresses, security policies, etc.)
- Manual setup of routes (in case automatic routing is not possible or desirable)
- Software updates (e.g., support for new protocols in data plane, new routing protocol in control plane)

This interface is the one that most people who have interacted with network systems are most familiar with since even simple router systems require some initial setup. This interface is typically implemented using a command line interface or a graphic interface (e.g., using simple Web server functionality). Unlike with the control plane–data plane interface, interactions across the administrator–control plane interface occur only occasionally and are not necessary during operation of the system (assuming the configuration is set up correctly).

With this broad overview on the software support for network systems in mind, we discuss more details on different types of control plane and data plane software.

OPERATING SYSTEM SUPPORT FOR NETWORKING

Simple router systems that do not use high-performance dedicated data plane processors are often based on conventional operating systems (e.g., embedded variation of Unix). In many cases, a single processor is used to implement both control plane and data plane processing (e.g., an embedded ARM or MIPS instruction set processor). The software in such a network system is often not too different from what can be encountered on typical workstations. The use of widely used operating systems simplifies the software development for these systems.

Networking software in operating systems

Practically all modern operating systems have built-in support for networking functionality. This functionality not only includes the protocol processing necessary to have a computer act as an end system (i.e., by implementing application and transport layer processing), but also the functionality that is necessary for router systems (i.e., packet forwarding).

Figure 14-2 shows the main software components related to networking in a typical Unix-based operating system (e.g., NetBSD, Linux). Above the network interface drivers, each layer in the protocol stack (link layer, network layer, transport layer) has its own processing component in the operating system kernel. If different protocol stack configurations are used (e.g., UDP instead of TCP or a different link layer), these processing components can be combined differently. For simplicity, we only show the TCP/IP stack in Figure 14-2. Applications, which

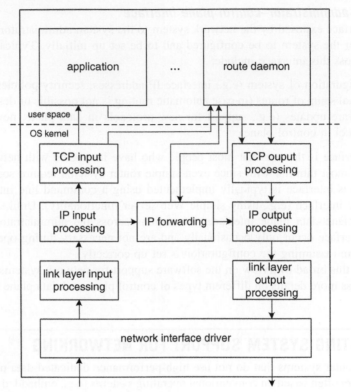

FIGURE 14-2

Networking support in an operating system.

are located in user space, use the socket interface to interact with the networking protocol stack. Also located in user space are some components of the control plane software. Route daemons handle route update computations and update to the forwarding table in the IP forwarding component. Other control plane software components (e.g., error handling in network layer) are part of the kernel.

In addition to networking software built into the kernel, operating systems also provide a set of command line tools for administrators to manage system configuration. These tools can be used to configure IP addresses of network interfaces, set up static routes, obtain monitoring information, etc. For a more detailed discussion of network software implementation inside the NetBSD operating system, see the excellent book by Wright and Stevens [189].

Software interactions

We illustrate the interactions among the various networking software components in an operating system using two scenarios: packet forwarding and route updates.

Data plane: Packet forwarding

Packet forwarding requires packet processing up to the network layer. Figure 14-3 shows the forwarding process on a router connected to two communicating end systems. The network layer modules used for packet forwarding are IP input processing, IP forwarding, and IP output processing. Packets are received from the link layer and processed by the IP input processing module. During this step, the IP header is verified and the destination address is extracted. If the packet is not destined for an IP address that is associated with the network system, then it is passed to the IP forwarding module. The forwarding module performs a destination address lookup to determine via which outgoing network interface the packet should be sent. The forwarding module also performs the processing that adjusts the time-to-live field in the IP header. Then, the packet is passed to the IP output processing module, where it is queued and scheduled for transmission.

On the end systems, the IP input and output processing modules are also used. However, because applications interact using a socket interface, transport layer input and output processing is also performed. For simplicity, only one direction of the TCP connection is shown. The forwarding module is present on end systems, but is typically not used, as traffic either originates from or terminates at the end system.

Control plane: Route update

Interactions for a route update between two software-based routers are shown in Figure 14-4. The route daemon on one router initiates the exchange of a route update. Route information is passed through the protocol stack on the sending router and the receiving router. Note that route exchanges typically use TCP and require bidirectional communication. For simplicity, only one direction of communication is shown. Once the route update has been processed by the route daemon, any potential update to the forwarding table is passed into the kernel.

Figure 14-4 also shows the conceptual separation between the data plane and the control plane (which is different from the kernel/user-space separation). Because the data plane is typically limited to forwarding at the network layer, TCP processing on a router is considered part of the control plane. Control plane information is

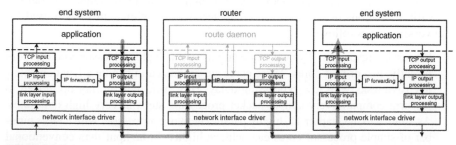

FIGURE 14-3

Packet forwarding in an operating system.

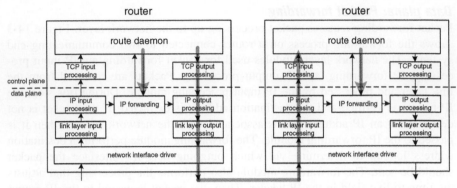

FIGURE 14-4

Route update in an operation system.

exchanged between routers via the data plane. There is typically no direct communication mechanism between control planes of different network systems.

Performance considerations

The use of general-purpose processors with operating system support for networking functionality is a straightforward way to design and implement a network system. However, the scalability of both hardware and software is limited. Therefore, the aggregate data rates that can be achieved by such network system designs are typically limited to a few gigabits per second. We briefly discuss some of the performance issues that arise in network systems that use conventional operating systems and how they can be addressed.

Hardware limitations

Use of a conventional workstation processor in networking devices typically implies that the overall system architecture is also similar to that of workstations. While workstation systems have experienced considerable performance improvements over the years, their inherent architecture is optimized for handling processing-intensive tasks rather than optimized for high-speed input/output operations. Specific limitations of conventional computer system architectures when used for networking are as follows.

- Processing resources: Typical workstations use a single processor core or, more recently, two or four cores. These cores are optimized to handle a few computer-intensive tasks with low processing delay. However, they are not optimized to perform comparatively simple packet processing steps at very high data rates. As alluded to in Chapter 11, highly parallel network processors with a large number of simple processor cores can achieve higher throughput than conventional workstation processors. However, such network processors are typically not able to run complex operating systems (see later). Therefore, general operating systems are used mostly on processing systems that have inherently limited packet forwarding performance.

- Input/output interconnect: The interconnect used for input and output is one of the key factors in determining the maximum data rate that can be achieved by a network system. In the case of conventional workstation system architecture, all I/O traffic traverses the system bus that connects the network interfaces to the processor(s). Each packet needs to traverse this bus at least twice: once to go from the input interface to the processor and once from the processor to the output interface. Typically, the bus is based on Peripheral Component Interconnect (PCI), PCI-X, or PCI Express technology, which can provide data rates ranging from several hundreds of megabits per second to several gigabits per second.
- Centralized design: The system architecture of a conventional workstation processor system is focused on a single central processing unit, a single system bus, etc. This centralized design leads to system bottlenecks (as discussed earlier for processing and I/O) and does not scale to high data rates. As discussed in Chapter 7, modern high-performance routers use designs where scalability can be achieved by replicating processing (and I/O) resources for each port.

These inherent hardware constraints have limited the use of general operating systems in the networking domain to systems where aggregate throughput demands do not exceed a few gigabits per second at most. But even in such systems, there are some important aspects to the networking software that ensure efficient operation.

Zero-copy packet processing

When performing the packet processing steps illustrated in Figures 14-3 and 14-4, packets are passed from module to module (e.g., input link layer processing to input network layer processing). In a straightforward software implementation, each processing module is implemented as an independent function that is called as the packet traverses the protocol stack. Packet data may be passed as a parameter in each function call. Such an implementation would be functionally correct, but would also lead to very low system performance.

When passing packet data as a function parameter, a copy of the packet is created on the processing stack. The process of copying the packet requires a large number of memory operations, as the entire packet needs to be read once and written once. In comparison to the amount of processing that is performed in each software module in the protocol stack, these memory operations can easily dominate the overall processing time. In addition, copying packets frequently may cause the memory interface to become a performance bottleneck as regular memory accesses for packet processing have to compete with memory accesses due to copying.

To counter this potential problem, most modern operating systems aim to minimize the number of times packets are copied while being handled in the protocol stack. In particular, two techniques are widely used.

- Direct Memory Access (DMA): In a straightforward implementation of packet I/O in an operating system, a network interface notifies the central processing unit when a packet is received. The CPU then reads the packet from the interface and stores it in system memory. This process has two key drawbacks. First, the central processing unit is involved in receiving the packet. During the time that the packet is copied from the input interface to memory, the CPU cannot do other useful processing (i.e., forward packets that have been received previously). In extreme cases, this can lead to live-lock where high input data rates can trigger so many system interrupts that the forwarding rate drops to zero. Second, packets need to cross the system bus twice—once from the input interface to the processor and once from the processor to memory. This step of indirection via the processor is not really necessary, as receiving the packet does not involve any actual processing. To tackle these issues, DMA can be used to transfer packets directly from the input interface to memory. The processor assigns a dedicated memory space to each input interface. The interface can manage this memory space and directly copy incoming packets without involvement of the central processing unit. Once a packet is completely received, a control signal is sent to the CPU to inform it of the available packet. The process for packet reception without and with DMA is shown in Figure 14-5.
- Zero-copy packet processing: Once a packet has been received by the operating system, several protocol processing modules need to have access to it. Instead of creating copies of the packet and passing it in function calls to these modules, many operating systems implement a zero-copy strategy. The packet remains in a fixed memory location, and only pointers to the packet data structure are passed among function calls. This process requires a data structure that allows headers to be removed from the packet (without copying the packet) as the protocol stack is traversed upward. On the downward traversal of the protocol stack, headers need to be added to the packet. One way to ensure that headers can be appended to the front of a packet without moving the actual packet data is to use a buffer chain as discussed in Chapter 7.

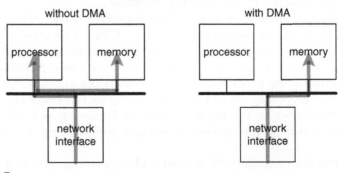

FIGURE 14-5

Packet reception without and with Direct Memory Access.

These two techniques of DMA and zero-copy processing support the efficient processing of network traffic in the operating system kernel.

Kernel vs user-space processing

Operating systems clearly separate processing that takes place in the operating system kernel and processing that takes place in user space. This separation is necessary to ensure isolation of individual computational processes and to protect the system in case of program failures. One important side effect of this separation is that data structures in the kernel use a different memory space than data structures used in user-space processes. Thus, when data move across the boundary between kernel and user space (e.g., to reach an application after completing TCP input processing as shown in Figure 14-3), it needs to be copied from one memory space to another. A zero-copy implementation, as it is done inside the operating system kernel, is not possible. Otherwise, a user-space process would have access to memory space that is reserved for the kernel, leading to potential vulnerabilities.

This copying step has important implications on packet processing in user space. Due to the overhead for traversing the kernel/user-space boundary, it is not practical to implement high-performance packet processing functionality in user space. While some networking functionality is placed in user space (e.g., route daemons), it is typically limited to slow-path and control plane processing. In contract, advanced packet processing functions require modification in the operating system kernel. These functions can be introduced either by recompiling the operating system kernel or by using loadable kernel modules that can be added to the kernel at run time. This need for pushing high-performance networking functionality into the operating system kernel makes the development of advanced packet processing functions a more complex effort.

SPECIALIZED ROUTER SOFTWARE

The use of general-purpose operating systems is a convenient way to implement router functionality on a workstation computer. For high-performance routers, this approach is not sufficient due to the performance limitations in the hardware and software design as discussed previously. In particular, the distributed design of high-performance routers with multiple independent ports with highly parallel packet processors does not mesh well with conventional operating system design, which is optimized for a single processing system (possibly with multiple processor cores). Therefore, specialized router operating systems have been developed.

Router operating systems

Router operating systems consist of software that handles control plane processing as well as data plane forwarding. Router operating systems can be based on open source operating systems or on proprietary implementations. In either case, the functionality of the router OS focuses on networking operations. Thus, there is little or no support for general-purpose processing tasks.

Software structure

The structure of a generic router operating system is shown in Figure 14-6. On the control processor, the router operating system performs processing for one or more routing protocols. These routing protocols have access to the routing information base to determine forwarding rules. The forwarding information base is replicated on each port of the router, where packet processing software performs the processing necessary to forward packets. Note that this software component is replicated across all ports and runs independently and in parallel. The output packet processors perform processing to queue packets and schedule them for transmission on

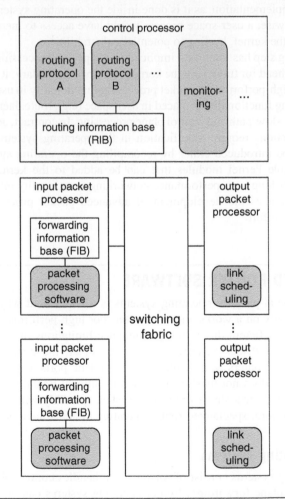

FIGURE 14-6

Structure of a router operating system.

the outgoing link. The control processor also may implement additional monitoring and management functions.

The key characteristic of router operating systems, by which they differ from conventional operating systems, is that networking functionality is distributed across multiple components. Conventional operating systems (Figure 14-2) implement control plane and data plane processing on a single processing system. In contrast, router operating systems (Figure 14-6) can separate data plane processing so that it can be implemented on processors on multiple parallel router ports. This approach has several benefits.

- Support for scalability: Separation of the data plane from the control plane allows data path processing to be replicated on multiple independent packet processors. This support for parallelism in the data plane presents the foundation for a scalable router design.
- Support for heterogeneity: Separation of the data plane from the control plane also allows for a range of router designs, where data path processing is implemented by a diverse set of packet processors. This flexibility to support heterogeneous processing platforms is useful for commercial routers, where a single system design can be configured with different data plane processors (e.g., low-performance single-core processor or high-performance network processor) to target different market segments.

The control plane software in a router OS is conceptually similar to that in conventional operating systems. In contrast, data plane software shows considerable differences that aim at achieving higher performance, as discussed later.

Example router operating systems

Router operating systems have been developed in the commercial domain as well as in the academic domain. Many of the commercial solutions are proprietary, and internal details about design and implementation are not publicly available. In contrast, the user interface for administrators is typically well documented, as it is in a router vendor's best interest to have a broad base of users who are familiar with their products. Academic solutions are often open source to allow other researchers to learn about the design and implementation and to contribute to improvements of the system. Examples from each domain include

- Cisco Internetwork Operating System (IOS): The IOS software is deployed in most modern Cisco routers and switches. It provides control plane functionality for routing and monitoring, as well as packet processing functions for the data plane. Administrators interact with IOS through a command line interface. More details on the Cisco IOS can be found elsewhere [30].
- eXtensible Open Router Platform (XORP): The XORP software is a Linux distribution that implements a router operating system, including several routing protocols in the control plane. The data path processing is implemented with Click modular router software, which is discussed later. More details on XORP can be found elsewhere [60, 193].

Both router OS examples can be used with different hardware solutions to implement packet processing functionality.

Packet processing software

Packet processing software is used in the data plane of the router to implement packet forwarding and any other processing steps necessary in the data plane. This software is a key to achieving high-throughput performance on the network system. As discussed in Chapter 11, different hardware platforms are used to provide the necessary processing power (e.g., embedded multicore network processors). The packet processing software needs to be able to exploit these available hardware resources.

Software abstractions

Performance in the data plane relies on parallel processing of packets. There are two models for how to exploit parallelism on packet processors.

- Run-to-completion: In the run-to-completion model, the entire packet processing functionality is implemented on each of the parallel processor cores. In Figure 14-7, this software model is shown for an example scenario with four processing steps and four processors. Packets are distributed to all processors (e.g., using round-robin). Once a packet is assigned to a processor, all processing steps are performed on that processor.
- Functional pipelining: In the pipelining model, different processing steps are placed on different processors and packets are passed between processors, as

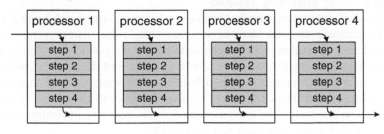

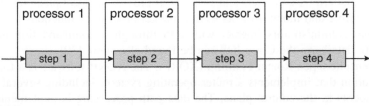

FIGURE 14-7

Comparison of run-to-completion and pipelining models for packet processing.

shown in Figure 14-7. In most cases, the pipeline is functional rather than physical, as most network processors use more complex processor interconnects. Note that when the number of processing steps does not match the number of processors, multiple steps can be placed on a single processor or multiple parallel pipelines can be used.

Several trade-offs need to be considered when deciding between these two processing models. The main benefit of run-to-completion is the simplicity of software development. Because all processing steps are located on all processor cores, the entire processing code can be developed as a monolithic application and installed on each core. However, this approach also puts high demands on the instruction store of the packet processing platform, as each core needs to have the entire processing application available. In systems where instruction store can be shared between processors, this problem can be alleviated. In the pipeline model, each processing step exists only once, which reduces the demands for instruction store. The main challenge with pipelining is that performance of a pipeline is determined by its slowest element. If processing steps are unbalanced, the most processing-intensive step determines system performance. Another benefit of having each processing step exist only once is that it simplifies the use of global data structures. In run-to-completion, duplicates of processing steps need to coordinate to ensure consistent use of data structures (e.g., when counting packets, updating queue pointers).

Modular packet processing

Even when using the run-to-completion model, packet processing software is structured internally into multiple processing steps. This structuring allows easier software development, as well as adjustment to new packet processing functions (e.g., for future network architectures as discussed in Chapter 15). Modularization can be achieved simply by using separate function calls for different packet processing steps. A more structured approach is to break packet processing into independent modules and provide a support system to combine different modules into a coherent packet processing implementation.

An example of a modular configuration of data path processing elements is shown in Figure 14-8. A packet processed in this configuration traverses one path from the input link processing to output link processing (unless it is dropped along the way). Note that different packets may traverse different paths (e.g., ARP responses are handled differently than IP packets).

One example of a modularized implementation is the Click modular router [91]. In Click, processing steps are implemented by modules implemented in C++. These modules are connected either directly or via queues, where packets can be buffered. Click provides a library of modules that can be used to implement standard protocols, but it is also possible to introduce new modules to extend the router's functionality. Once a click configuration is determined, the processing code can be installed in the kernel of Linux-based routers. There are extensions

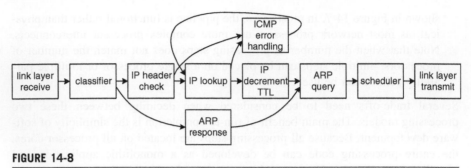

FIGURE 14-8

Example of packet processing modules in extensible router software.

to Click to support symmetric multiprocessing [26] and specialized hardware (e.g., Intel IXP network processor) [163].

Run-time management

As discussed earlier in this chapter, dynamic changes in workload are a fundamental aspect of network processing. Therefore, it is important to have a run-time management component in the data plane of routers. Because many specialized packet processing systems do not support full operating systems, run-time support is typically limited to a few target functions.

When considering modular router configurations as illustrated in Figure 14-8, it becomes clear that placing processing tasks onto processor cores is slightly more complex than illustrated in Figure 14-7. When using run-to-completion, all processing modules can be replicated on all cores, but the overhead for instruction store may prevent such a solution—in particular in systems where a large number of possible modules can be used by network traffic. Instead, it is more common to place modules onto different processor cores. Run-time management systems handle the assignment of modules to processor cores. For this assignment, several goals and constraints need to be considered.

- Load balancing: Changes in the amounts of network traffic that traverse different paths in the graph of packet processing modules cause changes in the amount of processing resources required for each module. Thus, a run-time management system needs to allocate processing tasks considering this load factor. In particular, the goal of allocation is to balance the processing load across processor cores such that there are no performance bottlenecks. Assuming that the processing load for each module is known (e.g., by measuring the amount of network traffic going into each module and by measuring the amount of processing necessary for each packet), the run-time system can attempt to balance the load evenly across cores. This balancing step can be trivial for some configurations (e.g., when using run-to-completion), but it can be computationally complex in other scenarios. In many cases, it is necessary to solve the equivalent of the bin-packing problem, which is known to be NP complete.

Thus, many run-time systems use a heuristic approach to balancing processing load across processor cores.

- Interconnect load: Depending on the placement of processing tasks, a packet may need to traverse the processor interconnect when moving from one processing step to the next. For example, pipelining as shown in Figure 14-7 requires each packet to traverse the interconnect between processing steps. In contrast, run-to-completion requires packets to be sent across the interconnect at the beginning of the processing and at the end. In some packet processing systems, the interconnect bandwidth is limited and thus the run-time system may need to consider this constraint when allocating processing tasks.

- Access to shared memory: Processing modules may need access to certain local and global data structures. Data structures shared between modules may require complex memory accesses and locks to ensure consistency. Thus, the placement of processing tasks that share such data structures may have an impact on system performance. Some run-time systems can consider these effects when making allocations of processing modules to processor cores.

Dynamic adaptation of module allocation is necessary to accommodate changes in network traffic. Thus, any allocation determined by a run-time system is only temporary. While the system operates, the run-time system continues to monitor network traffic and changes the module allocation as necessary. There are several example systems that implement dynamic run-time management for packet processors. In the system proposed by Kokku and colleagues [92], processing tasks can be duplicated across multiple processor cores. As processing demands increase, more processor cores are allocated to a module. While this system operates at a very coarse scale, it is one of the first examples of a dynamically adapting run-time system for network processors. A more fine-grained module allocation is proposed by Wu and Wolf [191], where Click modules are replicated based on processing demands. By achieving a balanced workload through replication of tasks, the run-time system can achieve load balancing without having to solve a packing problem where different-sized tasks need to be allocated evenly to the system's processors. This run-time system shows better performance than a Click implementation for symmetric multiprocessors.

SUMMARY

This chapter discussed the software that is used on network systems. This software can be structured into the control plane software that implements routing protocols and other control functions and the data plane software that implements packet forwarding operations. Router systems, where ease of code development is more important than high performance, may use conventional operating systems to implement control and data plane functionality. Most modern operating systems have support for efficient network processing. In high-performance routers, specialized router operating systems are used to provide support for scalable and heterogeneous router platforms. Data path processing in these systems may use modular router software, which permits dynamic configuration of data plane functionality. Run-time systems for packet processing platforms manage the dynamic module allocation process in response to changes in network traffic.

Next-generation Internet architecture

15

NEED FOR NEXT-GENERATION INTERNET

Previous chapters discussed many system designs and technologies that are or could be deployed today. These topics are important for understanding the needs of today's networks and for designing and implementing systems that can be deployed in the Internet in the near future. However, it is also important to look beyond this horizon and to be able to anticipate the developments in networking that will shape the medium- to long-term future of the Internet.

This chapter discusses some of the fundamental issues in next-generation Internet architecture. In particular, we focus on the following.

- Trends in networking: A number of ongoing and emerging trends change the way networks are used, what devices are connected to networks, and what functions are provided by the network infrastructure. These trends have considerable impact on the design of next-generation network architecture.
- Network virtualization: A key feature likely to be at the core of next-generation networks is virtualization. Using virtualization, multiple networks with different functionalities and protocol stacks can share a single physical infrastructure. This support for diversity in a single network infrastructure is essential to accommodate the demands placed on the network.
- Programmability: To support virtualization and the associated diversity in packet processing, programmability in the data path of routers is a necessary support function. This programmability is exposed to end systems to allow for a selection of packet processing functions at run time.

NETWORKING TRENDS

When Internet architecture was developed in the 1970s through the specification of core protocols (i.e., TCP/IP), it was hard to envision the vast success it would achieve in the 1990s and 2000s. It was an amazing feat to design a network architecture that could support a huge number of very diverse applications, ranging from Web browsing to email, online banking, interactive gaming, video distribution, voice communication, social networking, etc. The design principles that were the basis for this architecture are described in more detail elsewhere [34].

Limitations in the Internet

Due to the widespread use of the Internet for diverse applications, it has become clear that there are also a few limitations in the original Internet architecture. These limitations are mostly founded in the way the Internet Protocol (IP) operates. Because IP is the one protocol in the Internet that needs to be supported by every system and that is used every time data are communicated, these limitations impact the entire Internet. Examples of shortcomings in the Internet architecture include the following.

- Lack of inherent security: Security in the current Internet relies on the use of either end-system protocols (e.g., Transport Layer Security) or supplementary network devices (e.g., firewalls or intrusion detection systems). There is no inherent support for security, as IP addresses do not provide strong identities (they can be spoofed easily) and routers forward packets without performing any verification on traffic. As discussed in Chapter 10, this shortcoming of security support in the network has led to a range of attacks, ranging from denial of service (DoS) to phishing and end-system hacking.
- Lack of quality of service: While the IP contains a header field where packets should be able to indicate their quality-of-service needs, most routers do not consider these header values when making forwarding and scheduling decisions. Instead, all traffic is treated equally, which leads to potential problems when high-bandwidth connections share links with interactive traffic that has delay deadlines as discussed in Chapter 10. These problems are typically circumvented by overprovisioning networking resources. The network architecture itself does not provide any support for explicitly handling quality of service.
- Limitations in scaling: The Internet connects billions of end systems and thus has achieved a level of scalability that has been achieved by only few other engineered systems (e.g., telephone network). However, the number of available addresses in the currently used version 4 of the IP is not sufficient to provide a unique identifier to each end-system interface. This limitation has led to problematic fixes (e.g., use of private networks with Network Address Translation as discussed in Chapter 8) that violate the Internet architecture. A new version of the IP protocol has been proposed (e.g., IP version 6), but its global deployment would require a complete change in much of the physical networking infrastructure, which may be prohibitively expensive.
- Limitations to support emerging networking paradigms: As more diverse end systems are connected through the Internet (e.g., cell phones, sensors), the networking paradigms used shift away from classic connection-oriented client–server (or even peer-to-peer) communication. Some of these emerging communication paradigms, for example, content-centric networking, are difficult to implement using the existing IP infrastructure.

In particular, the lack of support for emerging networking paradigms is a problem that cannot be tackled easily by employing existing techniques. We discuss this issue further later.

Extended reach of the Internet

The number and types of end systems connected through networks and the Internet have continued to change over time. In the 1970s and 1980s, the first data networks connected a handful of large computers located at academic and industrial computing centers. The emergence of workstation computers extended the reach of the Internet to desktops in the workplace and later at home. In the 2000s, mobile wireless phones with data capabilities stretched the reach of the Internet to the point where an individual can be connected nearly at all times in nearly all places. This expansion continues with a rising number of embedded systems using the Internet for communication (e.g., home automation, sensor networks, cars).

The expansion of the Internet to a larger number of end systems stresses the scalability of the network design and its components. As discussed throughout this book, ensuring that network systems can achieve their maximum performance is an important aspect for ensuring that the Internet continues to handle this increase in systems and traffic. The types of systems used in the Internet have also increased in diversity. The following list provides a few examples of end systems that have been equipped with the ability to communicate via the Internet. Their introduction to the network has changed the demands on the Internet in terms of functionality and performance.

- Home entertainment: A large amount of entertainment media is available in digital format and can be accessed via the Internet. Types of entertainment media range from online radio stations to (free or subscription) downloads of movies and media service. This shift from physical media (e.g., video cassettes, DVD) to networked media has increased the demand on network bandwidth significantly.
- Mobile wireless devices: Many wireless cell phones and PDAs are equipped with data communication capabilities. Unlike conventional end systems, these devices need to change their access to the network as they are being carried around. This mobility implies that traffic needs to be routed differently as the receiving device's location changes. This functionality can be provided by mobility protocols, which are important for next-generation networks.
- Sensor networks: Sensors measure properties of the physical world and communicate their information via the network. Typical applications for sensor networks include surveillance, home automation, traffic control, environment monitoring, etc. Sensors are typically connected using a wireless ad-hoc network that may be severely constrained in transmission range and available power. Therefore, specific communication paradigms have been developed (e.g., in-network information fusion) to operate such sensor networks. There is a need for integrating such functionality into the Internet.

Demands on the Internet continue to expand. These new systems not only demand additional network resources, but also require changes in the way the network operates.

New networking paradigms

The trend toward heterogeneity in systems connected via the Internet has impacted the diversities of networking paradigms used in the network. While traditional communication principles based on client–server architecture still dominate the Internet, there are several other approaches on how to distribute information across the network. Some of them, for example, peer-to-peer networking, can be implemented in the existing networking infrastructure. However, others require a fundamental change in the way the network operates. The latter requires changes in the network that cannot be accommodated in the current Internet, but need to be considered for future Internet architectures.

Examples of communication paradigms that differ from client–server architectures are:

- Peer-to-peer networking: Peer-to-peer (P2P) networks combine the roles of the client and the server in each of the peer nodes [134]. Figure 15-1 shows client–server communication, and Figure 15-2 shows peer-to-peer communication in contrast. Instead of distributing information from a single centralized server, all peers participate in acting as servers to which other peers can connect. Using appropriate control information, a peer can determine which other peer to connect to in order to obtain a certain piece of information. This P2P communication

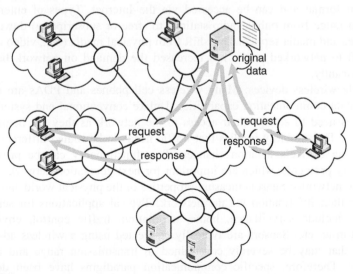

FIGURE 15-1

Client–server communication in network.

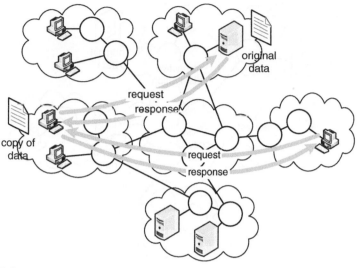

FIGURE 15-2

Peer-to-peer communication in network.

can be implemented using existing networking technology, as it simply requires changes to the end-system application.

- Content delivery networks: Content delivery networks aim to push content from the source (i.e., server) toward potential users (i.e., clients) instead of waiting for clients to explicitly pull content. Figure 15-3 shows this process. The proactive distribution of content allows clients to access copies of content located closer. Thus, better access performance can be achieved than when accessing the original server. The use of content distribution requires that the network supports mechanisms that allow redirection of a request to a local copy. In practice, this type of anycast can be achieved by manipulating DNS entries as described in Hardie [61].

- Information fusion in sensor networks: Many sensor networks consist of low-power wireless sensors that monitor physical properties of the environment [152]. These sensor networks communicate using wireless ad hoc networks that do not provide continuous connectivity. Sensing results are transmitted between neighbors for further relay, as illustrated in Figure 15-4. In applications where data collected by multiple sensors can be aggregated, information fusion is employed (e.g., to determine the maximum observed temperature, a node can aggregate all the available thermal sensor results and compute the results of the maximum function). In such networks, access to data is considerably different from conventional client–server architectures, as direct access to the source of data (i.e., the sensor) is not possible.

- Delay-tolerant networking: Delay-tolerant networks consist of network systems that cannot provide continuous connectivity [51]. Application domains include vehicular networks, where vehicles may be disconnected for some time, and

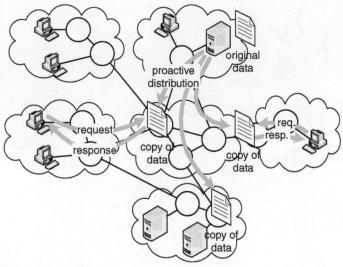

FIGURE 15-3

Content delivery in network.

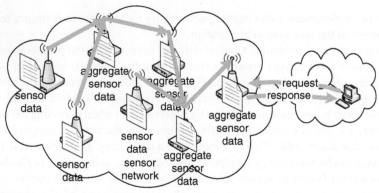

FIGURE 15-4

Information fusion in network.

mobile ad hoc networks in general. Protocols used in delay-tolerant networks are typically based on a store-and-forward approach, as it cannot be assumed that a complete end-to-end path can be established for conventional communication. Figure 15-5 shows this type of communication. The requirement for nodes to store data for potentially considerable amounts of time requires fundamental changes in the functionality of network systems.

These new communication paradigms shift the fundamental requirements of the network architecture.

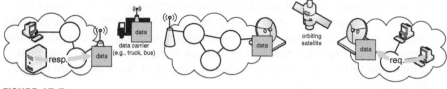

FIGURE 15-5

Delay-tolerant communication in network.

Implications

These networking trends clearly show that functional and performance demands on the Internet are increasing. The requirements for increasing performance can be met by higher link speeds and routers with higher aggregate throughput. However, the expanded functional demands cannot be met by the current Internet. The current version of the IP limits the functionality of the network to this one protocol. Even when using newer versions of IP (e.g., IPv6 [40]), the basic communication paradigms remain the same and some of the key issues in the network architecture remain unresolved (e.g., security).

A comprehensive solution to the weaknesses in the current Internet requires a fundamentally new network architecture. Many different proposals for such architecture have emerged from industry and the networking research community. However, there is no consensus on what the specific network architecture looks like. However, among all proposed solutions, there seem to be two dominating themes: network virtualization and programmability. We discuss each in more detail. It is important to note, however, that these two principles alone do not provide a complete network architecture. Many details need to be determined before a new Internet comes into existence.

NETWORK VIRTUALIZATION

Network virtualization is technology that allows the coexistence of multiple parallel network architectures on a single physical infrastructure. The support for multiple different networks ensures that the diversity in systems and communication paradigms can be accommodated.

Diversity of protocols

When considering the expanding demands on the network, one key observation crystallizes: It is very unlikely that a single network architecture fits all uses. The diversity of network use is so large that there are too many conflicting demands that cannot be brought into agreement in a single network. Consider the following three examples of application domains with conflicting needs for network support.

- On-demand video distribution: Online video distribution has very clear quality of service requirements for low delay and high bandwidth. This application domain requires a network where such requirements can be provided either through explicit QoS functionality or through overprovisioning. In some cases, it may also be beneficial to have multicast support to distribute video to multiple receivers in parallel.
- Secure banking: For secure banking (and many other security-related uses), there is typically an acceptable trade-off toward higher security guarantees at the cost of performance. This application domain may require heavyweight security protocols to provide authentication of end-system identities, privacy of communication, and defenses against DoS or man-in-the-middle attacks. The use of cryptographic functions in these protocols typically implies that the throughput performance is considerably lower than in conventional networks.
- Sensor network: Sensor networks are typically based on embedded nodes with a limited battery lifetime. Protocols for such systems aim to minimize the use of energy while providing near real-time access to sensor information. Nodes may be put into a sleep state to conserve their energy. Thus, the network protocols used in this domain are fundamentally different from the ones used in the current Internet, where continuous end-to-end connectivity is assumed.

These examples illustrate that it is extremely difficult, if not impossible, to design a single network protocol that can provide the performance and QoS needed for video distribution, as well as the security needed for online banking and the energy conservation needed for sensor networks. Therefore, it is desirable that the future Internet support multiple different networks in parallel. End-user applications can connect to the virtual network that is most suitable for them.

Single infrastructure

Despite the need for diversity in the protocols used in the network, it is highly desirable to use a single physical infrastructure to provide network connectivity. A single infrastructure allows the amortization of system cost over all networks deployed. This need for sharing cost becomes particularly apparent when considering that the alternative would require the deployment of separate sets of links and routers for each individual network.

Sharing of network infrastructure has been a crucial aspect of the current Internet. The use of statistical multiplexing for network traffic is at the core of the Internet design and has allowed the Internet to grow to its current scale. However, to support different network protocols, multiplexing has to happen at a different level in the system. Hardware resources need to be shared among networks with different protocols rather than packets within the same network. This kind of resource sharing can be achieved with network virtualization.

Virtualized networks

Network virtualization is a mechanism used to separate a single physical network into multiple logical networks. Virtual networks are often referred to as "slices." Each slice can be configured with different protocols and thus can be optimized for a different application domain. Figure 15-6 illustrates how two slices with different protocol stacks share a single network infrastructure. The virtual topology of each slice is also shown.

It is important to note that in the context of next-generation networks, virtualization refers to logical network configurations that span the entire protocol stack from the link layer to the application layer. This type of virtualization should not be confused with virtualization technology used in local area networks (LANs). Virtual LANs (VLANs) are used to configure logical subnets within a single physical local area network [65]. In such VLANs, the protocol stack is typically the same for all virtual networks. Thus, VLAN technology does not provide as comprehensive a virtualization solution as is necessary for next-generation networks. However, VLANs can be used as a partial solution for the link layer as discussed later.

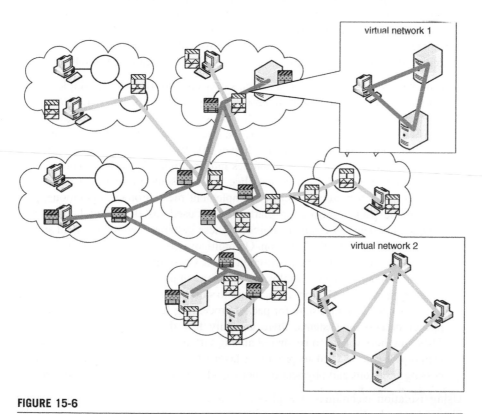

FIGURE 15-6

Two virtual network slices with different protocol stacks on a single network infrastructure.

The use of network virtualization requires that the physical infrastructure is able to split hardware resources among virtual networks and ensure isolation.

Resource virtualization and isolation

Virtualization in networks requires that multiple networks with different protocol stacks can coexist on the same physical infrastructure. To accomplish that, all resources used by the network need to be virtualized. These include link bandwidth, processing capacity on routers, packet storage on routers, etc. Instead of making these resources directly available to a particular network, they are managed by an intermediary layer of software (or hardware) that allocates them to different virtual networks. This process of platform virtualization is similar to what is done in workstations where multiple operating systems can coexist on the same physical computer. Virtualization software ensures that resources are shared among the virtual operating systems and that operations of one operating system do not affect another operating system.

When creating multiple network slices, it is essential to provide isolation between slices with respect to the physical resources in the infrastructure. Each virtual network has a certain amount of resources allocated and should not exceed its use (unless no other slice requires them). Resource isolation ensures that accidental or malicious attempts by one network slice to use resources from other slices can be contained. In particular, there are three types of resources for which isolation needs to be ensured.

- Link bandwidth: Because physical links may carry traffic from multiple virtual network slices, it is important to ensure that the amount of bandwidth available to each slice can be controlled by the network. In the simplest case, a time-division multiplexing approach may be used. It is also possible to use fair queuing approaches discussed in Chapter 10. Virtual LANs are one possible way to separate physical link resources into multiple virtual topologies.
- Processing resources: Each virtual slice requires some protocol operations (as defined by each protocol stack). To implement these protocol operations, programmable packet processing platforms are used (as discussed later and in Chapter 11). The processing resources of these systems need to be shared among all slices and thus require isolation. On multicore processing systems, individual processors can be dedicated to different slices. On single-core systems, operating system techniques can be employed to implement processor sharing.
- Memory resources: Memory is necessary to store packets (e.g., queue on outgoing interface) and program state for packet processing functions. Even in multicore packet processing systems, there are only few different physical memories. These memories need to be shared among virtual slices. Memory virtualization techniques can be used to provide a layer of indirection between packet processing functions and physical memories, where isolation can implemented.

Using isolation techniques, the physical infrastructure can ensure that separate virtual network slices can operate without negative interactions. Thus, from the perspective of each virtual slice, the network consists of the virtual topology of dedicated resources.

Dynamic network deployment

A key aspect of virtualization is the ability to deploy net virtual networks dynamically. As new application domains emerge and additional network functionality is necessary, a new virtual slice can be instantiated on the infrastructure during run time. Thus, it is not necessary to stop the operation of other slices to instantiate a new slice. Instead, each affected router and link reserves the necessary resources for the new slice and installs the necessary protocol stack functionality.

One important research question for dynamic instantiation of virtual networks is to determine how to map a virtual network's requirements to the physical infrastructure. Typically, requirements for the virtual network are given by

- The set of nodes that need to be connected by the virtual network
- The traffic requirements between nodes (e.g., as specified by a traffic matrix)
- The virtual topology providing the connectivity graph between nodes

For an example of the approaches that can be taken to solve the allocation problem, see Zhu and Ammar [197], where several heuristics and optimization strategies are discussed.

PROGRAMMABILITY

The use of virtualization to provide diverse network slices requires that the network infrastructure can implement different network protocols within these slices. Because slices may be deployed on-demand, it is not possible to know a priori what protocol processing functions are necessary on a router system. Thus, it is necessary for programmable packet processing systems to implement software-based protocol processing in these virtual networks. As discussed in Chapter 11, the use of programmable network processors provides a mechanism for dynamically changing protocol processing functions. Systems that are based on fixed function logic (e.g., ASIC) cannot provide such flexibility. Thus, programmability in the data path of routers is at the core of network virtualization.

Programmability in next-generation networks

The use of virtualization dictates that routers can be programmed to implement the protocol functions of virtual network slices. Thus, programmability of data path processing is a universal feature in virtualized networks. However, there are two fundamentally different ways of using this programmability in the network architecture:

- Programmability as a tool to realize virtualization: Programmability is necessary to implement dynamically changing protocol processing on the physical infrastructure. Thus, it serves as a tool to realize the functionality necessary to implement virtualization. In this case, however, programmability itself is not exposed within the network architecture of any particular slice. Thus, from the perspective of a virtual slice, operations implemented within that slice are as static as in the current Internet.

- Programmability as a networking function within a virtual slice: Because programmability is used in the infrastructure to implement virtualization, it is also possible to use this programmability within a slice. In this case, entities within the network slice can dynamically adapt network functionality by changing processing instructions used for handling network traffic.

For the latter case, there are several different approaches on how to expose this programmability toward end systems and applications. Many of these approaches have been considered as stand-alone solutions (i.e., without the use of virtualization) for next-generation networks. We briefly discuss several approaches to show the range of uses of programmability in next-generation networks.

Active networks

In active networks, packet processing functions are dynamically injected into the network [178]. Each packet may carry the processing code that routers apply to the network when they perform forwarding functions. For example, packets may carry information about when and how to duplicate them in case of multicast or packets may carry information on how to implement queuing to ensure that packets of high importance get dropped last. This approach to programming the network makes it possible that every packet could be handled in a different manner—although packets within one connection are likely to use the same processing. There are optimizations to cache processing instructions to reduce the overhead for carrying processing code.

While the active networks approach is very powerful, it is also extremely challenging to use in practice. The generality of the processing that may be performed on the router presents numerous challenges to reason about correctness and safety of processing code. It is also difficult to envision that end-system applications can utilize this powerful functionality to program the network in order to improve application functionality and performance.

Programmable router

A more moderate approach to programmability (compared to active networks) is that of using programmable routers [185]. This very general term implies that programmability is available in the data path, but is not controlled by end systems. Instead, the administrator of a router can install new functionality. Thus, the control path is used to change the functionality of the data path.

The programmable router approach is considerably more static than active networks. However, it provides greater control over the functionality that may or may not be provided by a router.

Data path services

An intermediate approach between the generality of active networks and the controllability of programmable routers is the use of data path services. A data path service is a well-defined function that is performed on packets (e.g., QoS scheduling, intrusion detection, transcoding). End systems can select the type (and order) of data path services that should be used on a particular connection, and routers in the network provide the requested service processing on demand [186]. As new networking functions emerge, new services can be introduced via the control plane of the network.

The use of predefined services limits the type of processing that may be performed by a router. Thus, it provides a level of controllability similar to programmable routers. However, instead of requiring that the same processing steps are performed on all packets, data path service architecture allows a differentiation by connection. Thus, a level of generality can be achieved that is near that of active networks.

Implementing programmability

To implement programmability in the data path, several different packet processing platforms can be used. As discussed in Chapter 11, these can range from single-core workstation processors to embedded multicore network processors. While next-generation network architectures rely on the functionality provided by these systems, there are still several ongoing challenges that need to be addressed before the widespread use of these systems becomes realistic.

- Performance: As more complex functions are implemented in the network, processing demands on these systems continue to increase. While current network processors can support aggregate throughputs of tens of gigabits per second, they are mostly optimized for processing packet headers and leaving packet payloads untouched. With more complex protocols, it is conceivable that more payload-processing functions are used. In such a case, the performance requirements would increase considerably, necessitating more advanced network processors.
- Programming abstractions: Current network processors use vendor-specific development environments. It is unrealistic to assume that customers who need a new virtual network slice would or could implement their specific protocol stack on the numerous network processors that can be found throughout the Internet. Therefore, it is necessary to develop new programming abstractions that ensure that a single implementation of a protocol can be compiled to most network processor systems.

While these challenges have not yet been fully resolved, it is clear that programmable packet processors provide a key piece of the next-generation network's infrastructure.

Deployment

When considering next-generation network architectures, it is important to take into account issues related to deployment of this technology at an Internet scale. Transition from the current Internet to the next-generation network cannot happen overnight. Our dependence on the availability of data communication requires that the current Internet continues to be available until users, end systems, and applications have transitioned to the next-generation network. Considering how many legacy-computing systems are still used today, it is likely that the current Internet will remain operational in its current form for a long time.

To introduce a next-generation network, it is likely that this network will be built up in parallel to the current Internet. Some of the existing Internet infrastructure can be used for the initial deployment (e.g., to tunnel traffic). Over time, more network traffic will shift to the new network and make the existing Internet increasingly obsolete.

One important requirement for this transition is that there is a clear goal on what the next-generation Internet architecture looks like. At this point, there is no definite answer. Instead, industrial and academic research is still exploring alternatives.

Experimental testbeds

Experimental validation of different design alternatives for the next-generation Internet is essential to argue for the deployment of a particular network architecture. However, experimentation with networks is challenging, especially when testing the scalability of protocols and systems. While a small network configuration with a few nodes can be simulated easily or set up in a laboratory environment, it is much more difficult to explore networks with hundreds or thousands of nodes. However, experimenting at this scale is often necessary to identify bottlenecks, find glitches, or observe unusual dynamics.

The networking community has developed several network testbeds, where experimentation at larger scales can be performed. These testbeds allow the dynamic deployment of experiments similar to how virtual slices are deployed in virtualized networks. Thus, these testbeds provide not only a basis for experimentation with next-generation network protocols, but also a system to study the use of a virtualized infrastructure. Examples of widely used experimental testbeds are as follows.

- Emulab: The Emulab testbed uses a large number of dedicated workstations and network links that are located at the University of Utah [182]. For experimentation, users can request a set of processing nodes that are interconnected with links according to users' needs. Emulab implements network virtualization, and thus the processing and link resources are shared. Emulab provides a high level of control over the experiment configuration and thus can be used to generate (mostly) reproducible results. However, this control also limits the realism of experiments to whatever the user configures.
- Planetlab: Planetlab is a testbed where participating users provide link and processing resources toward the shared infrastructure [141]. Experiments can be instantiated on Planetlab nodes across the globe. The connections between nodes are subject to the traffic conditions at the moment of the experiment.

Thus, Planetlab experiments are not reproducible, but show more realistic traffic behavior on links.

- Global Environment for Network Innovations (GENI): GENI is an initiative to create a testbed that supports network experimentation at very large scales [132]. The architecture of GENI is based on defining a single control infrastructure that allows the federation of existing testbeds (e.g., Emulab, Planetlab) as well as new ones. GENI is in the process of being developed.

These testbeds promise to provide the platforms to test the technology developed for next-generation networks.

Commercial incentives

In addition to technical concerns about correct and efficient operation of the network, it is important to consider the commercial aspects of network deployment. Deploying new infrastructure is a costly proposition and there need to be clear incentives for the parties involved. At the highest level, the following opportunities offer services and functionalities to other parties (and to be compensated for the investments necessary to provide them):

- Provide infrastructure services to network providers: Operators who manage the infrastructure of the network can offer virtualization services to network providers. These network providers can instantiate different virtual slices.
- Provide improved network functionality to application providers: Providers who have access to virtual network slices can implement novel network functionality that can be offered to application providers. It is also possible to offer general network functionality to the user directly (e.g., Internet access).
- Provide improved applications to users: Application providers can provide application functionality to users.

Using existing mechanisms for charging users (e.g., access fees, service subscription), providers can recover the cost for providing their own service and for obtaining services from other providers. Incentives for expending the costs for a new network infrastructure lie in the ability to provide (and to charge for) more innovative applications, services, and network functionality than possible in the current Internet.

SUMMARY

This chapter discussed why ongoing trends in networking point toward the need for a new network architecture to replace the current Internet. With more heterogeneous end systems and a new networking paradigm, new protocols need to be introduced into the network. However, no single protocol stack is likely to accommodate the needs of all possible new applications. Instead, multiple networks with different functionality are expected to coexist on a single infrastructure. Network virtualization is used to share resources among these virtual networks and to provide isolation. To implement virtualization, data path programmability is an essential functionality of next-generation routers. For testing of new network functionality, several network testbeds have been developed by the research community. The ability to offer innovative new services and applications is expected to present the incentives for providers to deploy the technology necessary for the next-generation Internet.

The layered Internet architecture and network protocols

The success of the Internet is in large part due to its well-designed network architecture. Internet architecture is based on a layered protocol stack that clearly isolates functionalities in different layers and allows for new protocols to be introduced in one layer without affecting other layers. In Chapter 2, we briefly introduced the International Organization for Standardization/Open Systems Interconnection reference model as one example of a layered protocol stack. For reference, this Appendix briefly reviews the main concepts of protocols used commonly in this layered architecture. Specifically, we focus on the protocols used in today's Internet.

This Appendix only touches on the main concepts within each protocol. A more thorough review of these protocols can be found in many computer networking texts, for example, the excellent book by Kurose and Ross [94].

LAYERED INTERNET ARCHITECTURE

The Internet architecture is based on the principles of the layered protocol stack described in Chapter 2. There are typically five protocol layers used in the Internet:

- The application layer uses application-specific protocols to implement distributed applications. This layer includes the session layer and the presentation layer, which are considered separate layers in other protocol stacks.
- The transport layer provides communication between different end-system processes. In most cases, the transport layer protocol implements reliable end-to-end communication.
- The network layer provides global connectivity between network interfaces. The network layer does not provide reliability or any other guarantees.
- The link layer provides point-to-point connectivity between neighboring network interfaces. This layer implements medium access control when the communication medium is shared.
- The physical layer provides the ability to send individual bits on the medium. The physical representation of bits depends on the type of medium (copper, fiber, wireless) and the physical layer protocols.

In this Appendix, we discuss more details on the operation and protocols of the link layer, network layer, and transport layer. The application layer is discussed in more detail in Chapter 9.

Hourglass architecture

An important aspect of this network architecture is that there is a single network layer protocol. Internet Protocol version 4 (IPv4) is the only network protocol used in the current Internet [with the exception of Internet Protocol version 6 (IPV6), which is being deployed incrementally]. This "hourglass architecture" is shown in Figure A-1, which shows the five protocol layers of the Internet and a selection of protocols for each layer. In the network layer, there is only one protocol—the Internet Protocol (IP). The restriction to IP at the network layer and the diversity of protocols in other layers give the hourglass architecture its "shape."

The restriction of using a single network protocol is necessary to ensure interoperability between all network systems in the network. With the layered protocol stack, however, it is possible to support diversity at layers above and below the network layer. For example, numerous different link layer protocols are in use to provide point-to-point connectivity between neighboring systems. Because the link layer is limited to neighboring systems, it is easily possible to deploy novel link layer protocols (e.g., wireless network access). As long as these systems are able to handle network layer traffic correctly, they do not impact the operation of other systems in the Internet. Similarly, different transport layer protocols use IP as the basis for their operation. Because only the connecting end systems need to be able to understand a specific transport layer protocol, new protocols can be deployed without problems.

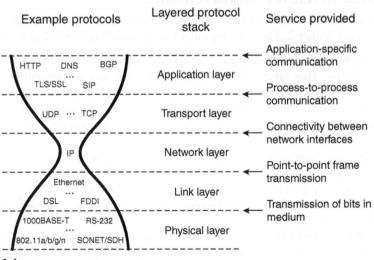

FIGURE A-1

Hourglass architecture of the Internet.

Protocol processing in network systems

The different types of network systems used in the Internet can be distinguished by the level of protocol processing they perform. Figure A-2 illustrates these differences.

- End systems (or hosts) process all layers of the protocol stack because they need to transform data sent from the application process all the way to physical transmission.
- Switches are devices that process link layer protocols (but not network layer or higher protocols). Switches are typically used to create local area networks (LANs). Because their processing is limited to the link layer, they can only handle communication between systems that are immediate (physical or virtual) neighbors.
- Routers are devices that process network layer protocols (but not transport layer or application layer protocols). Routers are the main components of the Internet and provide global connectivity between end systems.
- Transport layer systems process protocols up to the transport layer (but not the application layer). The transport layer focuses on connections. Transport layer systems perform connection-specific operations and thus need to process transport layer protocols.

As part of protocol processing, layers may use their own headers (and, in rare cases, trailers). As traffic moves down the protocol stack, more headers are added. As traffic moves up the stack, these headers are removed. Figure A-3 shows this process. Headers are denoted with "H" and trailers with "T."

The terminology for protocol data units at different layers in the protocol stack is also shown. When transmitting from an end system, data sent by an application are transformed into transport layer messages. These messages receive an additional

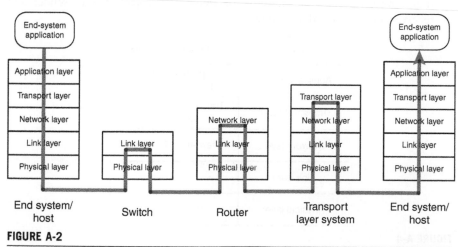

FIGURE A-2

Level of protocol processing on different types of network systems.

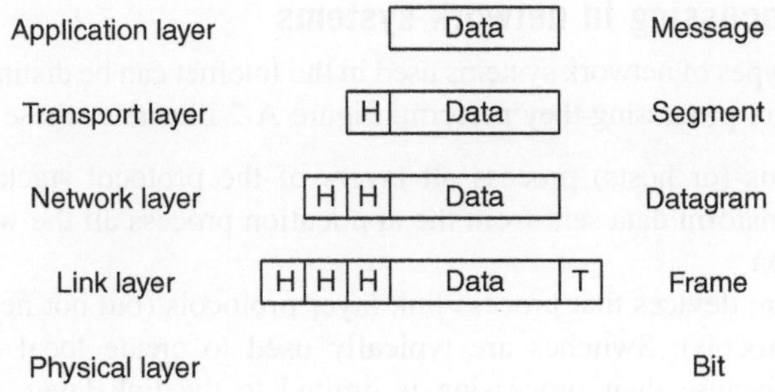

Application layer		Data		Message
Transport layer	H	Data		Segment
Network layer	H H	Data		Datagram
Link layer	H H H	Data	T	Frame
Physical layer				Bit

FIGURE A-3

Terminology of protocol data units.

header in the network layer and become datagrams. At the link layer, datagrams are transformed into frames that contain a link layer header and trailer. At the physical layer, bits of the link layer frame are transmitted. In some cases, the term "packet" is considered equivalent to "datagram."

Example protocol stack

An example of an Internet protocol stack with specific protocols is shown in Figure A-4. The protocols shown are typical and widely used representatives for their layer.

- Hypertext Transfer Protocol (HTTP): HTTP is widely used to request transfers of Web documents from servers. It is a typical example of client–server-style communication.
- Transmission Control Protocol (TCP): TCP is a connection-oriented protocol that provides reliable data transfer. TCP implements flow control and congestion control to adjust the transmission rate to the capabilities of sender and receiver and to network conditions.

Layer	Example protocols
Application layer	Hypertext Transfer Protocol (HTTP)
Transport layer	Transmission Control Protocol (TCP)
Network layer	Internet Protocol (IP)
Link layer	Ethernet
Physical layer	1000BASE-T

FIGURE A-4

Internet protocol stack with example protocols.

- Internet Protocol: IP is the network protocol used in the Internet to provide global datagram connectivity between network interfaces. IP requires routing to determine how to forward datagrams to the network interface.
- Ethernet: Ethernet is a link layer protocol that allows transmission of frames between two systems that are directly connected to each other. Ethernet handles medium access control to ensure that multiple systems can access a shared transmission medium.
- 1000BASE-T: This physical layer standard is used for gigabit Ethernet over copper wiring and determines the coding of bits in electronic signals.

We discuss the functionality and key concepts of Ethernet, IP, and TCP in more detail later.

Link layer

Link layer protocols assume that communication of individual bits is provided by the physical layer. The service that the link layer provides is to implement a protocol that allows point-to-point communication of entire frames between network systems that are directly connected to each other. That is, the link layer sends frames along a single hop in the network.

There are numerous link layer protocols in use and their specific functionalities differ. Some of the main services provided by link layer protocols include:

- Medium access control (MAC): Link layer protocols specify rules on how and when a station is permitted to transmit on a shared transmission medium.
- Error detection: Link layer protocols often use error detection coding [e.g., cyclic redundancy check (CRC)] to identify bit errors in the transmissions of frames.

In addition, some link layer protocols provide error correction (i.e., ability to recover from a limited number of bit errors), flow control (i.e., throttling of sender depending on receiver's buffer capacity), and reliability (i.e., local retransmissions of frames with errors).

Medium access control

The physical medium used for transmissions in the link layer can be a guided medium (e.g., copper wire, optical fiber) or an unguided medium (e.g., wireless spectrum). In many network deployment scenarios, multiple nodes share a single medium (e.g., single shared coaxial cable in old Ethernet deployments, single spectrum in modern wireless Ethernet deployments). When multiple nodes can access the same medium, it is necessary to have rules in place to avoid concurrent transmissions by multiple stations that lead to interference.

Medium access control protocol types

Medium access control protocols specify the rules for transmitting frames on a link. There are two principal types of MAC protocols.

- Channel partitioning protocols determine a priori how access to a link is partitioned between potential transmitters. Examples of channel partitioning protocols are time-division multiplexing, frequency-division multiplexing, and code division multiple access. For each of these partitioning approaches, a transmitter uses a specific time slot, frequency, or code to ensure that its transmission does not interfere with others.
- Random access protocols do not partition the medium. Transmitters can transmit (at the full data rate) whenever they are eligible. The basic components of a random access protocol are the ability to sense when one's transmission interferes with another transmitter's and the use of random back-off periods. When a transmitter determines that its transmission collided with another transmission, it determines a random back-off delay. After this delay has expired, the transmission is repeated. The use of randomization in this protocol ensures that repeated collisions by the same transmitters are increasingly unlikely.

There are many variations on the specifics of each type of protocol. Ethernet uses a random access protocol that is based on Carrier Sense Multiple Access with Collision Avoidance (CSMA/CD).

Carrier sense multiple access with collision avoidance

The CSMA/CD medium access protocol is a random access protocol, but uses several improvements over the simplest type of random access. The key aspects of CSMA/CD are:

- Carrier sensing: The transmitter monitors the link to determine if another transmitter is currently active. A transmission is started only when the medium is idle.
- Collision detection: While transmitting, a transmitter continues to monitor the link to determine if another transmission is interfering with its own. If such a collision is detected, the current transmission is aborted.

Using these techniques, the operation of a CSMA/CD transmitter is as follows.

1. Wait until frame is received for transmission from network layer. Reset retransmission counter.
2. Sense if link is idle. If link is in use, wait until it becomes idle.
3. Start transmission of frame.
4. Monitor link and determine if collision occurs (for duration of transmission). If collision occurs, go to step 6.
5. End transmission of frame and report successful transmission to network layer. Go to step 1.
6. Send jam signal to ensure that all receivers are aware of collision.
7. Increment retransmission counter.
8. If maximum number of retransmissions is reached, abort transmission of frame. Report unsuccessful transmission to network layer. Go to step 1.
9. Calculate random back-off period based on number of collisions.
10. Wait for duration of random back-off period. Go to step 2.

The random back-off period in Ethernet is based on a truncated binary exponential function. The back-off period is chosen randomly from an interval between 0 and $2^i - 1$, where i is the retransmission counter (i.e., the number of collisions experienced by one frame) bound by a maximum value. In Ethernet, the maximum number of transmission attempts is 16, but the value of i is limited to 10 to avoid very long back-off times.

By increasing the back-off interval with each collision, CSMA/CD can automatically adapt to the load on the link. If many transmitters want to use the link, more collisions occur and back-off intervals increase. With longer back-off intervals, the probability of collisions decreases and the probability of successful transmissions increases.

Examples of CSMA/CD operation are shown in Figures A-5 and A-6. These figures show space–time diagrams, where the link is shown horizontally and time progresses vertically (top to bottom). In Figure A-5, a successful transmission of a frame from station A is shown. The slope of the frame propagation through the link corresponds to the propagation speed within the medium (e.g., approximately two-thirds the speed of light when using copper wires).

Figure A-6 shows an example of a collision of two transmissions. Stations A and B both adhere to the CSMA/CD protocol described earlier. Note that only one transmission cycle is shown. Random back-off periods and retransmission attempts are not shown. There are several interesting observations for this example.

- Even though both stations perform carrier sensing, a collision can still occur. Because the propagation of a transmission takes some time, it is possible that a station senses an idle medium after another station has already begun transmission (i.e., B senses idle medium after A has already started transmission).

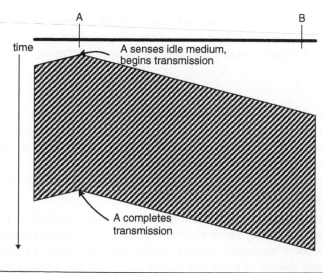

FIGURE A-5

Example of successful frame transmission in CSMA/CD.

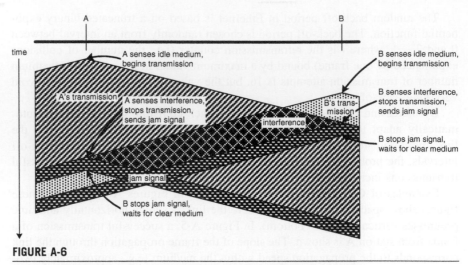

FIGURE A-6

Example of collision during frame transmissions in CSMA/CD.

- The time at which interference is detected may differ by station. In our example, B detects interference before A does. A transmits a large amount of data before the interference caused by B propagates back to it. This delay is the basis for the minimum frame length requirement in Ethernet (see later).
- After sending the jam signal, transmissions from other stations may still be received. Because transmissions that have already been sent continue to propagate, transmissions continue to be received after both stations have sent their respective jam signals.

The example of a collision shown in Figure A-6 can be modified by moving the stations and changing the starting times of the transmissions. However, the principal sequence of signals remains the same for all these examples.

Ethernet

Ethernet uses CSMA/CD as its medium access control protocol [122]. In addition, there are a number of details specified within the IEEE 802.3 Ethernet standard to ensure correct operation and interoperability. These details include specifications for the physical layer as well as the link layer.

The structure of an Ethernet frame is shown in Figure A-7. The frame contains the following important fields.

- Preamble and start of frame delimiter: These fields consist of a predefined bit pattern and are used by the receiver to synchronize its clock to the transmission. This process is necessary because sender and receiver use different clocks (which may deviate slightly and be out of phase) and because transmissions may start asynchronously.

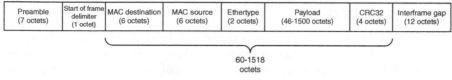

FIGURE A-7

Ethernet frame format.

- The MAC destination and source address: These 48-bit address fields identify the transmitter and the receiver. Each Ethernet device has a globally unique MAC address that is determined at manufacturing time. All receivers compare the destination address of a frame to their own MAC address to determine if they are the recipient. It is also possible to perform broadcasts to all receivers on a link using a special broadcast address.
- The Ethertype field identifies what network layer protocol should be used to process data in the frame. In a typical data transmission, IP is the recipient of the datagram within the frame. However, other protocols are also commonly used (e.g., Address Resolution Protocol (ARP) to associate IP addresses with MAC addresses).
- The payload field contains the datagram carried inside the frame. There is a requirement for a minimum payload size of 46 octets to ensure correct Ethernet operation (see later). If a datagram is smaller than the minimum frame size, padding is added to reach the minimum.
- The CRC32 field contains a 32-bit cyclic redundancy check code used to identify bit errors during transmission. If bit errors are detected, the frame is discarded. (For reliable transmissions, higher layer protocols, e.g., TCP, can detect this drop and initiate a retransmission.)
- The interframe gap is a required idle period at the end of a frame transmission to allow all receivers to reset before the next transmission starts.

One important aspect of the Ethernet standard is specification of a minimum frame size. Ethernet determines that a frame was transmitted successfully (i.e., without collisions) by monitoring for collisions during transmission. As shown in Figure A-6, collisions that happen at a distance from the transmitter require some time to propagate to the transmitter and be detected. If the frame transmission completes before the collision has propagated back, Ethernet would report (incorrectly) that the frame was transmitted successfully. Therefore, Ethernet requires that the transmission time for a frame exceeds twice the time it takes for a signal to propagate the maximum distance between two transmitters. By requiring that transmissions take at least this long, it can be ensured that collisions for any transmitter placement and transmission timing can be detected.

There are many more details about Ethernet, especially when considering higher data rates (e.g., gigabit Ethernet) or wireless Ethernet (IEEE 802.11 a/b/g/n standards). The reader is referred to the appropriate standards and textbooks that focus on these topics.

NETWORK LAYER

The network layer extends the ability of the link layer to send frames from one node to the next to provide multihop transmissions from one end system to another. The network layer requires a (possibly partial) global view of the network to make correct routing decisions and forward datagrams toward their destination.

The most important aspects of the network layer are:

- Addressing: Network interfaces on end systems need global addresses that allow other end systems to address traffic to them.
- Routing: Routing algorithms determine the paths that traffic takes through the network. These algorithms use local and global information to compute routes.
- Forwarding: The forwarding of traffic in a router uses the forwarding information base derived from routing to direct traffic from one router interface to another.

These three topics are discussed in the context of the Internet Protocol in detail in Chapter 7. Here, we discuss briefly how IP relates to other protocols in the protocols suite as well as the format of IP datagrams.

Internet protocol suite

The IP plays a central role in Internet architecture. As discussed previously, it represents the unifying aspect of the hourglass architecture and all network components that operate at the network layer or higher use IP.

To illustrate this importance of the IP, Figure A-8 shows its relation to several other protocols that are part of the IP suite. These protocols are:

- Address Resolution Protocol: ARP is used to associate the link layer MAC addresses of a network interface with the IP address used by it.
- Internet Control Message Protocol (ICMP): ICMP is used to handle special cases of IP traffic (e.g., TTL expiration or ping request).
- Routing protocols: These protocols (e.g., OSPF, RIP, BGP) are used to create and update the forwarding information base used by IP for forwarding datagrams.
- Domain Name System (DNS): DNS is used to associate host names (e.g., www.google.com) with IP addresses.

This is not a comprehensive list of related protocols, but is meant to show the influence of IP on other layers in the protocol stack.

Internet protocol

The Internet Protocol is specified in RFC 791 [144]. The IP is a datagram-oriented network protocol and provides best-effort service for datagram delivery. The format of the IP header is shown in Figure A-9. The main fields are:

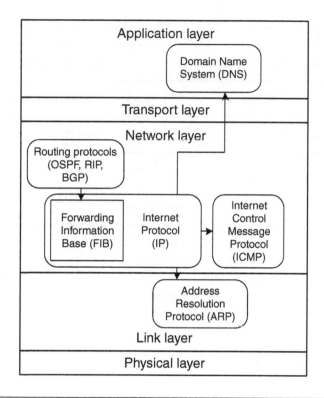

FIGURE A-8

Relation of Internet Protocol to other protocols in network stack.

- Version: The version field specifies how to interpret the protocol header. The current version number is 4, with version 6 being deployed.
- Header length: The header length field specifies how long the IP header (as a multiple of 32 bits) is. This field allows the use of options at the end of the IP header.
- Type of service (TOS): The TOS field could be used to specify performance requirements for the datagram that could help routers make improved scheduling decisions. This field is ignored by most current routers and there is ongoing debate about how to use these bits.
- Datagram length: The datagram length field specifies the length of the datagram, including header and data.
- Identifier, flags, fragment offset: These fields are used when a datagram needs to be fragmented. Fragmentation occurs when the size of a datagram exceeds the maximum size of the link layer on which it is to be transmitted. In practice, fragmentation does not occur very frequently.
- Time to live: The time to live field specifies how many hops the datagram may continue to be forwarded before it gets discarded.

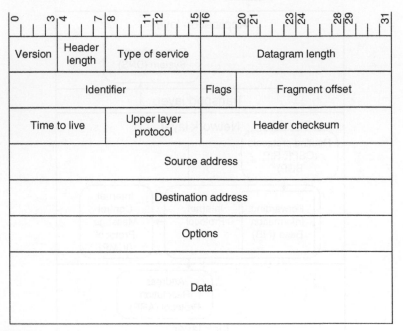

FIGURE A-9

Internet Protocol header format.

- Upper layer protocol: This field specifies the transport layer protocol used by the datagram.
- Header checksum: The header checksum is computed over the packet header and does not include packet data.
- Source address and destination address: These fields specify the interface address from where the packet was sent and to which interface it should be forwarded.
- Options: The option fields may carry special option headers.
- Data: The data field contains the transport layer frame carried in the datagram.

For more details on the operation of IP, the reader is referred to Chapter 7 and relevant literature.

TRANSPORT LAYER

The transport layer receives datagrams on the network interface of a system and provides process-to-process communication services. Because there are typically multiple end-system processes that may use a network interface, a transport layer protocol must provide at least one service.

- Multiplexing/demultiplexing: Transport layer protocols multiplex/demultiplex multiple connections to/from a single network interface. This functionality ensures that datagrams can be associated correctly with end-system processes. For more details, see Chapter 8.

In addition, a number of services may be provided by transport layer protocols:

- Error detection: Transport layer protocols can use checksums to verify the correct transmission of segments from one end system to another. This error detection covers the complete end-to-end path of a segment and thus is better at detecting errors than hop-by-hop solutions in the link layer.
- Reliability: The transport layer may implement a mechanism that ensures that lost or corrupt segments get retransmitted by the sender.
- Flow control: Flow control is used to communicate the available buffer space between the receiver and the sender. Using this mechanism, a receiver can throttle a sender to ensure that it does not get overwhelmed by the amount of data sent.
- Congestion control: This is used to throttle the transmission rate of a connection when the network experiences higher loads. Congestion control requires a mechanism for detecting or inferring congestion conditions, as well as an algorithm for determining the sending rate based on the conditions of the network.

As discussed in Chapter 8, there are two widely used transport layer protocols in the Internet, User Datagram Protocol (UDP) and TCP. UDP implements the bare minimum set of services, which are multiplexing/demultiplexing and an optional checksum. TCP implements multiplexing/demultiplexing, error detection, reliability, flow control, and congestion control. We briefly discuss the operation of reliable data transfer in TCP to illustrate one of the main features of TCP. We do not discuss the operation of congestion control in TCP, as this topic alone could be the subject of an entire book.

Reliable data transfer

Use of a protocol to achieve reliable data transfer over an unreliable network is a nice example of how one layer in the network stack can significantly augment the functionality of layers below. Several different possible protocol designs can achieve reliability under different assumptions about the network. Here, we focus on the techniques used by TCP to achieve reliability. For a more detailed derivation, see Kurose and Ross [94].

To achieve reliable data transfer, the transport layer needs to be able to do the following:

- Determine if a segment was transmitted correctly. TCP uses an error detection checksum to detect bit errors.
- Identify a segment. A reliable protocol needs to determine if a segment carries new data or a retransmission of previously lost data. TCP associates a sequence number with every byte of data that is transmitted.

- Notify the sender when retransmission is necessary. In order to recover from a lost segment, a reliable protocol requires a mechanism to inform the sender if segments have (or have not) arrived successfully. TCP uses an acknowledgment message to inform the sender of how far the sequence of bytes has been received correctly.

- Avoid deadlock from lost messages. Because the network layer provides unreliable service, any segment or request for retransmission (or acknowledgment) may be lost. It is necessary to design a protocol in such a way that any message can get lost without causing deadlock. TCP uses timers on the sender side to trigger retransmissions automatically in case there is no response from the receiver.

Using these principles, TCP implements reliable data transfers. In addition, TCP uses pipelined data transfers, where multiple unacknowledged segments may be transmitted to the receiver ("sliding window" transfer). When multiple segments can be transmitted in parallel, it is important that the receiver can acknowledge accurately what data have been received correctly. TCP uses a cumulative acknowledgment, where an acknowledgment of sequence number X implies that all bytes prior to X have been received correctly (i.e., X specifies the next byte that is expected by the receiver).

An example of a reliable data transfer based on the principles of TCP is shown in Figure A-10. The space–time diagram shows the exchange of messages. For

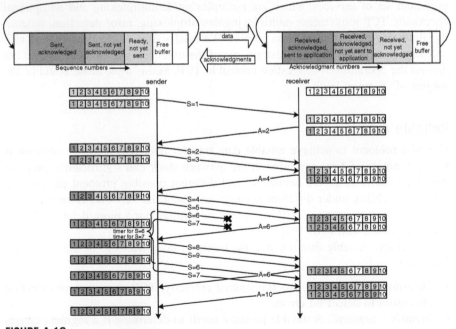

FIGURE A-10

Example of reliable data transfer.

simplicity, segments are assumed to carry a single byte (indentified by its sequence number). The example shows a transfer of 9 bytes. Acknowledgments from the receiver are cumulative and specify the next expected byte. Figure A-10 also shows the sender's and receiver's buffer (including the status for each byte in the transfer). Interpretation of the shading of a buffer cell is explained at the top of Figure A-10, where the progression of sequence and acknowledgment numbers are shown.

Initially, a single segment ($S = 1$) is transmitted. Because it is received successfully, the receiver sends an acknowledgment indicating which byte it expects next ($A = 2$). At this point, the sender transmits the next two segments ($S = 2$ and $S = 3$). The use of pipelined data transfers allows transmission of multiple segments in parallel. The congestion control mechanism of TCP, which we do not discuss here, controls the number of parallel segments allowed. When both segments are received correctly, the receiver acknowledges them both with a single, cumulative acknowledgment ($A = 4$). This acknowledgment illustrates another feature of TCP, which is the (intentional) delay of acknowledgments. By not acknowledging the reception of $S = 2$ right away with $A = 3$, the receiver can receive $S = 3$ and send a single acknowledgment for both segments.

During the transmission of $S = 4$ through $S = 7$, two segments, $S = 6$ and $S = 7$, get dropped (either due to congestion or due to bit errors). The receiver sends $A = 6$ to indicate the correct reception of $S = 4$ and $S = 5$. Reception of this acknowledgment advances the sliding window, and $S = 8$ and $S = 9$ are transmitted. The receiver continues to wait for an acknowledgment of the other two segments. After some time, the timers for $S = 6$ and $S = 7$ expire and trigger a retransmission of these segments. (All other segments also have timers, but they are not shown because they do not expire before the acknowledgment arrives.) When $S = 8$ and $S = 9$ arrive at the receiver, $S = 6$ and $S = 7$ are still missing and thus the only acknowledgment that can be sent is $A = 6$. When $A = 6$ and $A = 7$ arrive shortly after, then the complete sequence through $S = 9$ has been received and $A = 10$ is sent to acknowledge all segments cumulatively.

Transmission control protocol

The Transmission Control Protocol is specified in RFC 793 [145]. There have been several extensions to TCP relating to congestion control [82] and performance improvements. However, the header format for TCP shown in Figure A-11 has not changed. The fields in the TCP header are:

- Source and destination port: The 16-bit port number is used by end systems to multiplex and demultiplex TCP traffic to end-system processes.
- Sequence number: The sequence number indicates the position of the first byte of data in the segment within the stream of bytes transmitted from sender to receiver.
- Acknowledgment number: The acknowledgment number represents a cumulative acknowledgment of received data and indicates which byte is expected next by the receiver.

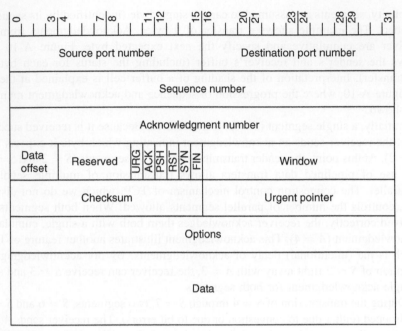

FIGURE A-11

Transmission Control Protocol header format.

- Data offset: The data offset indicates where in the data field the first valid byte is. This field is nonzero when TCP options are used.
- Flags: Flags indicate if urgent pointer is valid (URG), if acknowledgment field is valid (ACK), if data should be pushed to the receiving process (PSH), if connection needs to be reset (RST), if segment is used for connection setup (SYN), or if no more data will be sent from sender (FIN).
- Window: The window field indicates how many bytes can currently be received by the receiver (based on flow control).
- Checksum: The checksum is computed over the TCP header and data.
- Urgent pointer: The urgent pointer specifies the offset of the last urgent byte in data.
- Options: The option fields may carry special option headers.
- Data: The data field contains the application layer message carried in the segment.

The TCP header allows for duplex operation of a connection. That is, a segment may carry data for a connection in one direction as well as an acknowledgment for the connection in the reverse direction. In such a case, the ACK flag is set and the packet contains valid data. Note that sequence numbers used for the sequence number and acknowledgment numbers are unrelated because they refer to connections in opposite directions and each end system chooses its own starting sequence number.

There are many more details about TCP, especially relating to congestion control and various improvements (e.g., selective acknowledgments, window scaling for high-speed TCP). The reader is referred to the research literature and textbooks on this topic for more information.

SUMMARY

This Appendix briefly reviewed the layered protocol architecture of the Internet. We discussed how the hourglass architecture of the Internet, with IP in the network layer, ensures interoperability and the ability to introduce new protocols at physical, link, transport, and application layers. As examples of typical protocols in the network stack, we reviewed the operation of Ethernet, IP, and TCP. We discussed medium access control in the context of Ethernet and reliable data transmission in the context of TCP.

References

[1] Advanced Research & Technology for EMbedded Intelligence and Systems, ARTEMIS. http://www.artemis.eu/.

[2] M.J. Akhbarizadeh, M. Nourani, D.S. Vijayasarathi, P.T. Balsara, PCAM: A ternary CAM optimized for longest prefix matching tasks, in: Proceedings of the IEEE International Conference on Computer Design (ICCD), San Jose, CA, October 2004, pp. 6–11.

[3] T.E. Anderson, S.S. Owicki, J.B. Saxe, C.P. Thacker, High-speed switch scheduling for local-area networks, ACM Transactions on Computer Systems 1 (4) (1993).

[4] A. Andriahantenaina, A. Greiner, Micro-network for SoC: Implementation of a 32-port SPIN network, in: Proc. of Design, Automation and Test in Europe Conference and Exposition (DATE), Munich, Germany, March 2003, pp. 11128–11129.

[5] G. Apostolopoulos, D. Aubespin, V. Peris, P. Pradhan, D. Saha, Design, implementation and performance of a content-based switch, in: Proc. of IEEE INFOCOM 2000, Tel Aviv, Israel, March 2000, pp. 1117–1126.

[6] ARM Ltd., ARM Processor Bus Reference. http://www.arm.com/.

[7] ARM Ltd., ARM1136 Processor. http://www.arm.com/.

[8] ARTEMIS Strategic Research Agenda Working Group, ARTEMIS Strategic Research Agenda, first ed., March 2006. https://www.artemisia-association.org/downloads/SRA_MARS_2006.pdf.

[9] The ATM Forum, ATM User-Network Interface Specification Version 3.0, July 1993.

[10] F. Baker, Requirements for IP version 4 routers. RFC 1812, Network Working Group, June 1995.

[11] R.J. Baker, CMOS Circuit Design, Layout, and Simulation, second ed., Wiley-IEEE Press, 2004.

[12] H.B. Bakoglu, Circuits, Interconnections, and Packaging for VLSI, Addison-Wesley, January 1990.

[13] R.M. Batz, T.L. Sheu, F.Y. Lai, I. Viniotis, Y.C. Liu, D.N. Serpanos, Spatially-parallel router architectures with priority support for multimedia traffic, in: Proc. of Second IEEE International Conference on Computer Communications and Networks (ICCCN), San Diego, CA, October 1993, pp. 229–236.

[14] M. Becchi, P. Crowley, Efficient regular expression evaluation: Theory to practice, in: Proc. of ACM/IEEE Symposium on Architectures for Networking and Communication Systems (ANCS), San Jose, CA, November 2008, pp. 50–59.

[15] R. Bellman, On a routing problem, Q. Appl. Math. 16 (1) (1958) 87–90.

[16] J.C.R. Bennett, H. Zhang, WF^{2}Q: Worst-case fair weighted fair queueing, in: Proc. of IEEE INFOCOM 96, San Francisco, CA, March 1996, pp. 120–128.

[17] T. Berners-Lee, Hypertext markup language –2.0. RFC 1866, Network Working Group, November 1995.

[18] N.L. Binkert, A.G. Saidi, S.K. Reinhardt, Integrated network interfaces for high-bandwidth TCP/IP, in: Proc. of the 12th International Conference on Architectural Support for Programming Languages and Operating Systems (ASPLOS), San Jose, CA, October 2006, pp. 315–324.

[19] M. Björkman, Designing hierarchical hardware for efficient timer handling, in: Proc. of the Second IEEE Workshop on Future Trends of Distributed Computing Systems, Cairo, Egypt, September 1990, pp. 149–152.

[20] S. Blake, D. Black, M. Carlson, E. Davies, Z. Wang, W. Weiss, An architecture for differentiated services. RFC 2475, Network Working Group, December 1998.

[21] R. Braden, D. Clark, S. Shenker, Integrated services in the Internet architecture: An overview. RFC 1633, Network Working Group, June 1994.

[22] R. Braden, L. Zhang, S. Berson, S. Herzog, S. Jamin, Resource ReSerVation Protocol (RSVP)–version 1 functional specification. RFC 2205, Network Working Group, September 1997.

[23] The Broadband Forum, Broadband Forum. http://www.broadband-forum.org/.

[24] Cavium Networks, Mountain View, CA, OCTEON Plus CN58XX 4 to 16-Core MIPS64-Based SoCs (2008).

[25] V.G. Cerf, R.E. Kahn, A protocol for packet network intercommunication, IEEE Trans. Commun. COM-22 (5) (1974) 637–648.

[26] B. Chen, R. Morris, Flexible control of parallelism in a multiprocessor PC router, in: Proc. of the General Track: 2002 USENIX Annual Technical Conference, Monterey, CA, June 2001, pp. 333–346.

[27] T. Chen, R. Raghavan, J.N. Dale, E. Iwata, Cell broadband engine architecture and its first implementation: A performance view, IBM J. Res. Dev. 51 (5) (2007) 559–572.

[28] Y. Chen, O. Oguntoyinbo, Power efficient packet classification using cascaded Bloom filter and off-the-shelf ternary CAM for WDM networks, Comput. Commun. 32 (2) (2009) 349–356.

[29] G. Cheung, S. McCanne, Optimal routing table design for IP address lookups under memory constraints, in: Proceedings of the Eighteenth Annual Joint Conference of the IEEE Computer and Communications Societies (INFOCOM), vol. 3, New York, NY, March 1999, pp. 1437–1444.

[30] Cisco, Inc., Cisco IOS. http://www.cisco.com.

[31] Cisco Systems, Inc., Cisco 12000 Series Internet Router Architecture: Switch Fabric, July 2005. Document ID: 47240.

[32] Cisco Systems, Inc., San Jose, CA, The Cisco QuantumFlow Processor: Cisco's Next Generation Network Processor, February 2008.

[33] T. Chiueh, P. Pradham, Cache memory design for Internet processors, IEEE Micro 20 (1) (2000) 28–33.

[34] D.D. Clark, The design philosophy of the DARPA Internet protocols, in: Proc. of ACM SIGCOMM 88, Stanford, CA, August 1988, pp. 106–114.

[35] D.E. Comer, Internetworking with TCP/IP–Vol. 1: Principles, Protocols, and Architecture, fourth ed., Prentice Hall, 2000.

[36] W.J. Dally, B. Towles, Route packets, not wires: On-chip inteconnection networks, in: Proceedings of the 38th annual Design Automation Conference (DAC), Las Vegas, NV, June 2001, pp. 684–689.

[37] W.J. Dally, B.P. Towles, Principles and Practices of Interconnection Networks, first ed., Morgan Kaufmann, January 2004.

[38] C. Datsios, Network adapter architectures analysis. Master's thesis, University of Patras, Greece, February 2009.

[39] M. de Prycker, Asynchronous Transfer Mode: Solution for Broadband ISDN, third ed., Prentice Hall, August 2005.

[40] S. Deering, R. Hinden, Internet Protocol, version 6 (IPv6). RFC 2460, Network Working Group, December 1998.

[41] S. Demetriades, M. Hanna, S. Cho, R. Melhem, An efficient hardware-based multi-hash scheme for high speed IP lookup, in: Proceedings of the 16th Symposium on High Performance Interconnects HOT Interconnects (HOT-I), Stanford, CA, August 2008, pp. 103–110.

[42] W. Diffie, M.E. Hellman, New directions in cryptography, IEEE Transactions on Information Theory 22 (6) (1976) 644–654.

[43] E.W. Dijkstra, A note on two problems in connexion with graphs, Numer. Math. 1 (1959) 269–271.

[44] J. Duato, S. Yalamanchili, L. Ni, Interconnection Networks: An Engineering Approach, Morgan Kaufmann Publishers Inc., San Francisco, CA, 2002.

[45] J. Duato, S. Yalamanchili, L. Ni, Interconnection Networks: An Engineering Approach, IEEE Computer Society Press, January 1997.

[46] S. Dutta, K.J. O'Connor, A. Wolfe, High-performance crossbar interconnect for a VLIW video signal processor, in: Proceedings of the Ninth Annual IEEE International ASIC Conference and Exhibit, Rochester, NY, September 1996, pp. 45–49.

[47] R.J. Edell, M.T. Le, N. McKeown, The bay bridge: A high speed bridge/router, in: Proceedings of the IFIP WG6.1/WG6.4 Third International Workshop on Protocols for High-Speed Networks III, Stockholm, Sweden, 1993, pp. 203–218.

[48] K.B. Egevang, P. Francis, The IP network address translator (NAT). RFC 1631, Network Working Group, May 1994.

[49] Embedded Microprocessor Benchmark Consortium, EEMBC, http://www.eembc.org/.

[50] Embedded Microprocessor Benchmark Consortium, Networking—Software Benchmark Data Book. http://www.eembc.org/techlit/datasheets/networking_db.pdf.

[51] K. Fall, A delay-tolerant network architecture for challenged Internets, in: SIGCOMM '03: Proceedings of the 2003 Conference on Applications, Technologies, Architectures, and Protocols for Computer Communications, Karlsruhe, Germany, August 2003, pp. 27–34.

[52] R.T. Fielding, J. Gettys, J. Mogul, H. Frystyk, L. Masinter, P. Leach, et al., Hypertext transfer protocol–HTTP/1.1. RFC 2616, Network Working Group, June 1999.

[53] R.L. Fink, F.E. Ross, Following the fiber distributed data interface, IEEE Network 6 (2) (1992) 50–55.

[54] M.A. Franklin, T. Wolf, Power considerations in network processor design, in: M.A. Franklin, P. Crowley, H. Hadimioglu, P.Z. Onufryk (Eds.), Network Processor Design: Issues and Practices, vol. 2, Morgan Kaufmann Publishers, November 2003, pp. 29–50 (Chapter 3).

[55] P. Giaccone, B. Prabhakar, D. Shah, Randomized scheduling algorithms for high-aggregate bandwidth switches, IEEE Journal on Selected Areas in Communications 21 (4) (2003) 546–559.

[56] J. Greengrass, J. Evans, A.C. Begen, Not all packets are equal, part i: Streaming video coding and SLA requirements, IEEE Internet Computing 13 (1) (2009) 70–75.

[57] M. Gschwind, D. Erb, S. Manning, M. Nutter, An open source environment for cell broadband engine system software, Computer 40 (6) (2007) 37–47.

[58] P. Guerrier, A. Greiner, A generic architecture for on-chip packet-switched interconnections, in: Proceedings of the Conference on Design, Automation and Test in Europe (DATE), Paris, France, 2000, pp. 250–256.

[59] P. Gupta, N. McKeown, Algorithms for packet classification, IEEE Network 15 (2) (2001) 24–32.

[60] M. Handley, E. Kohler, A. Ghosh, O. Hodson, P. Radoslavov, Designing extensible IP router software, in: Proc. of the 2nd Conference on Symposium on Networked Systems Design and Implementation (NSDI), Berkeley, CA, May 2005, pp. 189–202.

[61] T. Hardie, Distributing authoritative name servers via shared unicast addresses. RFC 3258, Network Working Group, April 2002.

[62] C. Hedrick, Routing information protocol. RFC 1058, Network Working Group, June 1988.

[63] M. Hempstead, N. Tripathi, P. Mauro, G.Y. Wei, D. Brooks, An ultra low power system architecture for sensor network applications, SIGARCH Computer Architecture News 33 (2) (2005) 208–219.

[64] O. Hersent, D. Gurle, J.P. Petit, IP Telephony, first ed., Addison-Wesley, December 1999.

[65] IEEE, IEEE Standards for Local and Metropolitan Area Networks: Virtual Bridged Local Area Networks, December 1998.

[66] IEEE 802 LAN/MAN Standards Committee, IEEE 802. http://grouper.ieee.org/groups/802/.

[67] IEEE Standards Association, IEEE-SA. http://standards.ieee.org/.

[68] Institute of Electrical and Electronics Engineers, ANSI/IEEE Standard 802.4-1990—Information processing systems—Local area networks—Part 4: Token-passing bus access method and physical layer specifications (1990).

[69] Institute of Electrical and Electronics Engineers, IEEE Standard 802.1 Part D—Media access control (MAC) bridges, March 1991.

[70] Institute of Electrical and Electronics Engineers, IEEE Standard 802.1 Part G—Remote MAC bridging, October 1992. Draft 6.

[71] Institute of Electrical and Electronics Engineers, IEEE Standard 802.6 Part I—Remote LAN bridging of metropolitan area networks (MANs), 1993. Draft.

[72] Institute of Electrical and Electronics Engineers, IEEE Standard 802.6—Information technology—Telecommunications and information exchange between systems—Local and metropolitan area networks—Specific requirements—Part 6: Distributed Queue Dual Bus (DQDB) access method and physical layer specifications (1994).

[73] Institute of Electrical and Electronics Engineers, ANSI/IEEE Standard 802.5-1998E—Information technology—Telecommunications and information exchange between systems—Local and metropolitan area networks—Specific requirements—Part 5: Token ring access method and Physical Layer specifications, 1998.

[74] Institute of Electrical and Electronics Engineers, ISO/IEC Standard 8802-2:1998—Information technology—Telecommunications and information exchange between systems—Local and metropolitan area networks—Specific requirements—Part 2: Logical Link Control, 1998.

[75] Institute of Electrical and Electronics Engineers, IEEE Standard 802.3—Information technology—Telecommunications and information exchange between systems—Local and metropolitan area networks—Specific requirements—Part 3: Carrier Sense Multiple Access with Collision Detection (CSMA/CD) Access Method and Physical Layer Specifications (2008).

[76] Intel Corporation, Santa Clara, CA, Intel IXP2855 Network Processor, 2005.

[77] International Organization for Standardization, ISO. http://www.iso.org/.

[78] International Organization for Standardization/International Electrotechnical Commission, Geneva, Switzerland, International Standard ISO/IEC 10731—Information technology—Open Systems Interconnection—Basic Reference Model: Conventions for the Definition of OSI Services, first ed., December 1994.

[79] International Organization for Standardization/International Electrotechnical Commission, Geneva, Switzerland, International Standard ISO/IEC 7498-1—Information technology—Open Systems Interconnection—Basic Reference Model: The Basic Model, second ed., November 1994.

[80] International Organization for Standardization/International Electrotechnical Commission, Geneva, Switzerland, International Standard ISO/IEC 15776—VME64bus—Specification, first ed., December 2001.

[81] M.J. Irwin, L. Benini, N. Vijaykrishman, M. Kandemir, Techniques for designing energy-aware MPSoCs, in: A. Jerraya, W. Wolf (Eds.), Multiprocessor Systems-on-Chips, Morgan Kaufman, 2004, pp. 21–47 (Chapter 2).

[82] V. Jacobson, Congestion avoidance and control, in: Proc. of ACM SIGCOMM 88, Stanford, CA, August 1988, pp. 314–329.

[83] R. Jain, A comparison of hashing schemes for address lookup in computer networks, IEEE Trans. Commun. 40 (10) (1992) 1570–1573.

[84] F. Karim, A. Nguyen, S. Dey, R. Rao, On-chip communication architecture for OC-768 network processors, in: Proceedings of the 38th annual Design Automation Conference (DAC), Las Vegas, NV, June 2001, pp. 678–683.

[85] M.J. Karol, M.G. Hluchyj, S.P. Morgan, Input versus output queueing on a space-division packet switch, IEEE Trans. Commun. 35 (12) (1987) 1347–1356.

[86] R.M. Karp, U.V. Vazirani, V.V. Vazirani, An optimal algorithm for on-line bipartite matching, in: Proc. of the Twenty Second Annual ACM Symposium on Theory of Computing (STOC), Baltimore, MD, May 1990, pp. 352–358.

[87] S. Kaxiras, G. Keramidas, IPStash: A power-efficient memory architecture for IP-lookup, in: Proceedings of the 36th Annual IEEE/ACM International Symposium on Microarchitecture (MICRO), San Diego, CA, December 2003, pp. 361–372.

[88] S. Kaxiras, G. Keramidas, IPStash: A set-associative memory approach for efficient IP-lookup, in: Proceedings of the 24th Annual Joint Conference of the IEEE Computer and Communications Societies (INFOCOM), vol. 2, Phoenix, AZ, March 2005, pp. 992–1001.

[89] R.W. Kembel, Fibre Channel: A Comprehensive Introduction, Northwest Learning Associates, December 2009.

[90] M. Kobayashi, T. Murase, A. Kuriyama, A longest prefix match search engine for multi-gigabit IP processing, in: Proc. of IEEE International Conference on Communications (ICC), vol. 3, New Orleans, LA, June 2000, pp. 1360–1364.

[91] E. Kohler, R. Morris, B. Chen, J. Jannotti, M.F. Kaashoek, The Click modular router, ACM Transactions on Computer Systems 18 (3) (2000) 263–297.

[92] R. Kokku, T. Riché, A. Kunze, J. Mudigonda, J. Jason, H. Vin, A case for run-time adaptation in packet processing systems, in: Proc. of the 2nd Workshop on Hot Topics in Networks (HOTNETS-II), Cambridge, MA, November 2003.

[93] D.M. Kristol, L. Montulli, HTTP state management mechanism. RFC 2965, Network Working Group, October 2000.

[94] J.F. Kurose, K.W. Ross, Computer Networks, fifth ed., Addison Wesley, 2004.

[95] R.O. LaMaire, D.N. Serpanos, Two-dimensional round-robin schedulers for packet switches with multiple input queues, IEEE/ACM Transactions on Networking 2 (5) (1994) 471–482.

[96] R.O. LaMaire, D.N. Serpanos, A two-dimensional round-robin scheduling mechanism for switches with multiple input queues, United States Patent 5,299,190, March 1994.

[97]   J. Lawrence, How do you measure performance? Communications Solutions, November 2001.

[98]   M. Levy, MPF hosts premiere of ARM1136, Microprocessor Report 16 (2002) 26–29.

[99]   C. Li, S.Q. Zheng, M. Yang, Scalable schedulers for high-performance switches, in: Proc. of Workshop on High Performance Switching and Routing (HPSR), Phoenix, AZ, April 2004, pp. 198–202.

[100] D. Liu, C. Svensson, Power consumption estimation in CMOS VLSI chips, IEEE Journal of Solid-State Circuits 29 (6) (1994) 663–670.

[101] H. Liu, Routing prefix caching in network processor design, in: Proceedings of the Tenth International Conference on Computer Communications and Networks (ICCCN), Phoenix, AZ, October 2001, pp. 18–23.

[102] H. Liu, Routing table compaction in ternary CAM, IEEE Micro 22 (1) (2002) 58–64.

[103] P. Loshin, Essential ATM Standards: RFCs and Protocols Made Practical, John Wiley & Sons, November 1999.

[104] H. Lu, Improved trie partitioning for cooler tcam, in: Proc. of IASTED International Conference on Advances in Computer Science and Technology (ACST), USVI, St. Thomas, November 2004.

[105] H. Lu, On a trie partitioning algorithm for power-efficient TCAMs, International Journal of Communication Systems 21 (2) (2008) 115–133.

[106] W. Lu, S. Sahni, Low-power TCAMs for very large forwarding tables, IEEE/ACM Transactions on Networking 18 (3) (2010) 948–959.

[107] Y. Luo, J. Yu, J. Yang, L. Bhuyan, Low power network processor design using clock gating, in: Proceedings of the 42nd Design Automation Conference (DAC), Anaheim, CA, June 2005, pp. 712–715.

[108] Y. Luo, J. Yu, J. Yang, L.N. Bhuyan, Conserving network processor power consumption by exploiting traffic variability, ACM Transactions on Architecture and Code Optimization 4 (1) (2007).

[109] Z. Ma, W. Zhang, Dynamic power aware packet processing with CMP. Technical Report CS2006-0852, Department of Computer Science and Engineering, University of California San Diego, March 2006.

[110] K. Mackenzie, W. Shi, A. McDonald, I. Ganev, An Intel IXP1200-based network interface, in: Proc. of Workshop on Novel Uses of System Area Networks at HPCA (SAN-2), Anaheim, CA, February 2003.

[111] G.S. Malkin, RIP version 2. RFC 2453, Network Working Group, November 1998.

[112] A. Mallik, G. Memik, A case for clumsy packet processors, in: Proceedings of the 37th annual IEEE/ACM International Symposium on Microarchitecture (MICRO), Portland, Oregon, December 2004, pp. 147–156.

[113] E.P. Markatos, Speeding up TCP/IP: Faster processors are not enough, in: Proc. of 21st IEEE International Performance, Computing, and Communications Conference, Phoenix, AZ, April 2002, pp. 341–345.

[114] A.J. McAuley, P. Francis, Fast routing table lookup using CAMs, in: Proceedings of the Twelfth Annual Joint Conference of the IEEE Computer and Communications Societies (INFOCOM), San Francisco, CA, April 1993, pp. 1382–1391.

[115] T. McGregor, H.W. Braun, J. Brown, The NLANR network analysis infrastructure, IEEE Commun. Mag. 38 (5) (2000) 122–128.

[116] N. McKeown, The iSLIP scheduling algorithm for input-queued switches, IEEE/ACM Transactions on Networking 7 (2) (1999) 188–201.

[117] M. Meitinger, R. Ohlendorf, T. Wild, A. Herkersdorf, A hardware packet re-sequencer unit for network processors, in: Proceedings of the 21st international conference on Architecture of computing systems (ARCS), Dresden, Germany, February 2008, pp. 85–97.

[118] H.E. Meleis, D.N. Serpanos, Designing communication subsystems for high-speed networks, IEEE Network 6 (4) (1992) 40–46.

[119] G. Memik, W.H. Mangione-Smith, Increasing power efficiency of multi-core network processors through data filtering, in: Proceedings of the International Conference on Compilers, Architecture, and Synthesis for Embedded Systems (CASES), Grenoble, France, October 2002, pp. 108–116.

[120] G. Mercankosk, J.F. Siliquini, Z.L. Budrikis, Provision of real-time services over ATM using AAL type 2, in: Proc. of the 1st ACM International Workshop on Wireless Mobile Multimedia (WOWMOM), Dallas, TX, October 1998, pp. 83–90.

[121] Mesquite Software, Inc, Getting Started: CSIM 20 Simulation Engine (C Version). http://www.mesquite.com/.

[122] R.M. Metcalfe, D.R. Boggs, Ethernet: Distributed packet switching for local computer networks, Commun. ACM 19 (7) (1976) 395–404.

[123] P. Mockapetris, Domain names—Concepts and facilities. RFC 1034, Network Working Group, November 1987.

[124] P. Mockapetris, Domain names—Implementation and specification. RFC 1035, Network Working Group, November 1987.

[125] J.C. Mogul, Simple and flexible datagram access controls for UNIX-based gateways, in: USENIX Conference Proceedings, Baltimore, MD, June 1989, pp. 203–221.

[126] N. Mohan, M. Sachdev, Low power dual matchline ternary content addressable memory, in: Proceedings of the International Symposium on Circuits and Systems (ISCAS), vol. 2, Vancouver, BC, May 2004, pp. 633–636.

[127] G.E. Moore, Cramming more components onto integrated circuits, Electronics 38 (8) (1965) 114–117, April.

[128] J. Moy, OSPF version 2. RFC 2328, Network Working Group, April 1998.

[129] M. Naghshineh, R. Guerin, Fixed versus variable packet sizes in fast packet-switched networks, in: Proc. of the Twelfth Annual Joint Conference of the IEEE Computer and Communications Societies (INFOCOM), March 1993, pp. 217–226.

[130] National Institute of Standards and Technology, Data Encryption Standard (DES), October 1999. FIPS 46-3.

[131] National Institute of Standards and Technology, Advanced Encryption Standard (AES), November 2001. FIPS 197.

[132] National Science Foundation, Global Environment for Network Innovation. http://www.geni.net/.

[133] S. Nilsson, G. Karlsson, IP-address lookup using LC-tries, IEEE Journal on Selected Areas in Communications 17 (6) (1999) 1083–1092.

[134] A. Oram (Ed.), Peer-to-Peer: Harnessing the Power of Disruptive Technologies, O'Reilly & Associates, Inc., Sebastopol, CA, February 2001.

[135] J.D. Owens, W.J. Dally, R. Ho, D.N. Jayasimha, S.W. Keckler, P. Li-Shiuan, Research challenges for on-chip interconnection networks, IEEE Micro 27 (5) (2007) 96–108.

[136] R. Panigrahy, S. Sharma, Reducing TCAM power consumption and increasing throughput, in: Proceedings of the 10th Symposium on High Performance Interconnects HOT Interconnects (HOT-I), Stanford, CA, August 2002, pp. 107–114.

[137] D. Pao, Y.K. Li, P. Zhou, Efficient packet classification using TCAMs, Comput. Netw. 50 (18) (2006) 3523–3535.

[138] L. Peng, W. Lu, L. Duan, Power efficient IP lookup with supernode caching, in: Proceedings of the IEEE Global Telecommunications Conference (GLOBECOM), Washington, DC, November 2007, pp. 215–219.

[139] R. Perlman, Interconnections: Bridges and Routers, Addison Wesley Longman Publishing Co., Inc., Redwood City, CA, 1992.

[140] N.M. Piratla, A.P. Jayasumana, Metrics for packet reordering—A comparative analysis, International Journal of Communication Systems 21 (1) (2008) 99–113.

[141] Planetlab Consortium, An open platform for developing, deploying, and accessing planetary-scale services. http://www.planet-lab.org/.

[142] J. Postel, User Datagram Protocol. RFC 768, Information Sciences Institute, August 1980.

[143] J. Postel, Internet Control Message Protocol. RFC 792, Network Working Group, September 1981.

[144] J. Postel, Internet Protocol. RFC 791, Information Sciences Institute, September 1981.

[145] J. Postel, Transmission Control Protocol. RFC 793, Information Sciences Institute, September 1981.

[146] R. Ramaswamy, N. Weng, T. Wolf, Analysis of network processing workloads, J. Syst. Architect. 55 (10) (2009) 421–433.

[147] V.C. Ravikumar, R.N. Mahapatra, L.N. Bhuyan, EaseCAM: An energy and storage efficient TCAM-based router architecture for IP lookup, IEEE Transactions on Computers 54 (5) (2005) 521–533.

[148] Y. Rekhter, T. Li, S. Hares, A border gateway protocol 4 (BGP-4). RFC 4271, Network Working Group, January 2006.

[149] J. Rosenberg, H. Schulzrinne, G. Camarillo, A. Johnston, J. Peterson, R. Sparks, et al., SIP: Session initiation protocol. RFC 3261, Network Working Group, June 2002.

[150] F.E. Ross, An overview of FDDI: the fiber distributed data interface, Selected Areas in Communications, IEEE Journal on 7 (7) (1989) 1043–1051.

[151] M.Á. Ruiz-Sánchez, E.W. Biersack, W. Dabbous, Survey and taxonomy of IP address lookup algorithms, IEEE Network 15 (2) (2001) 8–23.

[152] S. Saroiu, K.P. Gummadi, R.J. Dunn, S.D. Gribble, H.M. Levy, An analysis of Internet content delivery systems, SIGOPS Operating System Review 36 (SI) (2002) 315–327.

[153] M. Sarrafzadeh, F. Dabiri, R. Jafari, T. Massey, A. Nahapetian, Low power lightweight embedded systems, in: Proceedings of the 2006 international symposium on Low power electronics and design (ISLPED), Tegernsee, Germany, October 2006, pp. 207–212.

[154] M. Schwartz, Telecommunication Networks: Protocols, Modeling and Analysis, Prentice Hall, January 1987.

[155] D.N. Serpanos, Protocol processing in communication subsystems for high speed networks, in: Proceedings of the IFIP TC6 Task Force/WG6.4 Fifth International Conference on Data Communication Systems and Their Performance, Raleigh, NC, October 1994, pp. 351–360.

[156] D.N. Serpanos, P.I. Antoniadis, Firm: A class of distributed scheduling algorithms for high-speed ATM switches with multiple input queues, in: Proc. of the Nineteenth Annual Joint Conference of the IEEE Computer and Communications Societies (INFOCOM), vol. 2, Tel Aviv, Israel, March 2000, pp. 548–555.

[157] D.N. Serpanos, M. Gamvrili, Randomized on-line matching (ROLM): Randomized scheduling algorithms for high-speed cell-based switches, in: Proc. of the Fifth IEEE International Symposium on Signal Processing and Information Technology (ISSPIT), Athens, Greece, December 2005, pp. 239–244.

[158] D.N. Serpanos, P. Karakonstantis, Efficient memory management for high-speed ATM systems, Design Automation for Embedded Systems 6 (2001) 207–235.

[159] D.N. Serpanos, P. Mountrouidou, M. Gamvrili, Evaluation of hardware and software schedulers for embedded switches, ACM Transactions on Embedded Computing Systems 3 (4) (2004) 736–759.

[160] D.N. Serpanos, W. Wolf, VLSI models of network-on-chip interconnect, in: Proc. of IFIP International Conference on Very Large Scale Integration (VLSI - SoC), Atlanta, GA, October 2007, pp. 72–77.

[161] A. Shacham, K. Bergman, L.P. Carloni, On the design of a photonic network-on-chip, in: Proceedings of the First International Symposium on Networks-on-Chip (NOCS), Princeton, NJ, May 2007, pp. 53–64.

[162] D. Shah, P. Gupta, Fast updating algorithms for TCAMs, IEEE Micro 21 (1) (2001) 36–47.

[163] N. Shah, W. Plishker, K. Ravindran, K. Keutzer, NP-Click: A productive software development approach for network processors, IEEE Micro 24 (5) (2004) 45–54.

[164] T. Shanley, InfiniBand Network Architecture, Addison-Wesley, November 2002.

[165] T. Shanley, D. Anderson, PCI System Architecture, fourth ed., Addison-Wesley, June 1999.

[166] M. Shreedhar, G. Varghese, Efficient fair queuing using deficit round robin, in: Proc. of ACM SIGCOMM 95, Cambridge, MA, August 1995, pp. 231–242.

[167] W. Simpson, Video over IP, second ed., Focal Press, August 2008.

[168] J.M. Smith, C. Brendan, S. Traw, Giving applications access to Gb/s networking, IEEE Network 7 (4) (1993) 44–52.

[169] V. Srinivasan, G. Varghese, Fast address lookups using controlled prefix expansion, ACM Transactions on Computer Systems 17 (1) (1999) 1–40.

[170] R. Steward, Stream Control Transmission Protocol. RFC 4960, Network Working Group, September 2007.

[171] D. Stiliadis, A. Varma, Rate proportional servers: A design methodology for fair queuing algorithms, IEEE/ACM Trans. on Networking 6 (2) (1998) 164–174.

[172] W. Timothy Strayer, B.J. Dempsey, A.C. Weaver, XTP: The Xpress Transfer Protocol, Addison-Wesley, August 1992.

[173] B. Talbot, T. Sherwood, B. Lin, IP caching for terabit speed routers, in: Proceedings of the IEEE Global Telecommunications Conference (GLOBECOM), vol. 2, Rio de Janeireo, Brazil, December 1999, pp. 1565–1569.

[174] A.N. Tantawy, H. Meleis, A high speed data link control protocol, in: Proceedings of the IFIP TC6/WG6.4 Fourth International Conference on High Performance Networking IV, Liège, Belgium, December 1992, pp. 81–99.

[175] A.N. Tantawy, M. Zitterbart, A method for universal MAC frame encoding, IBM Research Report RC-17779, IBM, March 1992. Also in document IEEE 802.6-92/9, March 1992.

[176] R.E. Tarjan, Data Structures and Network Algorithms, Society for Industrial and Applied Mathematics, Philadelphia, PA, 1983.

[177] D.E. Taylor, Survey and taxonomy of packet classification techniques, ACM Comput. Surv. 37 (3) (2005) 238–275.

[178] D.L. Tennenhouse, D.J. Wetherall, Towards an active network architecture, ACM SIGCOMM Computer Communication Review 26 (2) (1996) 5–18.

[179] J. Trodden, D. Anderson, HyperTransport Network Architecture, Addison-Wesley, February 2003.

[180] E.S.H. Tse, Switch fabric design for high performance IP routers: A survey, J. Syst. Architect. 51 (10–11) (2005) 571–601.

[181] N.F. Tzeng, Multistage-based switching fabrics for scalable routers, IEEE Transactions on Parallel and Distributed Systems 15 (4) (2004) 304–318.

[182] University of Utah, Network Emulation Testbed. http://www.emulab.net/.

[183] G. Varghese, T. Lauck, Hashed and hierarchical timing wheels: Data structures for the efficient implementation of a timer facility, SIGOPS Operating System Review 21 (5) (1987) 25–38.

[184] G. White, Internetworking and Addressing, McGraw-Hill, Inc., New York, 1992.

[185] T. Wolf, Design and Performance of Scalable High-Performance Programmable Routers, Ph.D. thesis, Department of Computer Science, Washington University, St. Louis, MO, May 2002.

[186] T. Wolf, Service-centric end-to-end abstractions in next-generation networks, in: Proc. of Fifteenth IEEE International Conference on Computer Communications and Networks (ICCCN), Arlington, VA, October 2006, pp. 79–86.

[187] W. Wolf, Modern VLSI Design, third ed., Prentice Hall, 2002.

[188] F. Worm, P. Ienne, P. Thiran, G. De Micheli, On-chip self-calibrating communication techniques robust to electrical parameter variations, IEEE Design and Test of Computers 21 (6) (2004) 524–535.

[189] G.R. Wright, W. Richard Stevens, TCP/IP Illustrated, Volume 2: The Implementation, Addison-Wesley Professional, February 1995.

[190] C.L. Wu, T.Y. Feng, Interconnection Networks for Parallel and Distributed Processing, IEEE Computer Society Press, 1984.

[191] Q. Wu, T. Wolf, On runtime management in multi-core packet processing systems, in: Proc. of ACM/IEEE Symposium on Architectures for Networking and Communication Systems (ANCS), San Jose, CA, November 2008, pp. 69–78.

[192] C. Xithalis, M. Gamvrili, D.N. Serpanos, Mutual priority: A scheme for effective and efficient distributed schedulers for high-speed cell-based switches, in: Proc. of Workshop on High Performance Switching and Routing (HPSR), Hong Kong, China, March 2005, pp. 63–67.

[193] XORP, Inc., eXtensible Open Router Platform. http://www.xorp.org.

[194] T.T. Ye, L. Benini, G. De Micheli, Packetization and routing analysis of on-chip multiprocessor networks, Journal of Systems Architecture: the EUROMICRO Journal 50 (2–3) (2004) 81–104.

[195] F. Zane, G. Narlikar, A. Basu, CoolCAMs: Power-efficient TCAMs for forwarding engines, in: Proc. of the Twenty-Second Annual Joint Conference of the IEEE Computer and Communications (INFOCOM), vol. 1, San Francisco, CA, March 2003, pp. 42–52.

[196] K. Zheng, C. Hu, H. Liu, B. Liu. An ultra high throughput and power efficient TCAM-based IP lookup engine, in: Proc. of the Twenty-Third Annual Joint Conference of the IEEE Computer and Communications Societies (INFOCOM), vol. 3, Hong Kong, China, March 2004, pp. 1984–1994.

[197] Y. Zhu, M. Ammar, Algorithms for assigning substrate network resources to virtual network components, in: Proc. of the Twenty-Fifth Annual Joint Conference of the

IEEE Computer and Communications Societies (INFOCOM 2006), Barcelona, Spain, April 2006.

[198] X. Zhuang, Compiler Optimizations for Multithreaded Multicore Network Processors, Ph.D. thesis, College of Computing, Georgia Institute of Technology, Atlanta, GA, July 2006.

[199] K. Zielinski, M. Chopping, D. Milway, A. Hopper, B. Robertson, The Metrobridge: A backbone network distributed switch, SIGCOMM Computer Communication Review 21 (3) (1991) 45–60.

[200] M. Zitterbart, Parallelism in communication subsystems, in: A.N. Tantawy (Ed.), High Performance Networks: Frontiers and Experience, Kluwer Academic Publishers, 1994.

[201] M. Zitterbart, A.N. Tantawy, D.N. Serpanos, Architecture of the high performance transparent bridge, IBM Research Report RC-17824, IBM, March 1992.

[202] M. Zitterbart, A.N. Tantawy, D.N. Serpanos, A high performance transparent bridge, IEEE/ACM Transactions on Networking 2 (4) (1994) 352–362.

Index

Note: Page numbers followed by *f* indicate figures and *t* indicate tables.

Printed and bound by CPI Group (UK) Ltd, Croydon, CR0 4YY

03/10/2024

01040310-0002